"*Village Idiot* is a story of struggles and triumphs that is engaging and riveting. David Sheinkopf uses his personal journey to teach us all about how to find our best selves with resilience, perseverance, and strength. As he overcomes the adversity he has faced, he continues to hold onto hope and a sense of humor. We can all learn a lot from reading this memoir."

—Stacy Kaiser, psychotherapist and television personality

"I was fortunate enough to live in Manhattan in the early to mid 1980s. Reading *Village Idiot* brought me back to when New York was leaving an indelible impression on me. The colorful, visceral, and truthful way David Sheinkopf captures the moments of his youth made me feel like a friend to the character and the Manhattan I knew! Though things don't always go his way, there's such joy and honest humor to the writing, I wanted to read more and more. He's a lovable person and a true hero. People will find different things in this book. I found, more than anything else, how inner strength keeps you going. A must read for anyone from the '80s and beyond."

—John Kassir, actor/voiceover artist, *Tales from the Crypt*

VILLAGE IDIOT

VILLAGE IDIOT

A Manhattan Memoir

David Sheinkopf

Full Court Press
Englewood Cliffs, New Jersey

First Edition

Copyright © 2022 by David Sheinkopf

Published in the United States of America
by Full Court Press, 601 Palisade Avenue,
Englewood Cliffs, NJ 07632
fullcourtpress.com

Paperback ISBN 978-1-946989-96-3
Hardcover ISBN 978-1-946989-99-4
Ebook ISBN 978-1-953728-74-6
Library of Congress Control No. 2021922489

This book reflects the author's present recollections of
experiences over time. Some names and characteristics
have been changed, some events have been compressed,
and some dialogue has been recreated.

*Editing, book design, and interior photo of the author
at 16 by Barry Sheinkopf*

*Cover art, Eighth Street in the 1980s,
by Robert Alan Clayton*

FOR ELIZABETH, AND FOR DEACON

ACKNOWLEDGMENTS

I would like to thank my family for always being there for me—my mother for being a rock my whole life, my father for always helping without question, and my sister for tolerating my antics with a smile. I would also like to thank the people in this book and the beautiful friends I have been lucky enough to have known. They are the color in the painting of my life.

"I am writing for myself and strangers.
This is the only way I can do it."

—Gertrude Stein

Deacon: Daddy, do you know why I am
    happy all the time?
David: No, I don't, but I would love to.
Deacon: Because I find happiness in myself.

—Deacon James Sheinkopf, age 7

TWELVE

(1982)

CHAPTER 1

O N THOSE CHANCE TIMES WHEN I DID WAKE UP, I always had a boner. I'd look down, and there it was—nothing exceptional, but a fact nonetheless; I was a pervert at twelve. The sheets on my bed hadn't been washed in a while and could've climbed down the ladder of my prehistoric bunk bed themselves, but I ignored that, rolled over, and stared out the window of my parents' fourteenth-floor apartment. I lay on my back with my head hanging off the bed. There was a radiator equipped with a large cover below me, so my bed butted up to it rather than the wall, which allowed a good eighteen inches of space. You'd think the manufacturer would have had some kind of child restraint to prevent me from being able to crawl down and come out under the desk below my bed.

Or if I felt so motivated, I could stand there on top of the radiator, hands pressed against the panes of glass that prevented me from falling out; I think every kid fantasizes about standing on a ledge that high. Feeling the blood seeping to my head, my nose

clogging up quickly—I had a crooked septum for a kid of my age—
I rolled over onto my stomach and propped myself up on my elbows.

She wasn't there. I rolled back and thought. She lived in one
of the many windows across the way that was cut off by louver
blinds; but there were times the blinds were open.

I had been maybe eleven and home sick the first time I made
this discovery. I was lying on the couch and staring at the nothing
on TV. A beam of sunlight made me cover my eyes, and in the
shadow of my palm, I noticed my bamboo shades, which weren't
working well. I propped myself higher on the couch. When I could
see clearly again, I did a double take at the sight of a middle-aged
woman standing in a bathrobe. I slunk to the ground, commando-
style, heart pumping, and crawled to the wall below the window.
Staying out of sight, I took a deep breath, knelt up to the window
ledge, and peered over, just catching her robe falling to the ground.
It wasn't the first time I'd seen a woman naked; my father had girly
magazines two feet high that I had looked at from a young age.
But nothing quite prepares you for the real thing. I felt my heart
race, and that's when it hit me: It was the anonymous voyeuristic
watching that excited me. As she rubbed lotion on her beautiful
round breasts, I looked down and felt it growing. I was smiling so
wide my cheeks cracked.

But it wasn't her I was thinking of that morning. I climbed
down from the bed and ran through the house, looking for my
father. This was going to be a unique way for a kid like me to get
a bike.

I'd had them before, but they hadn't been acquired in quite the same manner. I'd go down to Washington Square Park and walk around. Sometimes there was some strung-out, dirty white kid, or some Latino, looking to sell a stolen object in turn for a ten spot— now twenty dollars—that would buy him a whole jumbo of crack.

I sat on a bench, feeling the slats crack my back as I eased into it. I ran my hands through my slicked hair, wiping them on my sweatpants, adjusting the tongues on my Pony sneakers. I looked to my left and saw a black guy moving pretty quick, balancing a halfway decent-looking ten-speed around. It was green, kind of beat up. He stopped not ten feet from me and tanned for a moment. It was amazing to watch him in the vacation-like state he was in, as if he didn't have a care in the world. His mind jolted back as he shook his head—possibly feeling the urges of his addiction—and started in my direction. He rolled by, mumbling something about a twenty as he glanced from side to side, trying to get a visual fix on the cops he knew were somewhere. He sat down about three feet away from me and balanced his long-ass legs on the cross bar of the bike.

"You want a bike, man?" he said, leaning over and clearing his nose with a heavy inhale. It was perfect—I didn't need any stories, and he didn't offer; I just wanted the bike. I pulled a pilfered, crumpled twenty out of my pocket; I was eying him as I slid the twenty over to him on the bench. It wouldn't have been much for him to grab the cash, knock me down, and ride off, but I was prepared. I hooked my foot in the rear rim and in, one move, he threw his legs off the bike and was gone. I let the bike fall back into my hands and gave it a good once-over. It seemed all right—I was pretty short, and it seemed high, but I adjusted the seat so I could touch the ground. I hopped on, and off I went. I played with the handle-bars, shaking them left and right as I rode through the arch and hopped the curb, pedaling up Fifth Avenue.

I hadn't gotten ten feet when I felt no tension as I pedaled away. The chain had not only popped off but also broken in half, which sent me reeling into a car. There I'd been with a piece of shit bike on the side of the street, my hand bleeding. I had known it wasn't the schmuck that I'd gotten it from who caused that, but it hadn't been random either.

I pounded out of my room and found my pop in the kitchen. I tried to grab him in a half nelson, but he easily slipped out of it. I smelled his after shave, Paco Rabanne; he laughed.

I started to hound him to call—if we could just pick it up a *little* earlier. He started to box me, but I was single- minded. He gave up, walked over, grabbed the phone, and turned the rotary dial. I watched him, one hand on his hip, the other holding the instrument as he stared down at his Saturday shoes. He said a few word to the person on the phone, checked his watch, nodded, and hung up. "Okay—let's go. Guy said we could come up and wait. He'll *try* and get it finished ahead of schedule."

As we drove uptown, my hands were sweating. My heart was beating faster with every block that we drove, my eyes darting around.

The car barely came to a complete stop before I grabbed the handle, kicked the door open, and jumped out, clearing the side-walk in two big jumps. Even though it was actually happening, I still couldn't believe it. I turned around and around in the vestibule of the shop, getting psyched. I wrestled with the muscles on my face to stop a Cheshire grin from forming. I would truly succumb to the brain-numbing feeling only when I had the treasure safely in my hands. It wasn't every day a kid my age received a gift like it— not just some bike for a twelve-year-old (most kids who rode them were at least fourteen), but a gift from my pop, probably the most important thing I'd ever get. I hadn't even had to nag him or anything for it. He'd just offered it up, like some rite of passage.

The guy in the store had a professional way about him I hadn't encountered: quick moves, but every ounce of energy directed. Yeah, everything seemed just right as I passed my hand over the hard vinyl seat: would definitely take a while to get used to. Apart from that, the whole bike was gleaming chrome, right down to the pedals. It wasn't just a bicycle; it was my masterpiece.

I thought about the time I'd made the old man build a go-cart with me. No engine, of course—I was only six, seven. I'd never seen him so gung-ho, which'd brought what I thought would be a nice afternoon project to a much more heightened level. But though we'd spent days on it, after a few rides it'd become something the snow grew tired of, something that lived out its short life along the endless driveway in the corner of my yard.

This bike would be different, not momentary but something that lasted. *Some* of the kids I'd grown up with had drive, but very few seemed to have a sense of follow-through. It was a far cry from my Schwinn: banana yellow, a really long-ass matching seat, and ape-hanger handlebars that, when you hit the road, made it look like you weren't even steering.

I really wanted to ride the bike home, but we were far uptown, and to quote the man, "Like fucking hell you will."

"Do you think it'll, you know, be safe in there, Pops?" I asked innocently as we walked the bike outside to the car.

"Look, I know it's an expensive bike, David, I just started paying for it, but it'll survive in the trunk. You're not riding it downtown," he said without so much as looking my way or batting an eye.

"I *know!* Jesus, I just didn't know if you knew it would fit in there. I was just trying to help," I replied, rolling my eyes. It was tough to con an opponent that strong at his own game.

So we *gingerly* put the bike in the trunk of the car and set off for our own neighborhood. I loved looking out the window when we drove down Seventh Avenue. There were no lanes to speak of, only cars and cabs floating like geese on water.

Some people can't even sit in the driver's seat in the Big Apple. They don't realize, when they enter New York from Whereverville, that they actually have to *drive* in the city. It's not even actual driving: It's more like a telepathic defense virus taking over your body, and you becoming everything you always hated in a driver.

Not until the uninitiated get slammed behind a delivery truck or perpendicular to a cabbie do they realize: He's just munching his sandwich, minding his own business, and *you* had to go and ruin his day. Nor did they think they'd encounter guys on bicycles who purposely come within inches of their hood, messengers rolling, fast and agile as Mercury, in and out of the cars.

Before I knew it, we were downtown, nearing the apartment. It was a warm June day moving toward evening; I was sure I could manage to stay out till at least eight-thirty or nine. The air seemed still, though the warm breeze went through my hair like a ghost.

We pulled up next to the curb not twenty-five feet from the

front door of my building. I watched my pop open the trunk with the hidden button in the glove box. I hopped out, moved to the back of the car, and grabbed the bike—the grips tangible in my hands as soon as I reached for them and pulled the beast out. My mission was to ride the West Village in search of my friends or anyone who would appreciate it. But right before I left, my father looked me in the eyes as he held a handlebar with one hand and put his other one on my shoulder. He said in an optimistic tone, "You take care of this bike, alright, Dave?" He smiled, and I was off, guilt and all.

I couldn't believe the way it handled! And was it *light!* It was like riding on *air.* It was even more amazing than I remembered! At the bike shop you were only allowed to take it for a little spin up and down the cramped, car-lined street where the store was situated; it was nothing like the speed I was reaching now. Nothing was stopping me. *Whoosh!* I wove in between the cars and popped up on the sidewalk, unstoppable. I figured I'd mix it up a little and take Ninth over to the West Village. I got really low on the bike, resting my forearms on the handlebars, gliding silently. I'd commandeered a pair of old Vuarnet sunglasses—they were way too big for me, but they finished off the look and turned everything I saw a crisp and comprehensible green.

I came up to the light at Sixth Avenue and tried balancing the bike, focused, looking at the ground. As soon as the light turned, I sped up to get in front of the cabs that were looking for fares. I got a lot of looks as I coasted down the street standing on my pedals. The wind was slapping my shirt and pulling it up in the back; when I glanced at a couple walking down the stairs of a prewar brownstone to search for a cab, I laughed—*they* needed a bike like this.

Turning up Greenwich, I noticed the patches of cobblestone that remained under the asphalt looked like war-torn icebergs floating along in calmer water, which meant I was close.

A dog started barking. It lunged ferociously the length of its leash as I rolled by—expressing, in its own imprisonment, I knew, deep-seated feelings of jealousy and resentment toward me because of my newfound freedom. The owner just jerked the dog back, oblivious. I reached Bank Street and hung a left to take the long way to the entrance through the courtyard of Westbeth.

My friends and I had always played stickball and messed around on skateboards there. Because so many lived in the huge artists' community, I was there a lot; it was my home away from home. I rolled around, hooked my feet under both pedals, and yanked the bike upward, trying to land on a semi-circular concrete form in front of me. I glanced off it and continued to ride forward, up the ramp, past the theatre, reaching the inner corridor where I could do the whistle that called to arms all my friends within earshot.

Robin was the first to stick his head out the window. I was successfully doing loops within a large concrete doughnut that had actually been designed for sitting as well as staring off into space, a common occurrence in a community where creativity ran like water. I was glad it was vacant; I was sure it looked cool from my gang's windows high above.

"Yo, man! Yeaaah, buddy!" Robin called out from eight, waving his arms. I heard another window slide open and saw Arby and the neck of his Stratocaster sticking out his window. He was only on the third floor, so the conversation was easier. "*Davey! Nice ride!*"

"Thanks, man!" I screamed without looking up. In the zone, I felt my bottom lip droop in concentration. A few moments later Robin came down on his bike, rode over, got off balancing on one pedal, and laid it down like a feather. He loped around the bike and me with his hands on his chin in disbelief: virgin, not a scratch, not a decal out of place. It would take time to get all the battle scars and broken-in vibe it really yearned for. I was looking like a real BMX man: In a short-sleeved shirt that had the logo *P.K. Ripper* on the back, the parachute pants, and the Van slip-ons, all made up together, I looked authentic. Robin was in a similar ensemble, more worn-in and dirty white. I, who silently admired him and his dedication to the craft, was honored by the approval. Robin had to check out the bike and, of course, take a ride—you know, to *really* check it out.

The rest of my *compadres* came down to the courtyard one by one and were uniformly floored. They weren't jealous, they were happy; I almost felt equal. Not that I hadn't before, but this was different, as if a part of my life was just beginning; this bike was going to be the start of it all.

CHAPTER 2

THE FOLLOWING DAY I WENT TO SCHOOL without any discussions: The happier I kept my mom, the more reasonable she'd be about the bike.

She had this thing about bikes. Maybe it was on my mother's side, maybe my father's—some uncle had gotten hit by a truck while he was on a bike and killed instantly. It'd thrown a weird, black, biking cloud over the whole family. My mother never learned to ride. Couldn't say I remembered my pop on one much either, growing up.

So I got my things together and headed out. My mother had already left, but there'd be a note advising me of some bullshit sundown curfew or something. I had to come home at a reasonable hour—in case the need arose to use my own bathroom—so as not to disrupt her patients while they were receiving mental care in the living room from the bosom of my own. If only therapy rubbed off.

I'd walked to Chelsea a million times before. My hair was wet, but it dried quickly in the warm air; the light was bright and clean but not too blinding as I passed Ray's *Pizza* (*the* original one, if you could believe it, though it *had* always been there when I was a kid, so maybe). My mother had promised me that, when we moved to the city, she would put us within blocks of the place. It really meant a lot to her, a New York tradition. We were also situated within spitting distance of Washington Square. The friends I met there changed over time, though once you knew the Jamaican herb dealers, they always knew you.

I kept heading west on the sunny side of Eleventh, crossed Seventh Avenue—moved cautiously past the spot where a horrific accident had taken the lives of three children under the wheels of a Mack truck while their mother looked on in horror. I made my way across the street and successfully reached the other side; the accident had happened a year earlier, but it still gave me chills. I passed the Korean market on the corner. The sidewalk had been freshly hosed and had the musky smell of wet concrete when the sun hits it and it starts smoking with steam. I didn't know why they'd become known as Korean markets, or why Korean people owned the multitude of stepped-up bodegas in the city, but they did—an untapped resource until they came along. Fresh fruit lined boxes covered with ice, and they had nice flowers for a couple of bucks.

I headed up Eighth Avenue, entering the Chelsea of the Eighties. It was still mostly Puerto Rican and not quite as gay as it would later become when the neighborhood went through its complete gentrification. I glanced through the plate glass window of one downscale diner-like place where I could sit all day eating the rice and beans and all the mouth-watering dishes that the local restaurants had to offer, for cheap; even the *aroma* at that early hour was pleasing. The usual gang of kids was choking on cigarettes—the girls wearing really bad, fake-gold bamboo earrings, Adidas shell tops, and enough makeup on their faces to block out the sun. They were all piled next to cars on the avenue, and they all threw smiles at me, but most of them, I'd long concluded, would be pregnant dropouts in a few years.

Just before I reached the school gates, I passed my sister and her friends sitting in plain view of the guards. She and I were nice enough to each other—twenty months apart (i.e., too close in age to hang), though I had no problem pushing in the face of anyone who messed with her regardless of size. We caught sight of each other and shared a silent laugh, having mutually agreed to keep the lie of walking to school "together" between us. We figured what our mother didn't know wasn't going to kill her. Dana was much more of a goody two-shoes anyway, and I didn't need it weighing on *her* conscience when I took a different route to school altogether, via a cross-town bus, to a matinee.

We were enrolled in what was fondly known in the New York City system as a drop-in school. Not out, in. It meant any fuck-up who'd gotten kicked out of God knew where, for God knew what, wound up at I.S. 70—the O. Henry School, named for the author who had been a denizen of the broader district. The school was "racially diverse and exciting," some Board of Education flunky had written on a funding application (which had soon brought the school to the brink of utter demise but allowed for spanking new BMWs to select members of that very Board as Christmas bonuses).

Since the student population of Mr. Porter's namesake was about fifty percent Black, thirty percent Puerto-Rican, and twenty percent White, it *was* "exciting," to say the least. Someone usually got jumped in Gym. There were kids like the legendary Billy Fletcher, who was seventeen in the eighth grade; he looked like poverty and had a constant case of plumber's crack and an ever-flowing snotty nose. If someone his age still had snot running, you left it alone; he was a *big* kid. Punks like Teddy and Pedro, who haunted the halls, eventually ended up in jail for life or (probably better off) dead. But all in all, in such an atmosphere where individual achievement was encouraged, I'd managed to learn a few things—like how to have one of my friends breathe real heavy and then, pushing on their chest, cause them to fall down, hitting the ground with a thud, passed out cold; it was awesome!

The principal was an ex-pro-wrestling Orthodox Jew, a pretty scary individual in his own right. I couldn't even be seen *talking* to Freddy inside the building, or I'd immediately get sent to the main office. Freddy had problems of his own going to school or, more the case, not going. He had threatened a teacher too and did more socializing than school work, but the two of us together were serious trouble. We both found the fame amusing.

I managed to make my way through the morning, listening for the rarely functioning lunch bell and picking at a piece of the chipped laminate on the top of my desk. Oddly enough, the school let us out for lunch, hoping that at least half came back. If I didn't cut out to roam the endless city streets, it was only because I'd heard a good fight was going to take place right after school, and I always observed the first rule of cutting: Never Return to the Scene of the Crime, not even for a *really* good fight. I'd dash from here to there, trying not to get caught by the merciless truant officers who drove around in unmarked cars with nothing better to do then ruin a kid's day. My friends and I had all heard fables of others with tear-filled eyes being dragged to school kicking and screaming, to await their chastisement at the hands of our sadistic principal. But neither I nor any of my friends had ever been stupid enough to feel that first-hand.

Finishing the last of my slice that afternoon, I felt drawn to return to school. Could it be I needed emotionally to earn the bike waiting for me like a gallant steed in the foyer of my apartment? Or was it that I didn't want to slide into the mold set forth for me by the law of probability? Whatever the case, at a quarter to two I was sitting in my English class, lost in a daydream of cruising down the street while my teacher's familiar voice droned on about Piggy and islands and henchmen—from what I would only much later recognize as one of the greatest of all books.

After school I quickly went through the ritual *heys* and *laters*, and started home with a bounce in my step. I tried to mix it up a little on the route. My pop had once told me, "Never take the same way twice—keeps life interesting." Once I rounded the corner of Fifth Avenue, it was a quick run (with maybe a hot dog on Fourteenth), and I'd be safely home.

But Fourteenth Street in the Village was an animal all its own. Three-card monte games were usually proceeding in droves, and being a city kid, I was drawn to them. But I was more savvy then your average Joe Blow walking down the street, which translated into not joining the suckers losing twenties left and right, chasing the bitch, even if I had the money. I figured it was normal to want to watch, what the fuck; it was like a train wreck. It usually only took two or three minutes for me to figure out who was playing with the dealer—a glance that dragged for too long, or the inevitable cleanup that never happened to anyone else when they played; the bent corner on the card made me laugh. Monty isn't about watching where the dealer is going to throw the queen, or which card is bent; it's about knowing at what point he throws you the curve ball—flipping off the top card instead of the bottom one. The greatest feats of slight-of-hand occur in card selection.

I turned my attention to the watcher—some crackhead—who worked in cahoots with the others, watching the street for cops. I stayed for another minute or two, finished my hotdog, and headed down the avenue toward my apartment. My family and I had been lucky when we found our two-bedroom on Fifth Avenue in Greenwich Village; it looked great on paper.

When I got there, a daily face appeared before me: Pete the elevator man, a bona fide character. He had seemed, even on first encounter, at least a hundred and two. But over the years, he'd *gotten* really old and, at that moment, was sitting on the radiator by the door, gumming apple slices.

I realized that my mom was probably still in session with some freak (I had actually been walking in the park with her once when a bag lady called to her by her first name, so "freak" was, I thought, a suitable term). I threw my book bag on the floor and was sitting on the lobby seat that had accommodated my ass for nearly a decade—staring at the ceiling molding, making it shift around with my eyes. I had met Ed Koch in that lobby—and, more important, John McEnroe.

But I was impatient that day. I twisted in my seat when I asked, "How long they been up there for, Petey?"

It was a ritual. My mother didn't call for secrecy—no sneaking patients in and out or saying they were relatives who visited weekly and occasionally changed their gender. Jews and Italians share this not liking to talk about their business. I took pride in the way she'd gone for her master's when we were kids and changed the course of her life.

"Goddamit," the old man groused after a good long pause, running both hands over the pockets of his uniform jacket as if trying to frisk himself, "what do I look like to you, Davey? A friggin' *watch* dog?" Bits of apple flew from the corners of his mouth as he spoke. "I got *shit* to do!" he half-mumbled to himself. "Can't hang like some kind of a friggin' animal watching for some lunatic coming down from the fourteenth floor, now, can I?" He went back to gumming the bejeezus out of that apple.

When it seemed to me that a couple of minutes had gone by, I loped toward the elevator and waited for Pete to meander over, take his place by the brass throttle, and carry us toward my awaiting tedium.

I didn't dare knock—though it was great to see my mom come to the door with the phony what-are-you doing-here smile. I could've told her I'd just completed a high-speed police chase after knocking over a bank and was popping in to change clothes, and she wouldn't have cracked. Instead, I sat patiently on the steps of the stairwell next to my front door.

After what seemed like an eternity, I finally heard her voice coming closer and closer and echoing in the foyer. She invariably offered the same chitchat on the way out, the next weeks and the sounds greats. The patients looked at me weirdly, I assumed because of a curiosity they had about her private life. Or maybe they were wondering what a twelve-year-old degenerate snot-nose had done to incite regular sessions with a therapist. Whatever the case, I smiled at the nice lady in the hall and backed my way into the apartment.

My mom came to me with open arms and asked, "Where's my kiss, huh?"

I sheepishly sucked at my teeth and replied, "Come on! I'm not a baby, Mom!"

Whereat she laughed, and we got the hug over with as she grabbed my face and roughly but tenderly kissed my cheek. "How was your day?" she asked.

I described the trivialities of school and my walk home; but any day that there wasn't a message from the guidance counselor was a victory. I glanced at my pride and joy leaning in the corner. (*Gotta* lean, bro; only babies got kickstands. Or if you got the room, you flip it on its head so the wheels move freely. But my mother wasn't going to have it like that in her living room.) I got a rush, almost a loss of breath, every time I looked at it. But as I turned around, her look just completely shattered my mood. It was the look of *No*.

Parents have a lot of looks, but nothing quite matches the look of *No*. I got up and headed nonchalantly toward the bike, as if I hadn't even seen her. But that was like being outside and not seeing the sky.

"Where do you think *you're* going?" she asked. Her tone contained a suggestion of anger from which arose the slightest effervescence of sarcasm.

"What're you *talking* about?" I asked sluggishly, having led with naiveté, a poor choice.

"Don't get smart with *me*," she said. "You and I had a deal when you got that *thing* that everything else came first—including walking the dog—before you can even think of riding it!"

She was pretty easy to fight with, but I had learned (in one of the more thought-provoking moments of my life) to pick my battles wisely. I gave in quickly and, since the call of the wild and my bike were waiting, grabbed the family dog and left.

Tammy was an old girl by then. She had been more a gift to my mother before Dana was born, but that dog and I had a real connection. It isn't easy growing up with two kids constantly pulling and probing at you—but Tammy seemed to enjoy it. We waited by the elevator; I was peering through the crack of the door, watching the sparks fly in the shaft as the elevator came to life and drew closer and closer to our floor.

When Petey got there and opened up the door, it was as if we were truly messing up his plans by wanting to leave our apartment. "Aw, Jesus," he bellowed, "up and down—why don't you make up your mind?"

"Yeah, all right, Petey Boy," I retorted. "You just do your job, all right there, pally?" The condescending tone failed to show respect for the man's years, but hey—didn't I have to walk the dog in order to go out again not ten minutes from now with my *bike*? Didn't I? I wondered if Pete actually knew how much of a pain in the ass I meant to be, considering the circumstance I was in.

We headed up Eleventh Street, boy and dog, trying to get business done quickly, but Tammy wasn't one to rush. As we meandered up the block, I scoped out the streets for a place I and the Mongoose would ride. "Jump that curb," I said to myself, quickly turned back, and added, "Yeah, I think that can be done."

I continued talking to myself until the dog was finished. "Come *on*, girl!" I tugged at the leash, hoping that for once she wouldn't act like her usual self.

What happened next was utterly remarkable. Tammy looked up at me, somehow sensed this yearning to go and ride, to feel that pulse of life, and she began to trot. She was thirteen at the time, so breathing was an achievement, let alone such expenditure.

I ran just a bit in front of her as we headed back. The sideways jog, the leash dragging behind, had a rhythmic life of its own as it jangled over the cracks in the sidewalk. She really looked proud that afternoon, the expression on her face quite human, though her days in the sunshine were growing few.

When I got back upstairs, my mother was standing at the kitchen counter, reading a phone bill. "Did she do anything?"

"Yeah, well, kind of," I told her.

Seeming confused and, almost at the end of her daily rope, looked at me. "Why is it so hard for you to give me a straight answer?"

Admittedly I'd been rather vague. "She squatted half a dozen times, but I doubt if anything came out *all* the time. It's all about percentages," I immediately turned, avoiding confrontation, and hurried down the hallway to my room.

I quickly changed into my riding gear, took a once-over in the mirror, and headed out of my room and toward the steed. My mother stopped me in the foyer, looked in my eyes, and with both hands on my cheeks warned, "Be careful." She kissed me and stood back to watch her son grow up.

With a half-cocked smile I replied, "I will, Ma. I love you."

That was all she'd wanted all day; having given it to her, I headed out, standing on the pedals, and coasted to the elevator. Pete got there and gave me the usual business. "I'm not taking you back up, goddamn it."

We stopped on the eighth floor with a jerk; Pete, without moving his body, stretched out an arm to pull the gate and drop the mechanism to open the door.

"Hey, champ, what you got there? Wow! That's some sensational bike you got." Murray was an older gent with a wife half his age who you could tell found it tough to keep up with him. He wore his slacks with a great crease and had a sort of slide in his step. He was truly old school. We relished the look of the bike together; I thanked him and headed out.

CHAPTER 3

CRUISING AT LAST DOWN FIFTH AVENUE, I felt tireless that afternoon. I pedaled faster and faster in the street—where I wasn't supposed to, but nothing was like riding on smooth asphalt.

When I got to the park, I rode around the Arch standing on my pedals and looked for my BMX friends, some guys who weren't from the neighborhood and liked the park for its hills and possible trick spots. They were my first steps in a life of mixing circles. I saw a few of them and rode around, trying to learn the Ollie and End-os. I wasn't getting much height as I applied the front brake to bring the rear tire up, but that didn't matter; I was in a world of my own. My new bike wasn't such a big deal to that posse—they all had ones just like it. Sometimes they all left the park together, usually heading uptown to the East Side.

It was cool riding in a pack with them. There were at least ten of them that day as we rolled up Eighth Street to Third Avenue. It made my heart race to ride with that traffic. Up there, it was different—*so* different from my neighborhood. The cars seemed to move faster and were almost angry for having to work so hard. The smell of brake dust filled my nose, and the taste stayed in the back of my throat.

It wasn't as if I was scared, but the family thing did hang somewhere in the background: I was predestined to fuck up with a bicycle. I looked over at this kid Jayce, straight off the pages of some surfer magazine.

"How far up we going?" I screamed across the distance between us.

With the wind silencing every uttered word, he cried, "Maybe we'll hit that park up on Sixty-something—got some good jumps."

I was starting to feel the burn in my legs. I wasn't used to that much riding—but you couldn't just cut out and head home, that would really be un-cool. You had to go the duration. Heart racing, I felt the sweat pool on the back of my neck, roll down in tears, and well up on my lower back. We raced with the cars up Third, watching out for the yutz who didn't look up while stepping off the curb, cutting between the cars, crossing the street in kamikaze flight.

I started pedaling faster, and my mind jumped to when I was about nine or ten, walking on University Place, heading toward my house. It had been summer, and the street had had that stench of garbage that fills up your nose like ammonia. I'd seen Twelfth Street was being blocked off by a perspiring pig making overtime. I had speeded up toward the scene as most boys my age did, snuck between the whirling ambulance lights, and, passing the row of police holding back the crowds, come upon a biker who lay like a crumpled piece of paper on the hood of a taxicab, uttering screams one could only mimic if small needles were being shoved into their eyes. And then, when the biker's head, swinging back and forth from side to side, caught my glance, they locked and seared as he spoke a silent language to me clenching in pain. His side had been almost exploded, and what seemed like intestines and clotted blood had oozed out of it. "Don't ever ride a bike, kid! Not in *this* city!" he'd said, almost with the breath of angels.

When the biker passed out, some cop had leaned over in my face and said, "You can be arrested for even *being* here! It's a *crime* scene, you know!" The stench of coffee and what smelled like vomit on his breath had lingered in the air as I backed up, staring straight at him, and left.

When I slipped back to reality, the guys were already screwing around in the school playground up on Sixty-fifth. I was far away from any life I knew. We all messed around for a while, with me successfully completing some pedal grinds, feeling so good on my bike. It was more than anything I could've asked for.

After a while, it started getting late and we decided in unison to split up. In the city, it could take hours figuring out where to go. Everyone had a routine and seldom strayed. The one thing that leaned in my mind was the video games at Positively's, one of Eighth Street's finest pizzerias; plus it was close to home. I headed back down with a few of the crew who had to hit the hills in the park one more time.

By the time we got there, twilight was beginning to descend. We'd decided to coast down Fifth: cabbies mostly, with the occasional truck and the never-ending buses. There were always rumors of kids holding onto the backs of the buses while they rode their bikes. I had never seen such a thing with my own eyes, but in the city, anything is possible. At around Twentieth Street I felt my nose begin to run even quicker against the sleeve that wiped it, but I kept smiling.

We got to Eighth and headed down against the traffic. When we hit MacDougal, we all split up, with a couple of the guys going to the hills and Jayce and me going to the pizzeria. We headed down the street and reached Positively's. I coasted up, balancing on one pedal like a pro, put my bike up inside, against the wall, and looked to see which game machines were available while Jayce, always paranoid, locked up his outside.

Jayce headed to relieve himself while I considered my options. Dragon Slayer was an old favorite, but *man* did it eat quarters. I got change from Izzy, the only Albanian pizza arm I knew, and started playing. I'd been into it for a bit when I realized I was getting claustrophobic. A couple of kids who weren't locals were watching my every move. "Move *that* way, man!" said one young black kid, egging me on.

"I got it. Thanks, though." Sarcastic reply, I thought, but it *was* my game.

"Come on, man, I can play better—you wanna see?" The little black kid was practically grabbing the joystick as he asked. It took all my effort to maintain focus on the game.

All of a sudden, though, I felt the stares back off me.

I barely heard Izzy calling. "Hey, David, isn't that *your bike?*" I lifted my head up—staring at the screen, knowing exactly what was happening before I even turned. Izzy was halfway over the counter by the time I got to the door.

The oldest trick in the book, and I'd fallen for it: *Distraction and Collection.* I'd fucked up bad. My bike was long gone; I barely caught that same little kid flipping me the finger from a block away. All three kids were on my bike, a consortium of thieves. Forget calling the cops; it was my loss.

"Sorry, kid—looked like a nice bike, too," said Izzy, heading back into the shop and toward his station for flipping dough.

I sat down on the curb and held my head in my hands. All my dreams had vanished around that corner. I looked at the ground and cried angry tears, cursing anything I could think of. I was going to have to tell my pop—he was going to freak out, and I'd never be trusted again.

I got up and started walking almost instinctively toward the park, my mind so filled with hate and anger I envisioned those kids getting hit by a truck. Crushed under the wheels. But the snot kept running down my face, and there wasn't enough sleeve to wipe it all. I felt my walk turn into a trot as I picked up speed. I felt the blurring of spring pass my face, and the warm air on my cheeks. I could *see* the air as my speed picked up, till I was in full sprint. I entered the park. Birds and squirrels moved out of my way, almost in a flurry; they owed me. I felt blind but directed as I ran to the hills and up. I raced past as the snot on my face dried with my innocence. I was flying.

CHAPTER 4

I COULDN'T IMAGINE WHO'D COME UP with the chocolate racket, but someone in the Board of Education had managed to associate it with jerking people's heartstrings; thus the Chocolate Drive had been born. Here's how it went: The kids sold as many bars as possible and would be rewarded with crap jackets and t-shirts; the school would benefit from at least twenty-five percent of the actual adjusted net earnings of the said chocolate bars, with the rest falling through the cracks and into the coffers of the B-of-E bureaucracy.

But I knew there had to be *some* hustle room in there for us sweet enterprising children. I figured if I managed to pilfer at least a couple of dollars on the side, maybe it would be worth it. Besides, the project might momentarily appease my already fed-up mother. I looked at the thing as an exercise in giving back to the community.

After I got upstairs with my mistreated book bag and a stack of forms, I put my stuff down on the kitchen table and went to the

fridge to look for something to eat. I had just come from a modeling go-see strangely enough near my house. I had headed from
school, a little disheveled in my morning garb, to the East Side. The
place I was supposed to be going was nestled among commercial
restaurants and high-rises, which I thought a bit strange. I found
the address and buzzed the push button that looked like it'd had
the name changed a hundred or so times. Through the garble I
heard a voice ask, "Yes?"

I was astonished that a voice had come up at all. Crinkling my
forehead, I couldn't remember what I was there for. I looked at the
piece of paper I'd shoved in my pocket and saw a name on the bottom of it. "I'm here for Steve?"

There was a long pause that seemed like an eternity. "Come up
to five," the wary voice on the other end commanded. I heard an almost inaudible noise and felt a slight buzz in the hand holding the
bar on the door. I walked through a dimly lit hallway and saw an
elevator on my left. I pushed the call button and waited. Had I seen
a staircase, I would have surely taken it, since the elevator looked
like it hadn't been serviced since World War II. It came down with
a thud and the door opened. It was lined with that gray laminate
that had been keyed by many young passengers during their ride up.
The door closed with another thud, and I just prayed it would rise.

It was a very slow ride to five. After a moment, the elevator
jerked to a stop; I was extremely thankful. The door opened with
a thud and a bounce, and I got off. I looked to my left, pulled the
piece of paper out of my pocket again, but didn't see an office
number. This didn't seem to matter when I turned around and saw
a line of chairs to my right. As I walked over, I noticed an assort-

ment of guys my age sitting in them, trying to look cool. Some had their stage mothers with them: babies. The one thing my mother wasn't going to do for my chosen career was schlep me around to try to get a gig.

As I approached, I felt their eyes on me. I pretended I didn't see them. Just remain cool, I thought. I walked to the door next to the chairs and saw a piece of paper with names written on it, and a half-chewed pencil dangling from a piece of string; very classy. I chicken-scratched my name and looked for a chair (I still had no idea what I was there for but figured it would soon become clear). I found one near the end, next to some kid who looked Latino, nothing like me, and was wearing a pretty bad mullet, acid-washed jeans, and a denim jacket. He looked at me with a brace-filled smile. I hesitantly smiled back and sat down, chucking my book bag under my chair. I looked at the gray wall dressed up with a stripe in front of me. The whole place screamed *low-rent*. I looked back at the kid, who was now looking at me, seeming anxious to talk. "Hey, I'm Ruben," he said, sticking his hand out.

"Hey, what's up? I'm David." I grabbed the hand and felt a fish-like grasp—always a bad sign, my uncle had always told me. I gripped it hard but not in a menacing way. We sat there for a second or two in silence.

"So how'd you hear about it?" he asked in a roundabout way. I wasn't sure what he meant; I thought it was a regular modeling call.

"My agency just sent me up here. Isn't that the typical way?"

"Agency?" he said; his brow crinkled a bit, and his eyes widened in disbelief.

"Well, yeah—isn't this a modeling call?"

Ruben looked at me and shrugged. It appeared our young friend was crashing this one. I started to wonder what I was even doing there. The door at the end of the hall opened, and a Michael Jackson look-alike came out. What the fuck? He was followed out by a nerdy-looking guy with a clipboard, who looked up and down the hall. "Ruben Rodriguez?" he shouted as if there were a hundred people sitting there.

"Well, gotta go, I guess," Ruben said. He put a painter's hat on backwards, got up adjusting his jeans, and followed the guy into the room. I started to really wonder what in the hell I was doing there. I'd been to some crazy calls before but none so mysterious. I sat there for about five minutes and contemplated splitting but thought the better of it since I knew it would get back to Annabella. I could only imagine the shit hitting the fan.

I was staring off when the door opened again. Ruben came out grinning slightly and walked right past me. I looked up from my shrug with my elbows resting on my knees, just in time to see him walk by. He turned when he hit the elevators and, in a loud whisper, said, "Break a leg, man." Then he and his brace-filled face were gone.

The same nerdy-looking guy came out. "David?" he asked. I agree my handwriting wasn't the sharpest, but I thought it wasn't entirely illegible.

"Yeah, that's me. Sorry you couldn't read the last name, I'm working on it." The guy gave me a half smile for my attempted humor as I got up from the chair and followed him into the room. It was pretty big in there, kind of a dance class- looking space with mirrors lining one wall and a pretty large guy sitting behind a card table on the other side. He was wearing a safari jacket with a cheesy dress shirt underneath. His hair was in a bad fold-over, and his teeth, slightly yellowed, lay a bit bucked out of his mouth. There were about a million Styrofoam coffee cups scattered on the table and a legal pad sitting in front of him.

"So what do you do?" he asked to me, just long enough to take a slug of what I assumed was coffee.

I wasn't really sure what he had meant by that. "Huh?" I wasn't trying to be a smart-ass, but I was completely baffled. "What is this job for?" I asked.

The guy looked at me like he was the King of Sheba and I was supposed to know his family crest. "I'm putting together a world-class band made up of young entertainers. If you don't know what you're here for, you're probably in the wrong place," he added, with a trace of disgust in his voice. I thought for a second: I might not want to go to the party, but I'd certainly like an invitation.

I looked at the guy and put on a bit of a smile. "Well, I came here from my modeling agency, but I play guitar and sing." I had learned to play a year or so before, but he didn't need to know the details.

"Oh, really." He started running through some of his pad, looking for what appeared to be notes. "A modeling singer, huh? Who plays guitar. Very interesting." He continued to search, not seeming too impressed, but then suddenly stopped turning pages and closed the pad. "Okay, sing for me," he said, putting his hands behind his head and leaned back in his chair.

I hadn't expected to hear that. "What, now?" I said, surprised.

"Yeah, now," he said rather smugly, and waited. I thought about it for a second. I didn't think I'd want the job regardless, it looked like a pretty cheesy deal, but I wasn't going to let him scare me off either. "OK. Well I guess I'll have to sing it *a capella*, since I didn't bring my guitar," I said, trying to pump myself to get moving. He shrugged, not seeming to care much. I had a song in my head that my dad had taught me when I was little. It was a little corny but was the first song that I'd learned to play on the guitar, and I knew it all the way through. I belted it like I owned it. I had gotten about halfway through when he stopped me.

"Pretty good. You're not a bad-looking kid either. I may be able to use you." Use me? He stood up, and the first thing I noticed were a bad pair of polyester slacks. He walked around the table and picked what looked like a photo album off the floor, which he coveted as he walked over. "How do you feel about gold lamé shirts?"

"What's that?" I kinda thought they were the shiny ones Donny Osmond wore on his show. He opened the book, and lo and behold there were actual photographs of guys singing at what looked like bar mitzvahs or some sweet sixteen in cheesy gold shirts! I almost cracked up.

"I don't think this is for me, but thanks," I said as I turned toward the door.

"How do you think Menudo started out, huh?" he said, closing the book and loping back toward his seat. Comparing what he wanted me to do to some bad Latin boy band was more than enough glue to bind my decision. I smiled and turned, "Maybe being in a band isn't in the cards for me, but thanks for listening." I opened the door and looked at the row of saps sitting there salivating. I didn't think they would have turned it down, but then again, maybe if I looked like them, I wouldn't have either.

SINCE IT WAS MONDAY, SOME OF THE WEEKEND'S cold cuts should still've been lying on the middle shelf, but my view was temporarily blocked by something seemingly disgusting wrapped in tinfoil. When my mom was feeling especially kind—and eager to express her love in the Jewish way—she would go out to Bleeker Street and make the rounds on Saturday morning. She would first go to Fiacco's for all the deli meats—usually salami, turkey, and roast beef. When you walked into that store, it had the gamy smell of fresh prosciutto. All the women would stand on line after taking a number and kibbitz on a floor covered with a fresh coat of sawdust.

Then she stopped at Murray's Cheese Shop for some mozzarella and muenster. Old man Murray, one of the sweetest people around, took care of customers as people had in the old days, when those who worked in a place like that really cared about them.

Next, the illustrious Zito's for a loaf of the finest Italian bread. Antonio Zito, from Palermo, had opened the place in 1924 and still owned it. His grandson Anthony had run it for a while and had forearms like Popeye, which he told us kids he'd gotten from working too hard. We figured his wife just never gave him any. Freddy lived next door to Zito's—the yeast smell permeated his apartment all the time. After awhile, you just got used to it.

I fished arm-deep and grabbed the cold cuts; there was even enough of the good bread to make a sandwich fit for a king. After I cut off a nice hunk of the loaf and sliced it in half, I neatly stacked the meats on first, then the cheese, and at last the perfect combination of mustard and mayonnaise. After surveying the kitchen mess I'd managed to create in five minutes, I took my piled-high plate, grabbed the forms, and moved into the living room, where I started going through the television channels.

The door opened.

"Hey," I heard over my shoulder. I turned to see my sister, tired after her travel home.

"How long was it today?" I asked, taking a huge bite of my masterpiece. She'd gotten into an honors school and had to ride the train every day to Brooklyn. She was getting used to it, but it gave her a glaze. She dropped her book bag on the floor and kicked off her shoes before moving into a cross-legged position on the couch.

"It wasn't too bad today. I didn't get a seat on the way there. Some asshole snaked it right from under me! God! That fucking sucks," she said, moving for my sandwich as I recoiled, but with a smirk on my face I gave it to her anyway. She looked at the sandwich for a full thirty seconds before deciding where the perfect bite would be. *That* was my sister.

"I have to sell the chocolate again. It's so humiliating. Walking up and down those halls—you know how the building is." Since there were few kids in it, the neighbors didn't mind me hitting them up every couple of months for something or another, but the Stationery Fiasco had made people a little leery. Had it been my fault the company went bankrupt before they all got their orders filled?

My sister grabbed the remote and flipped to an old *Gilligan's Island* re-run.

"Just suck it up," she said with her mouthful and a bit of mayo on her chin. "Makes Mom happy when you accomplish something." Spoken like the true daughter of a therapist. She passed the sandwich back. Tammy meandered over to me and hung her head after sniffing the air, knowing my guilt wouldn't take long to set in. That dog had a look of starvation on her that could melt stone. I reluctantly ripped off a bit of the meat and gave it to her; she quickly retreated, swallowing it whole.

I finished the sandwich and thought over the situation as I walked to the window to consider tossing a water balloon. Was simple enough: You go around and hock chocolate. The bars had been floating around for a few years. *World's Finest*, they read right on the corner opposite the McDonald's logo, and your school's name slammed right in the middle. I didn't think it would be too hard a sell. Thinking better of the criminal act, I grabbed the forms, left my sister with the castaways, and went out the door.

There were only two floors above mine, so up I went, hitting the stairs two at a time. A woman named Jaclyn, who lived in the penthouse with her two kids, seemed nice enough—for a drunk. Maybe it was a Southern thing. I rang the bell and waited.

After a minute I heard some stumbling, and she answered the door with a look of hesitation on her face. It took her a moment to recognize who was standing there. She tried to stand up straight in the doorway and said, "Hello, David, how are you today? You want to come in for a drink?" She seemed to take pride in remembering my name, as if I was the newest delivery guy from the grocery store.

Contemplating this, I chuckled in embarrassment as I said, "Well, I would, if I wasn't twelve—but how 'bout a cigarette?" I suggested with a devilish grin.

She started laughing. "Of course you are, David, I know that. I was just joking. . . . A cigarette, you said?" Unsteadily handing over the pack, she struck the lighter to no avail. I grabbed it, lit up, and blew a perfect smoke ring. With the ever-flowing scotch glass in her right hand and a cigarette in the other that had an ash balancing as long as her pinky, she tried hard to focus on what I was saying.

I took another drag and started my spiel. "I just got this stuff from school, you know, sort of a drive to try to get stuff for the gym or something? Maybe you guys want to buy some chocolate?" Exhale. Her kids went to private school, where they didn't do "that" sort of thing.

"How precious! Children, would you like some chocolate?" she turned around and asked the kids, who didn't seem to be around. The airs she had about her were similar to the ones people have about feeding the poor. "Now—how much do they run?" she asked in a voice way too slurred for four-thirty.

"Only a buck apiece," I said. "But I get stuff depending on how much I sell, so the more the merrier!" I put on my best smile. The charm seemed to render her totally helpless; she handed over a ten dollar-bill.

"Thanks a lot," I said. "I'll be by in a few days with the —"

Slam! I laughed. She probably wouldn't even remember the incident.

I stamped out my cigarette, headed back down the stairs to 15, and looked around. That floor had a certain smell to it that came from one of the apartments—nice but distinct, a mixture of potpourri and pot roast. I went over and knocked on the door of a couple named Suzanne and Mark. They were nice Midwesterners, and she was the one who had convinced my father and mother a few years before that I could model. My pop, a photographer most of his life, had taken some sunset headshots of me at Morton Street Pier. We'd taken the photos to her friend Annabella at the Ford Modeling Agency, and I'd been signed on the spot. Believe it or not, I'd been turning quite a bit of cash from it for the last few years, but booking the jobs was a trip in itself. I was amazed when I walked into rooms filled with racks of expensive clothes from designers I'd never even heard of. Plus the chicks—man, I somehow managed to suffer through.

I had a special place for Suzanne. She answered the door with an unforgettable smile and a gratifying look of surprise. "And what do I owe this pleasure to?" she asked, almost knowing what to expect.

I looked at her, mentally adjusted my jive; she wasn't just run of the mill. I had a little difficulty looking her in the eye, caused by the crush on her I'd always had. "Hey, well, you know, I have this school thing, and there's chocolate, if you want, you know. It's just a buck. . .um. . . ." I usually played it much cooler.

She felt my nervousness and, without even acknowledging it, replied, "I'll take three. Would you like cash?" She smiled, so smooth.

"If you don't mind," I managed to get out, took the cash, and continued on my way.

After some banging, I concluded that either (a) no one was home at the next few stops, or (b) they knew I was coming and were avoiding me. By the time I hit the eighth floor, my legs were starting to give out. But my first knock, as always, was at Murray's, who was home as usual and opened the door with a bang. "What's going on there, kiddo?" He always seemed to be at the apex of a dance move.

I looked at the man in awe, for he was the very definition of life. The apartment behind him was invariably neat as a pin. I was never sure if that was Murray or his wife, but it was lovely: Sinatra in the background, the words floating in the air as if in a dream. "Come on in! What're you selling today?"

We moved to the couches, where Murray perched on the edge of his seat, hanging on my every word.

"Well, Murray, you know that school I go to in Chelsea. We sell this stuff to—you know, buy stuff, gym equipment, you know?"

"Sure. Yeah, sure, I get the picture." Murray raised and lowered his brow. "Good for you," he added with a finger pointing straight up in the air.

I was glad for the man's support; he wouldn't have wanted him to think I was doing anything babyish. "Yeah," I replied. "We can win some stuff if we sell, you know, a lot, or the most, or whatever." I laughed at my own redundancy. "The chocolate's pretty good stuff, too," I added, not that I actually knew: I didn't eat a lot of sweets, since I was hyper enough to begin with.

"Well, you know, as it happens I just might have to buy some for the girls down at the office," Murray said as he stood up to get his clip. I never was too sure what he did for a living except that it was definitely on the up and up. "How much these bars of gold gonna set me back?" he asked as he stuck his hand in his front pocket and pulled out a wad that could've choked a cow.

"They're a buck a piece, Murray, but I think I can swing you a deal on a whole box if you'd like," I said with a smile. Murray's face lit up with the pride of a *bubbeleh*—he had always appreciated my spunk—gave a quick chuckle, and flipped a few bills off the wad. "You take twenty for the school, and ten for an enterprising young man who can really make some moves!"

"I can't take the extra cash from you, Murray," I said sheepishly. "You know, it's not like I earned it. It wouldn't feel right."

"Nonsense!" Murray insisted as he stood up and ushered me to the door. "A man should be paid for a day's work, no? And I don't think the school's gonna pay for your hustling up and down those steps, am I right? You take the ten, and you buy something for your mom then, okay?" Succumbing finally to the wisdom of my elder, I walked out the door a little richer and a little wiser.

I figured it was late enough in the day to ring Jimmy's bell. I'd made the mistake some years earlier of ringing before noon, and what I'd seen was shocking. So an appropriate time had been arranged: anytime after sunset. When I turned toward that apartment on the other side of the floor, I starting smelling the familiar fragrance of Jimmy's place—a combination of patchouli oil and all the wonderful women I had seen parading in and out of the apartment over the years. Jimmy acted like a rock star, but he looked like Howard Stern: tall, thin, and fuckin' cool. He made the Eighties seem like the Twenties had in the Fifties: I could only *imagine* what went on behind that closed door.

I rang the bell, and when the portal creaked open, a blonde nymph barely covered in a man's dress shirt greeted me. Jimmy's apartment had northern exposure and hardly got any sun, so the only light in the whole place was from a lamp covered in a scarf that stood bearing witness in the corner of the room. She was absolutely beautiful. I couldn't remember if I'd seen her in a movie or *Playboy*, but she was unforgettable.

"Aren't you just the cutest?" She had a dynamite smile, and her cheeks were rosy, as if she'd spent the afternoon hiking on a mountain in Utah. And as she leaned over to speak to me, she revealed perfectly round and subtle breasts that were practically falling out of her shirt and within striking distance of my eyes. It took all my savvy not to get caught looking. As she turned to call to Jimmy in the other room, I caught her silhouette, which revealed an absence of underwear. I had died and gone to heaven. "Baby, there's some gorgeous kid here wants to see you?"

A rustling followed and, in an instant, Jimmy came around the corner in true form: black leather pants and a silk kimono too small and untied at the waist. Looking nevertheless like something that the cat had dragged in, he smiled a toothy grin and asked, "What's up, Davey boy? . . . Is this kid something, or what?" he asked her. He came around to me and tousled my hair as he dragged me inside. It always made me feel like an adult, being able to hang with older folks. "Sit down, man, take a load off. You what something to drink, maybe a Coke or something? Hey, Debbie, you mind getting the kid a Coke? You met David? This here. . .is David. Great kid." Jimmy was ADD. Debbie smiled flirtatiously at me as she got up to grab the soda as well as a cigarette for herself.

"I'm cool, Jimmy, really. You don't have to go to any trouble or anything."

Jimmy stood up, looking around for a cigarette for himself. "You *hear* that?" he yelled, although the kitchen was not ten feet away. "Such a kid, huh? . . . No trouble, Davey, she's up anyway. So what can I do for you?" he asked, lighting his butt as he melted back into the leather sofa, tuning into the almost inaudible music in the background. I quietly filled him in on the whole school fund-raiser thing, and not two seconds later Jimmy's hand was reaching back to his jacket to grab some bills.

"How's for twenty?" He wasn't up on the going rate of chocolate.

"Yeah, Jimmy, twenty is good! Yeah, sure, you'll get like twenty bars," I said, as if the calculations were difficult and I really needed to think about it.

"Great, but, you know, give the chocolate to Debbie or your mom or something, alright? I can't stand the stuff."

Realizing the beauty was nowhere to be found, I said my good-byes and left Jimmy floating away as I headed toward the door. My next score wasn't far off.

CHAPTER 5

S LEEP GREW MORE AND MORE DIFFICULT as I got older. If insomnia wasn't keeping me up, there were times when I was dead asleep but walking. That'd started when I was six or seven, at a farm camp in Vermont one summer with my sister, and the first time I can recollect having night terrors.

The place itself was out of some Hallmark card—kids swinging on ropes into ponds, horses roaming in green pastures. They had a spot the whole camp went to on Friday nights for an outing. Everyone slept in a lean-to—plastic and branches—and for me, although it might have been a mere mile from camp, it felt like the deep woods. After a long night of eating, all the singing ceased and everyone went to sleep. I fumbled for the spot where I'd been told to lay my sleeping bag and crawled in. Going to sleep like that was freaky. Noises that could only be paired with the most frightening thoughts imaginable seemed to be coming at me from every side.

I awoke to pitch darkness. I felt cold and wet everywhere as I turned. *All right,* I thought, *just crawl—you can feel the other sleeping bags around you.* But I couldn't see. *What's that? Why are there people up? It doesn't make any sense. Just follow the voices. . .that's it.* I started wandering farther and farther from my makeshift bunk. *No, I don't want to play piggyback—I'm tired, and I wanna go to sleep.* The entities around me weren't bothered by my lack of energy or not wanting to be there with them. *But where'd I put my sleeping bag?* I felt a desperate need to find my place. Everyone standing around me, everything spinning, turning faster and faster. . .I just wanted to find my place and curl up. My mind raced as the shock of the situation sank in. I fumbled in the dark. *Why is it so dark?* My eyes were wide open. Cold, *very* cold. Tears started rolling down my face: I couldn't tell where to go, the empty and alone feelings indescribable, an endless falling into a bottomless pit. I felt the cold moisture of a tree as I stumbled back. *Stay by this tree and wait till light comes,* I thought. I was so *scared.* I felt the need to crawl until I could feel something again.

There was no light at all in the woods. I couldn't even see my hands in front of me. *"Mommy!"* I screamed, but nothing came out. It was if my voice were being choked by the horror I felt. *Why can't she hold me now? Why is everyone laughing at me?* I wanted to scream at them to stop, but I still had no voice. My throat had closed with tears. Fumbling, falling all over, my eyes registered a murky false light coming over the horizon, but in reality it was only two o'clock in the morning. The ambient temperature was numbing; dressed only in a t-shirt, I was shivering and truly feeling the chill, and the metallic taste in my mouth was the proof.

Just when I seemed at my breaking point, as if I was going to really lose it, I realized I was back in my sleeping bag. But had I ever left?—down, falling down, empty, warm, and mine.

I fell back asleep in the fetal position. When I awoke the next morning, I remembered nothing except a feeling of being teased the night before, one more seemingly cursed phenomenon in a string that would follow. But I would never forget it.

Lying in my bed on Fifth Avenue was different from the forests of Vermont. Only it had in the interval been determined that I not only walked in my sleep but unlocked doors as well. It must have taken some real Einstein to let a kid who rang the elevator at two-thirty in the morning go down to the lobby in his underwear and a t-shirt. Or maybe some twenty-year-old Puerto Rican swing shifter who'd been unlucky enough to get the shift at all and didn't give a shit about some kid and his problems.

I continued to stare out the window, still smoking a freshly un-crumpled cigarette; I couldn't wait for the night to be over. If I got two hours of sleep, I felt lucky. I don't know why my mind wouldn't turn off—whether it was anxiety or some kind of cry for help; either way, it sucked.

When morning started to speak, I just couldn't get up. My mother had tried numerous means of encouragement: throwing water, a braid of curses, and threats, all to no avail. Going to school wasn't in the cards for me most mornings. My sister, heading off to that long train ride, stopped in on the craziness already in pro-gress. She saw the water seeping toward the door and the pot that had contained it turned over by the radiator. She looked at me—my baggy eyes, and the dark circles, were statements of inner tur-moil, plus it wasn't difficult when you shared a common wall and window that let the smoke of my cigarettes drift into her room; I even had to cross through her domain to get to mine. Watching her in the doorway, one of my eyes locked in her direction, the other falling shamelessly behind my pillow. "You feel bad this morning, bro?" she asked, adjusting the bag on her shoulder, trying not to sound like a big sister but just be there. I shrugged; being sleep-deprived made the sadness I felt overwhelming. All the while I was pulling the blankets tighter around my body like a protective cocoon.

"Ma!" she screamed from the door. "I think you should just let him stay home? He looks kind of sick." She turned her head back to me.

"*You* get to school, young lady, and I'll deal with your brother!" our mother bellowed from the other room.

Dana shrugged, palms up. "I tried," she said softly. I had already flipped onto my side.

I heard the door slam at her exit and, moments later, footsteps approaching as I mentally prepared myself. My mother came in sighing, arms crossed, one hand on her forehead, the other clutching the cordless phone to her chest.

"Here," she said. "Take this, David." She held the phone out. She was standing not three feet from me, but I would have to get up if I wanted the receiver.

"Who is it?" I snapped.

"It's just someone that wants to talk to you." She was trying her best to be nonchalant; I smelled a con coming.

"I don't want to talk anybody." I forced my face deeper into the pillow trying to shut out the world.

"David, *please* take the phone," she said through clenched teeth.

"Why won't you tell me who it *is?*" I demanded, my words barely audible.

"David, take the goddamn *phone!*" She had that fire in her voice that reminded me of where I got mine.

"*I don't want to!*" I was by then half-seated, red-faced, and staring at her.

"David," she said, taking a second to compose herself, wavering slightly, "it's Mr. Hand, and he just wants to talk to you." Her voice was softening, becoming therapeutic.

"Mom, he's just gonna scream his head off at me," I said, fighting the tears that were welling, wanting to fall back into her bosom.

"Sweetie, I just think he wants to help and figure this out," she said, moving closer, like a lion tamer. She was getting concerned about my inability. I hadn't mentioned my continuing bouts of sleeplessness: Stupidly enough, I felt ashamed and alone.

"You promise he won't yell?" I pleaded. She nodded—she wanted to believe he would be kind and gentle with her boy, but Mr. Hand was the guidance counselor at my school and a real piece of work. He was probably not the best choice of candidates for working with impoverished kids, more suited to a nice institution out on Long island. The worst thing was the two distinct faces he manufactured for the parents and the students.

I realized the only way I was going to get some sleep that morning was to talk to the guy.

"All right, give me the phone," I said with resignation in my voice. She tossed the phone up the bunk and into my lap. I picked it up, held it up to my ear, and said simply, "Hello?"

"David. Finally we're on the phone together. Maybe we can get something accomplished." For a second I didn't understand the tone in the man's voice, then realized Mr. Hand wasn't sure whether my mom was on an extension. "Is your mom on the phone as well?"

"No," I said, wishing I hadn't as soon as I opened my mouth. Now he was sure he had privacy, the situation broke wide open.

"David, let me ask you something. Who the hell do you think you *are?* Someone special? Get your ass dressed and get into school right now, do you *hear* me? You are no better than any of the other underachievers that waste time here while the real students are fighting to learn something. I'm not your mother, and *I don't care* if you're tired!" he screamed with utter disgust in his voice.

She meanwhile was standing by, not knowing what was being said, and I watched her face as the softened cheeks turned into the registered horror mirrored in my own, almost as if I'd seen death and was coming back from the other side. I threw the phone. It landed on the hardwood floor and broke into pieces. I put my face in the pillow and screamed. It was loud and primitive.

Thirty minutes later I heard the door slam, and I was alone. I stared silently at the ceiling and watched the morning turn into afternoon.

After a while, I got out of bed, stumbled into the living room, and counted the money I'd raised. Tammy came over to me, happy to have an unexpected companion for the day. I would have to go back to school at some point, at least to pick up the chocolate, but I prayed I wouldn't see *that* fucking psycho.

I went into the kitchen and sat at the table that overlooked the inner courtyard of my building. I had over the years thrown many things out that window, awaiting the enormous bang that came when they hit the ground. I liked the solace of the dining room— since it didn't get any direct light, it always exuded tranquility. I'd sit there and sometimes smoke pot when I couldn't sleep, trying to blow every bit of smoke out the window for fear of my parents awakening out to the familiar smell that, if caught, would seriously bring the house down; they wouldn't appreciate a twelve-year-old getting stoned.

My parents had smoked at different times during their lives, and I could remember the feeling I had when I was six or seven— after I had changed and washed for bed—being able to sit with the adults, trying to be unseen by my mother's eye, finally having to say good night to my parents' guests, going to bed, and within moments silently coming back out of my room—hovering hidden in the doorway and hearing the sounds, smelling the decadence. But the watching was almost as fun as the being. Or so I'd thought at the time.

I figured I'd get dressed and try to collect a few more dollars before returning to school the next day—I might be able to get out of going one day, but two in a row? I wouldn't push it. I left my apartment and rang for the elevator. To my surprise, when it arrived, Eddy was on shift—a Yugoslav smartass.

"Hey, hey!" he said, with a fairly heavy accent. "What, you don't have to go to school anymore?"

"Wasn't feeling good today, Eddy," I said, knowing it wasn't going to end there.

"Sheesh, that is some kind of bullshit you got there." Eddy was pretty wise to my shenanigans by then. "If you were my kid, ha, I'd beat you with my belt if you didn't listen!" he said, sucked at his teeth, and laughed. Eddy was as strong as bull, and you could tell he'd had his share of beatings in life. "You need to go into the army, like *me!*" he continued as he turned a toothpick in his mouth. "In my country, everyone has to go to army. Makes you a man."

"You never know, I might just join up sometime." I had no intention of ever doing such a stupid thing, but it got Eddy off the subject. "Can you let me off at 3?" I added, hoping I'd be able to find people home.

"What, you want to bother the nice people?" Eddy said, sounding like a security guard at a club.

"I'm trying to sell candy bars for school. You want to buy some for your kids?" I asked with little optimism in my voice; he was a cheap fuck.

"My kids are selling the same shit in Queens, and I had to buy a box of it to make my wife happy," he told me as he dropped the throttle and opened the gate.

"Thanks anyway, Eddy. Wish me luck, okay?" I asked as I left.

"You don't need luck, kid. You some hustler!" he exclaimed as he closed the gate and headed down to the lobby, where he would sit and wait for his life to slip by.

The first door I rang on 3 was Stella's. She was a model, and breathtaking. She'd been around town with sports stars and celebrities, and had a freshness to her that reminded me of spring. I rang the door and waited, nervously fidgeting, staring at my shoes. The striped wallpaper threw me into a hypnotic trance when I stared at it long enough. The familiar blue door opened, revealing Stella in a black pantsuit. Hands on hips, she said, "Hey there, you! What you doing all the way down here?" She had always joked with me about how it was better to live higher up; I didn't get it.

"Hey, Stella," I retorted, trying not to look into her beautiful eyes that exposed a bewildering innocence. "I'm selling this chocolate. Do you eat chocolate? Anyway, it's for school, and we're supposed to sell so much, and. . . ." I drifted off as I tried not to stare but simply watch her eyes light up and dance with the thoughts she had.

"That reminds me of when I used to sell Girl Scout cookies back in D.C., when I was a little girl!" The thought of her in that cute little outfit was too much for me to bear.

"I *love* those cookies!" I said. Jesus Christ, had I really just said that?

But she replied, "Why don't I buy a box from you, and I can sell them to my friends and kind of help you out?" She continued, "It would kind of be like selling cookies." I was about to close on another whole box.

"Yeah, okay," I said quickly before she changed her mind. "That will be twenty bucks, okay?" I said with hesitation. I didn't want to shock her—it was a lot of money to me.

"No problem," she said, walked over to the closet, grabbed her purse, and pulled out her wallet. It seemed to be stuffed with cash. I later learned she was one of the biggest models of her time, that the love I felt for her was shared by millions; but she made me feel special. She rustled through, looking hard for such a small bill, and handed it over.

"There you go. Thanks!" She smiled and kissed me on the cheek.

In heaven, I walked to the other side of the floor and rang the bell of the legendary Max Gordon, a jazzman from way back who owned a little club in town called the Village Vanguard. The hunch-backed Mr. Max was only about five feet tall, had huge feet, wore an old fedora, and he always seemed to be smiling.

"Yes?" he said, with a voice made scratchy from too many years of cigarettes. He was speaking through the locked door—no fear, just old-school habits.

"Hey, Mr. Max. It's David from 14. I don't mean to bother you. I'm just selling chocolates for school—thought you might like to buy some." I heard the myriad of locks rattling as they were being opened, and then the old man appeared in all his glory.

"Well, don't just *stand* there. Come in, son, come in," he mumbled, as if life was one long scat. I entered an apartment piled with newspapers, all with the worn-out look of having being read through. The walls were adorned with images of places in Europe and the States where Gordon had played, some of which I hadn't heard of. He sat down on the couch just as a new record flipped onto the already spinning turntable. Thelonious Monk came up softly, and I watched Max fall into his chair and drift under a spell that time could not break.

"I played with him in my club, back in '74," he said as he lit another Nat Sherman. "One of the best on the keys in the business, if you ask me, and I know a thing or two," he added, exhaling smoke. I was too young to realize I was watching him grieve the loss of an old friend who had died tragically only a few nights before. Max had survived all the greats—Coltrane, Ella, and now the immortal Monk. He spoke about them with a heavy heart that could only be remedied by death. We think of death as an end; for some, it's a relief.

"Listen," he said. "You hear the way he switches keys? Like it was supposed to happen?"

I did have a great love of music but couldn't comprehend what Gordon was saying, so I nodded and replied, "Yeah, Mr. Max, I hear it." His eyes were closed, his fingers jamming to the music. He was too old and didn't have enough steam to play the many woodwinds he once had, but he could always jam in his mind.

I didn't want to interrupt, but I had to get moving. "So what do you think, Mr. Max, you want a couple of bars?" I asked, waving the forms in the air.

"Huh?" he said, startled, as if had forgotten why I was there. "Oh. Yeah," he said. "I'll take a few for the grandkids. They love chocolate."

He gave me some crumpled-up dollars, fell back, and was once again consumed by memories. "I played with him, you know," he called out to me as I was walking toward the door.

I turned back with a sharp feeling of sorrow in my heart. "Really? I never knew that, Mr. Max—that's wonderful." For a long moment I watched the old man who had long since become a friend, and listened to the effortless sound that sang out, and was reminded of the importance of walking to the sound of your own music.

CHAPTER 6

OVING OUT OF NEW JERSEY into Manhattan had made it easier for my mom to finish graduate school. But though I had spent the first few years of my life in Brooklyn, I wasn't prepared for Greenwich Village. I never felt adjusted; my parents thought I might have a learning disability.

I found being a latch-key kid strange, too. If my mother was heavily into her studies and my father was teaching in New Jersey, I was supposed to come directly home. I usually didn't. I found the streets a new place of comfort. I would roam the parks or go to Eighth Street. Whether they came from comfortable families or were runaways, kids were equals there. Of course a hierarchy existed, and there were certain places you never sat and people you didn't mess with. I felt like a doe in the woods.

I was ten the first time I did nitrous oxide. It was an easy escape from reality, but it didn't last long. I liked the feeling of time slowing down and the occasional fleeting loss of consciousness. I was taken under the wing of some older kids, possibly to my detriment. I was having a good time, so I didn't care.

I made some friends who were in a similar situation. I had started smoking cigarettes pretty regularly by the time I was twelve. It was a thing to do to be cool, but then it became a habit. I didn't have a job, so I took to stealing from my mom or dad if there was a purse or wallet around. I spent more and more time hanging around and getting into trouble.

The first time I met Jim, I was playing a video game at a place called Mamie'e Ice Cream Parlour. It had a few machines, and there was a place to sit and eat in the back, but I only went there to use the bathroom. The owners hated all the kids hanging out there but didn't mind us pumping whatever money we had into the Stargate Machine or Tron. There was even a Pac-Man. It got really cramped toward the front with all the kids pushing and shoving to jockey for a game. If you left a quarter, it was a marker to know you had next up, and people respected that.

I was playing Stargate. I wasn't the best at it, but I was doing pretty well when I crashed. The counter came up for extended play if you stuck another quarter in. I searched my pockets quickly but came up empty. That's when I heard a voice say, "Here—you seemed like you were doing pretty good," from behind me as he fed the machine. I kept playing on his quarters for a while. I figured it was nice of him to give them to me.

When I was finally done, I turned around to see the voice that was egging me on. He was a lot older than me and wore wire-rimmed glasses. He had his hands jammed in his coat pocket and a crooked smile. I noticed he had dark circles under his eyes.

"Hey, thanks," I said walking by him.

"Aw, that's no problem. You looked like you were professional at it or something." He told me his name and chuckled at his own comment. I laughed; I was okay at the game, but there were kids a lot better than me. I barely made the high scoreboard.

"Ah, I'm David, and nah, I mean I'm okay, but I could get a lot better if I had more quarters. But money doesn't grow on trees," I concluded. My dad said that all the time, and I had finally found a way to use it.

"Well, I might be able to help out. I like watching you play, and if I can give you a roll of quarters now and then, it isn't a big deal," he said as I walked out past him. I looked back and smiled awkwardly. He nodded and gave a half wave. No one had ever offered to give me money before for anything, so I wasn't sure what to say.

A few days later, I was at Positively Pizza, down the block from the ice cream place. It was crammed with kids as usual, especially since it was cold outside. I was waiting in line to play the Donkey Kong machine when I heard my name from across the way. I turned around and saw Jim sitting in a booth with a few older kids I had seen—they might have even been in high school. The booths at the pizza place were kinda cool they way they were shaped—you stepped down to the lower ones and stepped up to the top. I walked over. They had what was left of a whole pizza pie sitting on the table.

"You want a slice?" one of them asked me. I hadn't gone home, so I was pretty starved.

"Yeah, I mean if you have extra or something," I said sheepishly. I didn't want to seem like I was begging for it. I reached over, took a slice, and laid in on my palm before folding it in half; it was still warm. I sat on the stair happily munching my slice.

Turned out the guy was named Bob, and his girlfriend was Nat. She had gone to school with me but was a few years older; I didn't know how old Bob was, but he had a beard, so he must have been in high school at least. I could tell he was a huge guy from the way he was crammed into the booth.

I finished my slice and headed back over to the game. It was finally free, and I had a few quarters. While I was playing my game, I felt someone watching; I saw the reflection of Jim standing there in the screen. I heard a jingling sound and turned to see his hand in his pocket. "I'm ready to hand you quarters if you need," he said with a closed-mouth smile, adjusting the glasses on his face.

I played that machine for a while and finally lost interest. When I walked out, he walked with me. I headed up the block toward Fifth Avenue to get home. When we turned the corner, his building was on the left.

"I live right here. I actually have an Atari set up if you want to see it," he asked, holding the door open. I know my mom wouldn't want me to go in to someone's house, but he was from Eighth Street, so I figured it was okay. I went through one glass door into a little hallway that had another glass door leading to an elevator in the back of the lobby. It wasn't big, and the lift looked like it couldn't have fit more than three people at a time.

He led me down a hall—it looked like it could have been offices at one time. He unlocked one of the identical doors, which opened into a studio apartment that wouldn't fit more than the couch and a television. It was really hot in the apartment.

"They turn the steam on at Thanksgiving and they don't turn it off till Memorial Day," he said with a grin. I took my scarf off but kept my jacket on. I went over to the couch and sat down.

I saw an Atari on a shelf, with a bunch of dust on it, balancing on a wire TV stand. There was one door for a bathroom, and an opening for a kitchen the size of a closet.

"This is what you call an efficiency unit," he said, sitting on a folding chair in front of a window that overlooked Fifth. "Location, location, location!" I didn't understand what that meant, but if this was location, I thought, I would like a different one. He turned on the television and flicked a switch in the back to make the game console work. I sat cross-legged on the floor in front of it. He had a few games I had played, Asteroids and Mario Brothers, Warlords. I put the Mario in first. With his eyes glued to the TV, Jim moved backward and sat on the floor next to me. I played for a bit, but he talked so much it got annoying. He got up, walked over to the window, and sat on the folding chair.

"You want to see a movie? I think I have something in the VCR," he said, getting up again and moving toward the TV without hearing my response. I guess the video game was boring anyway. He fumbled with something in the back of the TV while I shuffled toward the couch behind me and leaned against it.

"I don't know what's in there—it's been a while since I turned it on," he said, grabbing a remote from the top of the set, and pushed a few buttons.

I heard the moaning first before the picture came on. Then came a poor-quality video with lines down the middle. It was some girl on her back having sex with two guys.

"Oh, how did that get in there?" I heard him say. ". . . Well, as long as it's on, you want to watch it?" I didn't know what to say. I felt my chest go *ba-boom ba-boom.* He was smirking when I looked at him.

"I mean, it's already on—we might as well watch it," he said, leaning back in his folding chair. We watched in silence. I felt like I couldn't speak. I felt myself growing as I watched the video in front of me. The woman on the bed had her legs in the air. There was some bad music playing along to it. I had seen Channel J on the cable box—they played short sex clips and had weird talk shows like *The Robin Byrd Show* or *Midnight Blue.* I know I wasn't supposed to watch them, but I did. This was much longer.

"Wow, that guy has some big dick, huh?" Jim said, moving over to the far end of the couch. "Mine isn't like that at all," he said with a guffaw. He started rubbing himself over his pants. I felt frozen. I didn't look his way. I wanted to run but couldn't stand up. The music and the moans became a drone I heard over my pounding heartbeat.

"I bet yours isn't that big either," he said with a laugh. "I even have a tape measure over here."

I looked over at him for the first time. "I'm just kidding," he said, laughing it off. "But I bet yours is still bigger than mine. I mean, mine is just average."

I hadn't thought about my size. I was still shorter than most of the guys in my class, but I didn't know about in our pants. I had learned to play with mine about a year before. But I hadn't done it with anyone else.

"I don't know," I said, staring at the images on the screen.

"Well, I mean if you want," he said hesitatingly, "I can just measure it for you," he continued. "I mean, it's no big deal, lots of guys do it," he said.

Maybe I was just being paranoid? Maybe this is what guys do with each other? I didn't want to be thought of as a little kid.

"Come on," he said, "it's no big deal," he continued, picking up the tape measure sitting on the radiator by the window. "Guys do it all the time, I swear," he said, and crossed his heart with his finger. I suddenly felt like I was making more of a big deal out of it. I stood up and walked over toward him. He pulled the tape out of the little metal case. He said, "You can pull your pants down, I'll measure it," very matter-of-factly. I unbuttoned my jeans and pulled my zipper down.

"Here, let me help you," he said grabbing both side of my jeans and tugging down all at once till they were at my thighs. I was fully erect and embarrassed. He nodded at what he saw, held my penis while he got the tape measure to the bottom, and pulled it to the tip.

"Yep, almost seven inches, definitely bigger than mine," he said, holding it for a moment longer before letting go with a chuckle. I grabbed my pants by the side and went over to sit back down on the couch. *Ba-boom ba-boom*: I sat there staring at the television again. He stood up, moved over to the couch, and sat on the far end. The film on the set seemed endless. "You don't mind if I jerk off, do you?" he said, opening his pants and pulling his dick out. *Ba-boom ba-boom.* I stared at the television, trying to be cool. Kids did this all the time. Even he said so. I tried to focus on the scene that was playing out before me. I couldn't hear anything. I felt the couch move as he went *whap, whap, whap*, pleasuring himself. There was sweat on my brow from the steam heat that hissed in the background.

"You can touch mine if you want," he said, again chuckling to himself. "I would even give you a hundred dollars to," he said, now openly laughing. I looked back at him. "It really isn't a big deal," he said, all the while playing with himself. He reached over and took my hand. I withdrew it and pulled away.

"You don't have to do anything you don't want to. I'm not going to tell anybody. Believe it or not, people you know have done the same thing," he said, bouncing his thighs together. I didn't know that *my* friends had done it. Maybe it *wasn't* a big deal. My mind was spinning. I felt him move closer to me.

"Okay, how 'bout if you don't move it means you want to," he said, still jerking on himself. I felt frozen and didn't know what to do as the moments ticked away like the sweat dripping down my back. I felt his hand grab mine. I hesitated, but he pulled it toward him. He put it on his penis and moved it up and down.

"Now, that isn't so bad is it?" he said, I looked over for the first time at what I was doing, and I saw the smirk on his face. I jerked my hand up and down. He took my hand and moved it faster all the while the moans from the television continued to play.

"Tell you what—if you let me suck on your dick, I will give you another hundred," he said, trying to make it sound again like it like it wasn't a big deal. I didn't say anything or move, other than my hand going up and down. I just heard the hiss of the heater in the corner. I didn't know people did this. I felt his penis in my hand for the first time and felt like I was doing something wrong and felt like crying.

"If you want me to do it, just pull your pants down," he said, again moving my hand up and down faster. *Ba-boom, ba-boom, ba-boom, ba-boom.* I didn't dare move.

"You know Rob, from Mamie's?" he said. I tried to draw my focus to what he was saying and running in my mind. Rob was older than me and more of a punk rocker, and we didn't talk much, but everyone on Eighth Street knew each other. I nodded silently. "Well, he does this with me all the time," he said, now nodding in affirmation. "It isn't a big deal for him," he said, moving his hands to his sides while I continued to robotically move my hand up and down. He moved his hand over to my thigh and held it there. I felt the sweat drip down the side of my face. We sat there for a few minutes in silence.

"Here, stand up for a second," he said. I let go long enough to rise. It was then I realized my jacket was still on. He slid over the couch a bit and in one move pulled it off, and he was right—even at twelve, mine was bigger than his. *Ba-boom, ba- boom.* He took it in his hands.

"If you don't say anything, I'm going to put it in my mouth," he said, daring me. I had no voice—the light was murky as I stood looking out at the building that I could see under the half-drawn venetian blind. There were people moving about, going from room to room, not knowing what was going on across the street. I felt his mouth on me and stared out the window. I felt sad that I could-n't speak up for myself. I had never had anyone do that to me. I felt his teeth ride from the bottom to the top like it was supposed to give me some kind of pleasure. He pushed me down and continued to suck on me. I just stared at the television unable to move or say a word.

He asked if I had come. I had climaxed a small drop that sat on the back of his hand. He got up and went over to the bathroom and washed his hands. I felt so disgusting, I still couldn't say a word as I sat up closing my pants.

"So Rob has done this with you?" I asked curiously.

"No, I was just kidding. You're the only one," he said, laughing again slightly at his own joke. "Just so you know, if you tell anyone about this, I have friends. Guys that will kill your family," he said very matter-of-factly.

"I won't say anything, I swear," I said, moving toward the closet-sized bathroom. I went in and took a pee, trying not to look in the mirror at myself, and felt tears well up in my eyes. I wiped away any sign of pain before I opened the door. I looked at Jim numb. He stuffed a bunch of twenty-dollar bills in my pocket. I took the two or three steps to the door.

"Let me know if you want to do it again," he said, opening the door, sticking his head out to see if anyone was around, stepping to the side to let me out.

I went down the hall from which I had come and pushed the button for the elevator. When it came, I stepped inside. Turning around to push the ground-floor button, I saw him standing in the doorway, staring at me. He was smiling and waving as if nothing had happened; to him, it hadn't. I rode down the elevator in silence.

A FEW DAYS LATER, I WAS STANDING in the hallway outside Room 304 right after the bell rang. The line of kids with their forms filled out, waiting their turn, was already running the length of the hall.

I'd barely made it back to school at all, but I had to pick up the chocolate. It was one of the days when I was "taking a long lunch," trying to fit in another modeling go-see. You had to hit a lot of those to finally get a job; it was all odds. I'd gotten off the train at Fifty-seventh Street, climbed to the surface, and got my bearings.

I'd felt a hand graze my shoulder, causing an immediate jump to the side while I pulled off my book bag and cocked it back like a weapon. But it'd turned out only to be some yokel in a jogging suit who was feeling the burning desire to be a Good Samaritan.

"Are you lost, son?" he had asked, taking his own pulse while jogging in place.

I'd done a double take after realizing the guy was even talking to me. "Do I *look* lost?" I had replied with all the sarcasm a twelve-year-old could muster. "Why don't you go and cruise in the park? *Capisce?*" I had turned east, leaving him stunned and bewildered in my wake.

I had known it was a pretty big job that I was going for, major label or something, to be a fit model; I'd figured I should at least show. I had reached to the big red 9 and swung a left into the lobby with really high ceilings and marble everywhere, checked the directory, and headed up to the eighteenth floor.

When I got off, I'd seen the hallway littered with beautiful women leaning against what I assumed was the wall leading to the office door. I'd gotten a smile from a brunette with turned-in knees, a short skirt, and way too much make-up for somebody who looked sixteen but was probably eleven. When I walked through the door, I'd seen more piles of women staring at me in chorus.

I had approached the desk. "I have an appointment, but I'm a little late. My name's David," I had said quietly to the receptionist, giving her my best smile but setting my sights low.

She had checked through her list and looked me up and down before uttering a word. "A little late? You were supposed to be here between eleven and twelve." The numerical clock behind her clearly read 12:45. She had turned back to me.

"Yeah, well, I couldn't get out of school till lunchtime, and that was at noon, and you know, catching the train? It never runs on time, and I go to school in Chelsea, so. . . ."

She'd put up a hand and risen without saying a word, then crossed the room to a pair of double doors. Not knowing quite what to do, I had looked at all the pretty girls now engrossed in magazines.

The receptionist came back after a minute or so. "This is a meeting to be a fit model. It is a *very* serious and special job. They've already started with the next category, but after I talked with R.L., he said he'd take a quick look at you. Come with me."

She had dragged me by the hand through the double door, which hadn't even stopped swinging. Inside, the three half-naked women who glanced my way had not been bothered by the disturbance; they'd been more focused on the man sitting in a leather club chair in front of them, smoking a cigarette and looking as if he'd just stepped off a beach in the Hamptons.

The woman had handed me a sweater and a pair of slacks off a rack in the corner. "Here," she'd said, physically turning my head back to her as she spoke. "Just put this on and walk toward him, wait a moment, turn, and walk back."

I had taken the clothes. "Where can I change?" She'd looked at me like I was an alien. "What, you mean change right here?" The girls had looked my way and smiled: Ah, how the tides can change.

"Your group was here forty-five minutes ago. You're lucky you're being seen at all."

I had dropped my bag and stripped down to my tighty-whities and socks, staring at the girls the whole time; luckily, modesty wasn't a part of my nature. The clothes had fit perfectly. I had done my dance and, believe it or not, got a steady job in the process. Sometimes it didn't matter when you got there, as long as it was the right time.

THE CONTRAST BETWEEN WHERE I'D JUST COME from and the hallway outside Room 304 at school blew my mind. I wasn't paying attention when the kid started talking to me. "How many did you sell?" he asked with an over-zealous smile that made me think he'd probably been dropped on the floor at birth. His glasses were horn-rimmed, black, and thick as brick. Under normal conditions, he wouldn't even have spoken to me; he must have had some notion that we were equals in line.

I looked at him and quickly said, "I don't know, I lost count." This was total bullshit—I knew every bit of the seventy-five dollars that was burning a hole in my pocket—but I had to be cool.

"Between my mom and Granny, I got almost twenty dollars collected!" said the boy with the eagerness of a puppy. There were kids in the public school system who seemed to slip through its proverbial fingers. This one was beckoning to be held back a year or two.

"Yeah? Really? You don't say," I replied as I scoped out the scene, not making eye contact. Looking left, I saw serious trouble coming down the pike. Billy Fletcher seemed to be shaking down people in line. Of course—the perfect situation. No teachers around but the one in the room, and students just lined up for the pickings; who would hear their muffled screams? Who the fuck had thought of this idea?

Billy was still way down the hall but quickly making his way forward. The corridor had the usual disinfectant smell, but it hardly covered up his stench. I grabbed the cash I had in my pocket and stuffed it in my sock. The other kid, completely clueless, asked with the innocence of a child in a sandbox, "What are you doing that for?" They should give sixth-graders an instruction booklet on survival in the real world of school.

"I'm doing exactly what you should be doing, if you know what's good for you," I said, straightening my pants so they didn't look like I'd been messing with them. I stood up, confident of circumventing any problem that might arise. The kid saw Billy and his crew making their way to the front. He turned to me and said, in a very matter-of-fact way, with a small grin curling up in the corners of his mouth, "He won't touch me—there's a teacher right in the next room!"

I was hoping the kid was well versed in karate or judo or had a machine gun in the back pocket of his Garanimals, because he was a sitting duck. "Suit yourself," I said. The feeling of the bullies getting closer and closer to me made the hairs on the back of my neck stand on end.

"Well, if it isn't young David. Hello, David, and how much

money did *you* raise for our piece-of-shit principal and his crooked school?" asked Billy, sauntering up to me in a shirt that was so tight the wads of stretch-marked flesh seeping out looked like Hefty bags filled with water. His walk had a shuffle to it, his arms propelling that massive form forward. The sneakers he wore had holes down to his sockless feet.

"Not me, Billy. You know, couldn't get anything together—just look." I shoved the blank form in Billy's face. Regardless of how much of it we sold, we had to turn the form in, blank or not. I hadn't filled out any paperwork, and I wouldn't until I was safely in the room with someone in authority. Getting out of the building with the goods—well, *that* presented a whole different set of problems.

"Now, come on, David, you didn't raise any money at all? What kind of a kid are you? You don't support your *school*? This boy is truly a menace," Billy added, nodding and looking for verification from his crew. With mock consent, he and the flunkies had a good laugh as they continued looking for someone to heist. Just as Billy was moving up the line, he spotted the kid behind me, and the laughter ceased.

"What about you?" Billy said, snatching the form out of the kid's hands, and ran his slimy fingers up and down the pages, figuring how much the kid was worth. "Well, well, well," he said almost disappointedly. "Only twenty-two dollars for your school? You should be ashamed!" He crumpled up the paper, grabbing the kid by his throat, and in an instant had him a foot off the floor against the wall. "Give me the money!" Billy said with a stench like still water on his breath. The look of terror that filled that kid's

eyes was hard to watch; he was gasping for breath and in total disbelief. Billy reached down and ripped his pockets open, revealing
a stack of singles. He took the money, dropped the kid at the same
time, and started to walk away.

"Come on, Billy, he's just some putz," I said in utter disbelief
that the words were coming out of my mouth at all. What was I,
fucking crazy? I didn't even *know* the kid.

More surprised still was Billy. "*What* did you say, Davey boy?"
he barked as he slowly turned around, his shifting mass of polyester
and blubber shaking with every move. The only thing more dim-
witted than confronting Billy at all was doing it in front of a crowd.
"You want to maybe stand up for your little boyfriend?" he
sneered.

I could feel the public confrontation being thrust upon me. In
the hush that fell on the hall and the eyes turning to look, I could
almost read the yearning for a fight.

In school, there were two kinds of fights: The first was the kind
that started after a few words were exchanged on the sidewalk—
each side egged on by the crowd and actually forced by them into
violence, so that, if you didn't get beaten to a pulp by the other guy,
you would most likely get crushed by the enormous weight of the
bloodthirsty crowd moving in.

And then there was the David-and-Goliath saga (much more
common in the school systems of greater New York), which consisted of a large bully and a much smaller and obviously weaker
opponent. Usually David didn't win, and with luck the bully didn't
maim him for life. But I wasn't stupid enough to take it there—
not in this lifetime anyway. I had to back down no matter how

bad it felt. If a coward dies a hundred deaths, and a hero dies just once, how bad does that one time *feel?* Like your body being ripped apart by horses tied to your arms and legs?

"No, Billy," I said with both palms facing him in surrender trying hard to diffuse the tense situation. "I don't want nothing from you." I was completely relieved to see Billy's hands slowly unclench and start to walk away, mumbling about the next time. You could hear the disappointment that escaped from the crowd like a hiss when they found out blood would not be shed.

Heart racing, I looked back at the kid lying on the ground like a rag doll. I helped him up; the kid tearfully thanked me for trying to help. If only he'd listened in the first place—but at least I was in one piece.

I finally got inside Room 304 and looked in the corner, where the teacher was. Standing behind her were boxes and boxes of World's Finest Chocolate. They looked like cardboard suitcases stacked in a pile, just waiting.

"Well, how much did *you* raise?" she asked condescendingly as she removed the form from my hand and looked it over in disapproval.

"Almost four boxes worth." I threw my foot up on the chair in front of me and reached down to pull the money out of my sock. The teacher looked at me, puzzled.

"It shows on the form here that you didn't raise anyth—"

"You didn't grow up going to a New York City public school, did you?" I pulled a piece of paper out of my book bag, transcribing amounts as I filled out all the forms completely, took my four boxes, and left.

After a quick look around in the hallway (you never really know if one of Billy's friends was standing lookout, like mold spores on the wall), I took the three flights two steps at a time to the lobby. I chose the side door for my exit; it also happened to be the closest to Eighth Avenue. When I got outside there were mostly stragglers smoking cigarettes, guys with their girlfriends—who were dressed (even though it was September) in identical dyed sheepskin jackets that turned your skin blue as the dye wore in—as well as some kids with suitcases identical to my own. I saw my friend Paul. He was a couple of years older than me and looked Puerto Rican, but his parents owned a little French café on Greenwich. When I saw him standing there with his girl, who was not only in the same jacket, but in Adidas shell top sneakers matching his, he signaled me with his cigarette hand to come over. "Whoa, little man! Very nice!" He held his cigarette in his mouth with the smoke curling in his eye as he said this and extended a very blue hand. "Don't worry, it doesn't rub off," he snickered as I slapped hands and curled our fists together.

"I ain't worried, bro," I said, and put my other hand on top of our union. He was a big guy, maybe six foot, and one of the nicest cats I ever met.

"Hey, man! You got a lot of that chocolate, huh?" he said perusing over my cartons.

"Yeah, a few. I pretty much sold them all to a few people." I wasn't ashamed but didn't want to seem like a goody-two-shoes either.

"That's cool, man! Hey, you need like a bodyguard?" Paul said, puffing his chest out. His girlfriend smacked his stomach, which made it stick out even further than before. "Why did you have go and do that?" he said, pushing her head in disrespect.

"Oh, no, you *didn't!*" she said, and backed him up into the garbage cans. She was all of five-two but very Puerto Rican and very ornery.

"Okay, okay!" Paul said running to the side to avoid her punches. "Hey, you need me, I'm here, Davey boy," he screamed as he ran down the street, for the moment being chased by the one he loved.

I walked to the Mr. Pizza on the corner and quickly checked my pockets to see if the change in them would add up to a slice. It wasn't one of my favorite places, but it was on the way. People in New York are serious about their pizza, completely loyal to their spots, almost as serious as they are about baseball. As I said earlier, my favorite had always been Joe's, right next to Rocco's Bakery on Bleeker Street.

I was about thirty cents short. The guys in that place didn't give credit either, not with hundreds of little con artists running around. I took the east side of Eighth Avenue, so I could look in the window of the army and navy shop. The sun that was bouncing against the building forced me to almost squint when I heard, *"Que pasa, Davide,"* coming from the doorway.

Fifteen years earlier, Manny had floated, blistered and half-dead, across the ocean from Havana on a makeshift boat contrived of plywood and a few tires, and never looked back. He worked the bodega on the corner of Fifteenth. He had on one of the guayabera shirts the Cuban barbers wore, and shoes with the gleam and shine that fit a pimp, not a grocery clerk. I had always assumed that his family owned the joint, since Manny wasn't the swiftest guy, but he had heart. He stood about five foot nothing and had a gut that hadn't allowed him to see his toes in at least ten years.

But he would kill for the country that had made it possible for him to have the great life he did, clutch his heart and sing the "Star Spangled Banner" while he was watching a Yankees game in the store; he would even cry. He also had the knack of seeing people coming from behind him, a power he swore Jesus had given him for taking the sight from his eye during a fight.

Just then he made this noise with his hands that seemed to send the pigeons on the street flying.

"*Nada, me amigo, nada,*" I said as we moved shoulder to shoulder for an around-the-world high five. Manny stepped on his cigarette and flicked the butt into the gutter with the tip of his shoe.

"What you doin' wit all de boxes? Jou moving out?" he said, smile revealing the sparkling gold bridge in his mouth.

"Nah, Manny, this is all the *chocolate* that I sold. We had to pick it up today, so we can give it to the customers," I said, proud of the responsibility that came with sales.

"You sure sol' a lot, Davide." Manny was looking over the case. "You musta sol' like a million bars. I bet you like the bes' guy dey got selling dat chocolate," he concluded with the seriousness and admiration of a true hustler. "You eat that crap pizza fron' dow' the street after school?" he asked, turning toward the kitchen of the bodega. "That shit will kill you, *mange!*" That a guy carrying fifty pounds of excess weight was concerned about a little cheese baffled me.

"Now, you take some of this nice pork," he said, pointing.

"You sit down, and we make you a nice *sanwich Cubano*."

Cuban-mix sandwiches were like the Latin version of grilled cheese. Some sliced pork shoulder lay on one half of a buttered roll. You piled ham, Swiss cheese, and sliced pickle, covered this with the mustard-coated other half, spread butter on the outside of the whole thing, and set it in a pressing machine that grilled the sandwich and flattened it to an inch thick.

"I'm a little light today, Manny. You want to split a Cuban?"

Manny shook his head. "You a good boy, Davide. I make you a sanwish, okey, thas the bes' jou ever eat, okey? Okey." He slipped into the makeshift kitchen and went to work.

I made myself comfortable in the compact dining area of the store, which consisted of two metal lawn chairs and a garden table. A few minutes later Manny came back to the table with the sandwiches on oval plates. The first bite was by far the most incredible. The sandwiches were always cut on an angle, so you *had* to bite off the corner. Just glorious.

CHAPTER 7

I WAS FEELING THE WEIGHT OF THE CHOCOLATE as I made my way down Eighth Avenue. A few kids were hanging around the Twin Doughnuts on the corner of Fourteenth Street, playing video games or waiting for the bus back to their world in the projects on the East Side. I started up Fourteenth but thought twice—the chocolate might be too tempting to some schmuck— turned around, and headed back to Eighth and over to Greenwich toward Eleventh Street, a safer route, where I'd make the left and head east.

The change from Chelsea to the Village, which began at Fourteenth, came suddenly. If you were Puerto Rican, so it seemed, you weren't allowed to venture below Fourteenth; they pretended they didn't care, but the invisible handcuffs that tied them to their area were tight and made the shift in racial diversity from one neighborhood to the other drastic.

I stopped for a second and considered going to Westbeth to see if anybody was hanging out—just to make sure I wasn't missing out on anything. I passed Horatio Park at the intersection and looked in on nothing—a scrawny New York pigeon was fluttering its wings, bobbling by in hope of food.

I stepped up my pace when heard a rumble of footsteps from behind me—but before I had time to run, I was in a choke-hold and flying to the ground. My face was pushed into concrete, and the chocolate flew out of my arms as I struggled like mad. I felt my breath shorten as the arm grew tighter and another went over my eye; the thought that it was my friends playing around was gone. In a few quick moments it was all over. I spun around to see two older-looking kids running down Horatio toward Ninth, laughing and shouting bullshit with my chocolate in hand.

"*Nooooooo!*" I screamed from down on the ground. Anger filled every crevice of my body; overcome by the sheer mass of it, I sat facing the street and cried.

A car rolled up. "I saw the whole thing, kid! Don't you worry—I'll get 'em!" I heard from the inside of a beat-up Caprice. In the driver's seat, leaning over and talking out the passenger window in a white overcoat you'd only wear in the meat market, was an Irish-looking guy probably heading to work.

I didn't think much at all as I watched the car speed off, barely catching the green light. I didn't know what I was gonna do. My knee was pretty fucked up from going down, and the blood in my mouth reminded me that it was reality. I'd been fucking *mugged*; I was so pissed.

I figured the school would think I was lying, since I didn't have a stellar record on that front. Maybe if I told everyone I'd tripped while running in the subway—that's how I'd messed my knee up—and the chocolate had fallen on the tracks of the A line! My parents might believe me and show some sympathy—after all, I was their only namesake heir—but it hadn't been that long since the bike.

Being a city kid, I never thought of calling the cops; that option didn't even enter into my mind. But my parents. . .huh, my mother, she'd want to call every fucking precinct all the way to the Bronx. I stood up and took inventory. My pants were pretty ripped from where I'd gone down; my knapsack lay in the gutter, and the extra bars strew across the sidewalk. I grabbed my bag and headed east. I imagined staggering into St. Vincent's with a gunshot to the gut.

The other guy was lying dead on the sidewalk as I side-stepped my way up the street, nine-millimeter in one hand and the other clutching my belly; I was keeping the blood from seeping out of the hole where I had been gut shot. I grabbed the first orderly I saw, making a fist out of his tee-shirt as I said, "You can rip the soul out of my chest and send me down to hell itself, but the gun stays with me!" I pushed the orderly away and moved forward, lighting a smoke. The doctor who came crashing though the double doors that helped restrain the screams was in my sights before they had even swung shut. I dropped the gun arm down when I saw he wasn't a threat, and leaned against the wall.

"That looks pretty bad," the doctor whispered in a tone you would only use with a dying man.

"It's only a scratch," I said with a sneer. "You can't imagine what I've seen." I flicked my cigarette to the floor and climbed onto the awaiting gurney.

"All I want to know is," asked the doctor with a disgusted tone,

"was it really worth it?"

I looked him straight in the eye; I heard the hum from the motor, in the clock on the wall. And with a cockeyed grin on my face, I said, "Nobody steals my chocolate. Nobody."

I stumbled past Ray's Pizza. If I'd only taken a different way, I thought, but that didn't matter. I'd have to explain to everyone what had happened. But would they actually believe me?

I continued up Eleventh Street, past the brownstone where, in the Sixties, members of a revolutionary group called the Weathermen had toyed with explosives and blown themselves, and it, to pieces. Now it was the only brownstone on the block with part of the façade at right angles to the street. When I got to my building, I passed it up and sat on the steps next door to figure things out. After a while I got up and headed off to face the music.

Ralph, who smelled of Old Spice, was a man of few words. He and his well-kept hair and gleaming ruby pinky ring were on the elevator when I walked in. He was a tall Puerto Rican with a meticulous mustache that reminded me of my grandfather's. We rode up to my floor in silence; I wasn't eager to start a conversation, and Ralph wasn't the kind to start one on his own. I got off, crossed the hallway, and opened the door.

THAT EVENING, I RELIVED THE STORY for my pop when he got home. Both of my parents were, of course, glad I hadn't been seriously injured, but to my shock and surprise I wasn't yelled at for losing something or for not being careful; the conversation turned instead to innocence lost and when my folks had been kids. Parents can really surprise you sometimes. They told me that the police had to be called, it being a mugging. And when my father got off the phone with the Sixth Precinct, he was angry.

"They can't do a damn thing!" he said as he slammed the phone down, causing Tammy to actually lift her head from her slumber. He was pacing back and forth in the living room, looking out the window, seething. I wasn't surprised by the cops' reaction. My mother didn't want me going to school the next day, but I thought differently.

"I'll be fine, Ma," I said reassuringly. "Don't worry about me."

As I REACHED THE BLOCK THE NEXT MORNING, I saw the usual faces and, when I made my way toward the gates, I heard someone calling, "Yo, David, come here!"

It was Camacho and his crew. I'd never had any beef with them or any reason not to go over.

"What's up, man?" I asked.

"I heard you got rolled yesterday, got your shit taken." George had a certain smirk in his voice and a bob in his movements. I wondered how the news had traveled that fast. "You wanna know who took it?" The crowd started to snicker.

"Why? You know, bro?" I responded, as if I would *do* something if he did.

"Yeah, but I can't tell you!" When George broke out in laughter, I understood: It was a big joke to them.

"Whatever," I said, and turned toward the gates. When I was a couple of feet away, I heard a voice over the crowd blurt out, "*Yo! I* took your shit." I couldn't fucking believe it. I heard George tell the guy to keep cool, but the kid didn't care. His name was

Santiago, and he was a few years older than all of them. I walked back. He was leaning loosely against a car. He looked familiar, but it'd happened so fast.

"*You* took *my* chocolate?"

Santiago was a tall Dominican kid from the neighborhood who had one of those baby-fine mustaches that only Latinos grew. He looked me right in the eyes. "Yeah, I took it. What, you gonna do something?" He stood up. He was a good foot taller than me.

When he spoke, that voice came back—oh, yeah, it was him. I was seething but thinking, always thinking. "No, man, I'm not going to do shit." I turned away. When I got inside, I felt warm with anger. I spotted the familiar face of Mitch—a thirty-something guard who had worked in the school for a while and actually lasted longer than any of the others, a big black guy with a well-kept beard.

I walked straight up to him. "Hey, Mitch," I said, trying to be collected, "you see that guy standing outside by Macho?" Mitch looked through the gate. "That kid jumped me yesterday and took all my chocolate."

Mitch looked back at me and repositioned the Gazelles on his brow. "You sure?" Mitch was always fair, so the question didn't shock.

"He just *admitted* it to me!" I said, almost stammering in a loud whisper.

"Alright, let's go." We reappeared to an awaiting crowd. Mitch went straight up to Santiago and asked, "You mug this kid?" He had a booming voice that would scare the shit out of most.

"I don't go to this fucking school, so I don't have to tell you shit." Santiago began to turn.

Mitch grabbed him by the collar and dragged him back. "*You* might not go here, but *he* does, so we need to talk now!" Macho and his crew started laughing at Santiago this time, turning their backs in disrespect.

In utter shock that it was going down like that, I watched Mitch drag the kid through the school and right into the principal's office.

"What's going on here?" the principal demanded as he downed the last of his wine and coffee. Mitch filled him in. I stood in the doorway and waited.

"So it was you," he said to me as he came out into the main room. "We got a call from a guy in the meat market trying to return some chocolate he found in a garbage can."

The guy had not only corroborated my story, but when the people at his job found out what had happened, they'd put together a kitty and bought a hundred and sixty dollars' worth of the chocolate in my name—it was *unreal*.

Santiago, on the other hand, was in deep shit. "Call David's father. I'm sure he'll want a word or two with this kid," the principal said, as he went back into his office. "And get this punk into the nurse's office. Good work, Mitch. You watch him."

Mitch smiled at me as he took Santiago away. I called my pop, who was just leaving the house on the way to his office in Jersey but, after hearing the news, made a beeline to the school. I figured I'd get picked up and taken home or something as a treat for my troubles. I sat in the hallway outside the nurse's office and waited for him to show.

I couldn't believe how lucky I'd been. I wasn't sure if there would be any repercussions over telling the guard, but fuck it, I did-n't care; what goes around comes around. I also had a different feeling about the streets. Even though snitches should get stitches, there *was* no fair fight on the streets, figuratively speaking. I could-n't have let it slide with Santiago after he admitted it. Besides, I had a responsibility to see that all the people who'd given me money for the chocolate got what was coming to them. I'd proven myself to be a man of my word.

I was sitting on the floor, staring at the glass-topped door of the gym and watching the dodge ball pop into view every few seconds, when I first caught a glimpse of my dad, in a well-pressed madras shirt, denim jeans, and a pair of loafers, checking in at the main of-fice at the far end of the hall. He was escorted to the nurse's office by the assistant principal, who had caught wind of the whole scene only moments earlier. When he got there, I stood up, and he gave me a long hug.

"Well, David, your father and I are going to go and talk to San-tiago. Why don't you go to your next class?"

I couldn't believe it. "What are you talking about? I want to go in," I said.

"I don't think it's a good idea for you to—"

"He *mugged* me, for fuck's sake!"

"Hey, knock it off, David," my father threw in.

"Pop, I just want to see his face. Don't you understand what this all means?" I felt my eyes starting to sting. "This kid jumped me and thought he could get away with it, but he didn't, all right?"

My father nodded.

The nurse's office was only a ten-by-ten room with an exam

table on one wall on which Santiago was sitting when we came in. Mitch was perched on a chair against the opposite wall; Santiago sat on a gurney with his head down and didn't raise it. "All right. Which school you go to. . .Santiago?" the assistant principal asked, looking down at a sheet of paper stuck on his clipboard. Santiago mumbled something about midtown without lifting his head.

"You like picking on little kids?" my pop suddenly snapped. He stopped right in front of the exam table, hands in the air. "What if I pick on you, would you like that?" He bent down to force Santiago to look him in the eyes. "You're some tough kid, aren't you? You and a few other guys jump someone half your size and you call yourselves hoods. I should kick your ass, you little fuck!"

Santiago, tears welling up in his eyes, stared straight ahead of him at the wall above the guard's head. I couldn't believe my dad, a man who had been in the presence of poets and aristocrats, was going Bronx on the kid.

They wound up calling Santiago's parents—after he quickly gave up the number—and headed back into the main office. The principal was standing in the doorway of his office in the usual manner, arms folded, large rod lodged in his ass.

"Well, it's all here." He stepped aside and revealed, not only the four original boxes that were a little tattered from the garbage can, but the eight others—compliments of the meat market—sitting like gold on the conference table in his office. I was completely awestruck by the pile. "It looks like we know who sold the most this year," the principal said with a grin.

When I crossed the street with my pop and Mitch, it was like having an armored transport going out. None of the kids could believe anyone had sold that much of the finest; I was smiling, because *I'd* finally heard the music.

FOURTEEN

(1984)

CHAPTER 8

BEFORE I LEFT FOR CAMP, I had to say goodbye to an old friend. My family had taken a practically translucent dog to the vet to give her a respectful end. But my sister'd lost it, so the vet had decided to give it another week.

It'd been hard enough for me to un-wriggle my hand from her tail as I walked out of that office without her; I hadn't thought I could do it twice. But with my mother sobbing, they'd of course agreed with the doctor, and we had dragged Tammy home.

It was really hard for me that week; I could barely look at her. When that fateful Friday finally came, my mother asked me to take her down for a walk. I looked at Tammy, who had chosen a sunny spot in the corner of the apartment since she'd been back and seemed quite happy basking away as the family pet for another spell. I went over to her. She looked at me with her eyes first—her tail paddling a quick thud on the ground as she lifted her head. She sighed and lay her head back down. I tried to help her up—she would stand, head sort of swaying from the weight, as she got her bearings, and make her way to the front door. I opened it at just the right time so as not to hinder her flow, and when we reached the elevator, she looked up into my eyes and, like falling snow, collapsed where she stood.

In one move I scooped her up in my arms. "*Mom!*" I screamed, "Tammy isn't moving!" As my whole family arrived in an instant and put their hands on her still-warm neck, the elevator arrived, unusually fast, but speed didn't matter anymore. She died in my arms as a friend should; she just knew. It was the first death I had faced in my life.

WHILE I WAS AWAY AT CAMP THAT YEAR, my friends found a new kind of enjoyment. I called my crew when I got back in town, but no one seemed to be around. After what seemed like hours, I gave up and headed out for a walk. Sporting the new pukka beads my parents had brought me from Key West, I felt older. I strolled down Fifth and went to Washington Square Park, and under the Arch, and leaned on one of the railings.

"Where you bin, yout?" asked the large figure next to me, a Rastafarian named Gemini. "I haven't been able to win a game witout you."

I slapped palms with him.

"You bin practicing ya foot bwal?" he asked comically as he threw a ball from nowhere that I began juggling on my thighs and feet like an old pro. "Ya, man! Respect, son. Nice!"

A large crowd had soon gathered to play a ritualistic game of pass around. Even though I was the only white kid there, I hardly noticed. The crowd was enormous, my acceptance remarkable.

After a while we sat down, drinking sodas in the summer heat. "What happened to the *dreds* you had, man?" I asked, but as the words left my lips a moment of clarity came over me that I shouldn't have said anything.

Gemini's demeanor changed, his head dropped, and his eyes locked on the cobblestones at his feet. But in a second that familiar grin came over his face as he looked from left to right, leaned in, pulling slightly at the sunglasses he was wearing to reveal his blood-shot eyes, and whispered, "The bumbaclot five-o is lookin' for a ras wit da dreads, not a soccer-playing Jamaican man wit out!" We started to laugh; I watched the dealers making moves right before my eyes. I knew one day they would catch Gemini, but they hadn't yet. I stood up, said goodbye, and moved on. I appreciated that Gemini had always looked out for me—as well as a drug dealer could.

I headed toward the hills to see if any of the BMX crew was around but only found a few kids on skate boards, riding down on their bellies, feeling like experts every time they got to the bottom without wiping out.

I left the park and turned toward Cornelia. When I got to Freddy's place, I yelled down the grate to the subterranean part of the apartment, "Yo, Freddy!"

I saw movement but from my angle couldn't identify anything below, probably for the best. I listened; just before I bellowed out another round, I heard his mother scream, "He's not here! I don't know where the hell he is and frankly don't *care*. But if you find him, tell him to pick up cat food on his way home!"

"No problem!" I shouted back. I strolled toward Bleeker and Joe's Pizza. I hadn't had a slice in two months.

The shorts I was wearing were sticking to me by the time I got to feel the hot air blowing from the ovens as I entered Joe's. The place was so small, the outside was in. I saw Sal cleaning the counter. "What's going on, Sal?" I asked with a smile, rubbing my hands together in anticipation of getting my paws on a slice.

He wore a hat that he constructed daily out of the morning paper. He glanced at me out of the corner of his eye and sucked his teeth as an answer.

I didn't get it. " Hey. . .Sallie boy, what's up?" I waited for a reply as I dodged and weaved boxing my shadow.

He crumpled up the paper he had been using to clean with, threw it on the floor, and put both arms down of the counter in front of me. He was a big boy and, though he was in his fifties, looked like he'd seen some shit; my attention was warranted. He looked me in the eye, nodding slowly. "Whassa matta, you don't come by no more? Some pretty girl, she make you feel like you gotta go to *dat* place, maybe? Wha? Wha happened, Davey boy? You breaka my heart!" He slapped his chest and turned his head indifferently.

"Sal?" I said in complete bewilderment, but all he did was wave me away and flick his fingers off his chin. Had he just told me to go fuck myself?

I couldn't believe it. I would *never* go someplace else, but I guessed he didn't understand that. I moved gingerly around to the other side of the counter, crept up before his vast bulk as I dodged my head around to catch his glance, and with my hand over my heart spoke, "Sal, I went away to *camp*. I was gone all *summer!* I swear! That's why I wasn't here. The day before I left, I came to say goodbye to you, but your brother told me you were with your wife. She was having gallstones removed, right? I told him to tell you, but. . .I guess he didn't." I paced by the prep table and continued, "I would never eat somewhere else, Sal. You are, and will always be, the man."

I turned to leave, feeling defeated. Just then a smile appeared on his face as he said, "Why didn't you just *say* so, Davey boy! Huh? Who knew? Come on, I make a calzone for you that you can't believe! You a good boy, Davey."

He slapped my shoulder, moving me aside as he walked over to his prep table and clapped a huge cloud of flour in the air; I was just happy to be that much closer to a slice.

"You mind if I have one of those to start with, Sal?" I asked cautiously, pointing to the pizza, not wanting him to think I didn't want the calzone, but I had been dreaming of a slice.

"A slice? Of course you can have a slice, Davey boy! Warm, just the way you like it! Then, me an you, we kick the crap out of this calzone that I make, alright?" I looked at him and smiled.

WHEN WE FINISHED, I HEADED OUT with an Italian ice running down my arm. I still wasn't sure where my crew was, so I headed down Bleeker toward Westbeth, just on the verge of puking. I slurped down as much of the ice as I could stomach and threw the remains in an overfilled garbage can on the corner of the street as unyielding as the parking meters that stood like sentinels for as far as the eye could see.

I got stared at when I walked past Christopher Street. I didn't know why they were staring—at *me?* I was just a kid, old for my years but still fourteen. I kept on moving, past a new Chinese restaurant that smelled bad—the rotten vegetables just being sprayed with a hose to the gutter. Up the block, I heard screams that sounded like wounded kids. I ran up the street and turned the corner only to find a middle-aged guy kneeling next to an opened-up hydrant, making a huge mess on Tenth Street. I ripped off my topsiders and paraded into the cool water.

"Enjoy it, it won't last for long!" he said, unscrewing the rest of the valve on the side. The police usually shut it down pretty quick.

I looked around for something. Some kids were playing in the water, but it didn't have a good pressure. I found an old soup can in the garbage and asked one of the old ladies who were hanging out the first floor window to cut off the bottom with a can opener. She smiled a toothless grin, returned with can opener in hand, and handed it over to me, not wanting to be a party to criminal behavior. I opened up the bottom and smoothed out the edges with the handle. I went over to the hydrant and, holding the can tightly in front of the gusher, sprayed the water all the way across the street. It was beautiful! All the kids were running back and forth, happy for the relief from the muggy heat of the afternoon. The man tapped me on the shoulder and said, "Give me the can, kid. Go on." When we switched positions, I felt the cool water first-hand. I ran around like a freak in that afternoon sun, my clothes clinging to me like a second layer of skin as I imagined the sky high above going on forever, like the Twin Towers behind me.

Suddenly, it stopped. I looked back and saw a couple of cops from the Sixth Precinct shutting it down. I was suddenly alone. One of the cops waved a finger at me.

"You open up this hydrant, kid? What if there was a fire and we couldn't put it out because you used up all the water to play in, huh? You gonna pay for it?" I glanced at him pulling up his plumber's crack as he rose from the hydrant and, in one fluid motion, grabbed my shoes and ran barefoot down the street. I continued to run as I saw the cop take one step, laugh, and bend down to finish the job.

When I felt far enough away from the scene, I slumped onto a stoop and started putting my shoes back on. City kids will practically eat dogshit off the floor, but walking those nasty streets in bare feet. . .ahh, no. I stared up at the sticker-bug tree looming overhead, providing some protection from the sun. I pulled my shirt off and tried wringing it out, but it didn't matter; it would dry from the heat soon enough. I got up and kept on walking. I thought about trying to get in touch with my agent, Annabella, who had called me at camp over the summer to tell me she'd left the Ford agency and was starting a young adult division at a talent agency. She asked me if I wanted to come along for the ride. Why not? Acting had always been something that came natural to me. It was like a filmed hustle.

I stopped at a phone booth at Abington Square Park. Realizing I didn't have any change, I walked past the stinking bums lying on the bricks.

"I could have been president," I heard one beckon almost soberly as I passed. I looked back at the blackened, dirty figure on the ground, huddled in old newspaper, and thought how quickly life could change. I stopped for a second to look at the park where I had played with my friends, but it was for little kids, so we didn't hang there anymore.

I got to the south entrance of the building and walked into the courtyard, hoping to find someone playing ball or a familiar face, but only found Bruce strolling across the yard in a fog-like state. He was a few years older than me. His father had taken the Green Slide of Doom a few years before and landed flat-backed in the courtyard thirteen stories below. Thankfully, Bruce had been away. But he had been right there when his mother did the same thing a year later—awoke one morning, got out of bed without a word, and silently headed off to the roof. Bruce had to be pulled physically off the corpse that lay in severed sections, in her nightgown, on the cobblestones. He'd clung to her body and the only connection he would ever have thereafter with reality. When the state later came to claim him, they heard him muttering something about fishing. Mental illness is genetic, and unless you have the power inside to fight it, you've already lost.

CHAPTER 9

RTISTS SEE THINGS IN A DIFFERENT WAY was instilled in my brain at a very young age. I thought of that line as I watched a fifteen-foot sculpture of an abstract penis being erected in the inner courtyard of Westbeth as the sun started to fade into the west. I headed into the building, strolled past the guard desk, and continued on to the elevators with a few other people slowly merging together like lambs to the slaughter.

My first stop was always the third floor: Marlon and Remy lived there, and it was the obvious route to the G section, a stairwell that was on the east side of the building.

Marlon and his family lived in what was considered a "smaller" Westbeth apartment, a mere thousand square feet. Marlon's father, a painter, had made it really modern, with a loft bed in the living room that his parents shared. The main room was divided into two spaces: one for socializing, the other an art studio. Paint was strewn all over the floor and walls in a methodical way. He taught art to the blind, which for my friends and me was a constant oxymoron.

I rang the bell a few times but got no answer, so I stared up at the wavy ceiling as I walked. The hallways were endless and without windows—except by the elevators. Very eerie. Maybe it was the fluorescent lights that cast a murky haze over the whole place.

I hit Remy's doorbell, admiring the small wooden tree that stood above it. I heard footsteps as I leaned against the wall opposite the door and waited. "Hello?" It was Frank, Remy's father.

"Hey, Frank, it's me, David." After what seemed like an eternity waiting for the door to open, I saw the man standing before me in all his glory. Frank had a cognac snifter in one hand and, in his green pants and matching shirt, looked like a gas station attendant from Oklahoma.

"David," he said, kicking at some piece of flooring peeling up slightly at his feet. He was not only a painter of true merit but a sculptor as well.

"I was looking for Remy. . .how you doin'?"

"Not bad, David. How was your summer?" he replied, the ash on his cigar seemingly halted.

"It was good, you know, getting out of the city and all." The fact that I'd had gotten my lips around the nipple of Brigette for the first time would not enter *this* conversation.

"Come on down, David. I want to show you something," he said, inviting me downstairs, where his work was ongoing.

The stairwell down was narrow and steep, with pictures adorning both sides of the walls. When I reached the bottom of the stairs, cigar smoke was rippling through beams of light from the windows. Musical instruments sat cluttered everywhere. Frank was playing on the newest toy he had been given by the college he taught at, where he was a full professor of art. On a computer monitor, he had transposed a painting into lines running to and fro across and down the screen. "When Jean-Baptiste Chardin painted this in the eighteenth century, he really knew what he was doing; it's called *A Green-Necked Duck with a Seville Orange.*" Frank invariably spoke to me as if I understood every word. He just shifted his eyes off the work as he spoke with his thumb and forefinger holding his chin.

"Yeah. It looks like triangles, Frank."

"Exactly, geometry. Take a look at this," he went on, got up, and moved to an easel covered with a floral sheet. He whipped it off in one tug and revealed an interpretation of the painting, which consisted of a freshly killed duck hanging on a wall with a gun at its side. Only his had been devised in an abstract form with bent wood in different colors and shapes, pieces of mirror here and there, mystical in its subtlety. It captured the very essence that I felt looking at the painting, but even more in its three-dimensional state.

"*Wow!*" I said, trying to be cool but finding it hard. "I can't believe this. It's incredible!" I said, moving in to touch the curves in the piece, completely awestruck.

"It's all math, David, in its root form," Frank remarked as he went into the back of the apartment to relight his cigar and finish the cognac he had started. "Make yourself a sandwich if you're hungry—and you can let yourself out if you don't mind, okay? I'll tell Remy you stopped by. It's good to see you," I heard from around the corner as he collapsed back into his chair.

I left the apartment, headed back down the hall, and hung a right, winding up at the G section. I opened the door leading in but found no one, only the smell of piss permeating the air. I decided to take the two flights to five and Zed's apartment. I knocked on the door, rang, and waited. Above the guitar playing in the background I heard footsteps. Eddy opened the door. "Dave *Rave*! Where you been? Come in!"

Eddy was a cross between Al Pacino and a Tibetan monk. He was wearing shorts and an Indian sari that revealed the Buddha hanging round his neck, as well as a huge smile. Zed's house was the most unwatched, and we all seemed to congregate there. Eddy's philosophy was a simple one: He'd rather have his kid doing whatever at home then out on the street. He hugged me, then sat me around the kitchen table and said with a smile, "So what are we going to do with my boy, Rave?" He seemed to be at a loss.

I wasn't sure what to say other than, "He's cool, Eddy, he's all right." We sat there together drinking some cold tea and talking about girls.

Eddy always had some young chick in the wings. I told him about Brigette and the tit, and he commended me on my triumph. After a minute, I remembered why I was there and asked where Zed was.

Eddy, who seemed to be looking around in a haze, suddenly focused when he heard his son's name. "He's been hanging around with a kid named Jean." I hadn't heard that name before.

The phone rang.

Eddy walked over to the rotary, which sat on a bamboo table separating the kitchen and hallway, and grabbed the receiver. "Hey, babe, what's going on? . . . Yeah? You'll never guess who's here. Hold on." He motioned for me to come over and handed me the receiver.

"Hello?" I said, trying to hear the voice on the other end over the loud street noise.

"Hey, man! What you doin' over there?" It was Zed, his voice echoing over the phone like a fog in the mist.

"I was looking for you, dude! Just got back. Where *is* every-one?"

There was a brief silence. "Is my dad near you?"

I quickly caught on. "Nah, he went into the T.V. room. Why?" I started to get excited when deceit was in the air.

"Call your parents and tell them you're sleeping at my house, and I'm gonna do the same, okay? Don't call from there. Use the pay phone downstairs, okay? And meet me at Horatio in twenty minutes, got it?"

I couldn't believe I was already lying to my parents. "Yeah, dude, I'm in. See you in a sec." I hung up, said my goodbyes, and left.

I jumped down the stairwell three at a time, wondering what was going on, but when I hit the street and saw a pay phone on the corner, I fished for a dime to call home. The phone rang. Finally my mother answered, sounding tired from the summer heat.

"Hey, Mom," I said, trying to play it cool without acting too cool, "Zed asked his Dad if I could stay over and he said it was cool, so I was calling to tell you—"

"What do you mean, 'tell me'? You just got *home*, David. Can't you stay in *one night*? I haven't even seen you for more then five minutes."

In the ensuing silence, I had to change gears and re-think the matter. "Ahh, I'm sorry, Mom, I was so excited when I finally hooked up with Zed I completely forgot about how you'd feel. Do you mind if I stay at his house tonight? I *promise* I won't go out much this weekend. Please, Ma?"

I heard her sigh on the other end and could tell she had been taken off guard. After a long moment, she answered in a hushed tone, "Whatever you want David. Fine."

Now, usually, the guilt would have overcome me to the point of folding and giving up, but Zed's plan sounded too good.

"Thanks, Ma!" I said, knowing she would be surprised at me calling her bluff. "I'll see you in the morning, alright?" Silence. Sigh. Deep breath.

"Alright, David, be safe, and. . .I love you."

I was free to roam the streets and dying for a smoke I was hoping Zed was holding. I headed up Bank Street to Eighth Avenue and took a left uptown. I was running late. Every time I got near the park where I'd been mugged (which seemed like years ago by then), I carefully checked over my shoulder in search of an assailant waiting to jump me.

I saw Zed a block away in his black wife-beater tee and shorts, pacing, smoke dangling out of the corner of his mouth. Thank god he's got smokes, I thought.

He was the first kid I'd had ever seen when I moved into the city. I entered the fourth grade class that morning, sat down, and was told to talk about myself. A kid named Gabe, with snot dripping from his nose and hair that had a look like it had been combed with a shell, had asked me if I was from Jersey. I, somewhat intrigued by this psychic ability, had replied in the affirmative, only to hear Gabe say, "Figures." I'd been left totally deflated—I'd been there five minutes and was already looking like a schmuck. But this kid Zed had stuck up for me and reminded Gabe that I was much further ahead in math (for some reason Jersey had a more expeditious curriculum that left me in the know), and that he should shut the fuck up and maybe he'd learn something. From then Zed and I had been friends.

"What's *up*, dude! Fresh pukkas!" he said, high-fiving and reveling in my tan. I'd been assistant water-ski instructor all summer, so my tan was deep and my hair was really sun-bleached; I looked like I belonged in Maui. "You're not going to believe what's been going on," he continued. "Jane and Pamela met this dude named Jean, whose father is this art dealer and has this fresh like penthouse on Gramercy Park, right? And Jean knows these people, or this girl name Kathy, who have this stuff called 'acid,' and it's been a constant party over there, and Freddy did it with Marlon and some of the girls, and I was going to do it tonight. . .and I can't believe you're *back!*" He was going a mile a minute as he handed me the pack of Marlboro and squeezed my shoulder. I fished one out, hanging on his every word, and lit it up with a sigh.

It had been nearly a month since I'd had a smoke. "So you wanna take it tonight?" I asked almost hesitantly, nonchalantly, although I knew the answer before I finished my sentence. Zed wasn't the kind to shy away from new experiences and, as expected, had already called home, spinning tales of crashing at my house.

We walked side by side up the avenue, talking of the summer and what'd been accomplished; as Zed continued filling me in on the drug experiences of his friends, Brigette's tits seemed like small potatoes.

CHAPTER 10

I WAS THINKING ABOUT THINGS, my mind racing a mile a minute, as we made our way over to Jean's. Zed filled me in on how the situation had been developing for the past few weeks. Since the girls met Jean, it'd been an ongoing party at his house. We'd been smoking pot for a while but nothing harder. I got a rush at the thought of doing acid. There was no comparison to that after-school movie where the kid, all strung out, jumped into a swimming pool without the water in it; he'd been doing PCP. Our parents had done psychedelics in the Sixties, and *they'd*—for the most part—turned out okay. So my friends and I felt entitled.

We passed a Sabrett stand as we were turning east on Seventeenth Street. "What can I do for you boys?" asked the hot dog man, who looked like he was set for an icy winter in the Arctic, which included a plaid coat, a hat, and fingerless gloves to match. It was a little strange for the middle of August.

"Ahh, I think, I'll have—think! Think! Think! Maybe, um. . ."

Zed mumbled, hitting his palm to his forehead in a rhythmic beat. His indecisive behavior was typical and didn't bother me in the slightest, I actually expected it, but I could tell the vendor was getting edgy.

"Come on, come on. If you don't know what you want, step back! You're blocking the customers!" he snapped, looking up and down the empty street.

"Gimme a break, alright! It's a tough choice, you know?" Zed barked. The vendor folded his arms and began to hiss.

"I'll have a knish with mustard and a grape soda," I said quickly, moving in to get mine before the guy's frustration made him up and move his cart. I grabbed the proffered knish, handed him a buck, and started eating. I cracked the tab on the can and took a slug. The grape soda was so cold it practically closed my throat as it slid down.

"Yeah, give me one of those," Zed said. "Only ketchup—no, make that mustard and ketchup." The man had started to prepare the knish just as Zed, practically grabbing the man's hands, said, "I'm sorry, I'm sorry, fuck it, make it a hot dog instead, alright?"

Thank fucking god! Zed had finally settled, but the man had lost his patience. He threw the knish back, grabbed his fork, and flipped open the steamer compartment, eyeballing Zed the entire time. "You're sure you want this, right?" he asked condescendingly, stabbing a frank from the murky steaming water with his fork. "You're not gonna change your mind?" he went on, shaking the pierced dog at him.

"Yeah, yeah," Zed said. "Gimme mustard, some ketchup, kraut, and onions, and an orange soda. . .no, make it a root beer." He grinned at the last part.

The man finished making Zed's mess on a bun and handed it over. Zed stared him down as he gave him the buck, and we headed over to a stoop.

I couldn't help but laugh at the whole thing. Zed always wanted what he didn't have. "What?" he asked like a rabid animal, chomping off the end of his dog; he was in some fucking mood.

"Nothing, man," I assured him. "You crack me up. How's your dog?"

He was already eyeballing my knish. "It sucks!" he said. "Maybe he'll change it if I go over there?" He was beginning to get up.

"You never know," I said drily, though it was obvious the guy would sooner cut off his own prick and stick it in a bun than give away food for free. "Look, you want a bite of mine, just to make sure before you go over there and start some shit?"

Zed leaned over. I held the knish out, and he bit off a piece. "Yeah, I think I'll stick with the dog." He sat back down, satisfied.

It was getting dark, and by the time we hit Gramercy Park, we were beat. We crossed the street in front of awning-covered door and went in. I thought it looked pretty swanky. "You sure this is the place?" I asked, my intuition tingling. I was imagining a huge hoax: But this was *Zed* with me, not Freddy, who was more the type to pull some shit like that. Zed looked up and down the buzzer list, put his finger on one, and rang.

"Hello?" replied a voice, slightly drowned out by music, from the intercom.

"Hey, Jean, it's me, Zed, and my boy, David."

"Who?" the voice replied sarcastically.

"Come on, man, let us up!"

"All right, all right," the voice chuckled as the buzzer sounded, and the locked door opened like a vault. We jumped down the few steps to the lobby and rang for the elevator.

Waiting for it, Zed got panicky. He turned to me. "Just be cool, right? Jean threw out a few guys the other day that were acting stupid."

"Yeah, yeah, I know. Come on. No prob, man, I'll be cool." I didn't know what that would entail, but I adapted quickly to situations. The elevator arrived, and a man in a brown suit and matching hat, with gleaming shoes, asked us our destination in a rough German accent.

"Ah, fourteen, please—Jean's house," Zed told him. We got in. The elevator car reminded me of a museum as I sat on an engraved bench built into the side.

When the doors slid open noiselessly, there were only two apartments, A and B, and that's when it dawned on me: This was serious money. We turned to the door on the west side of the hallway and rang the bell. I could hear noises and partying in the background. A moment or two later, the door opened to reveal Jean.

He was *black*? At about five-ten and skinny, he looked more like a transient then the son of an art dealer. He had slightly bloodshot, bugged-out eyes, and he reached for Zed's hand with long, slender fingers; but he had a great smile. "What's up, Zed! Good to see you back! So this is him?"

I felt out of place for a second as he waited. "Yeah, Jean, this is David. David, Jean."

Jean looked me up and down he shook my hand with barely a

grip. We were still in the doorway, so anything could have happened. "So you're David. I heard about you. How was summer camp?" Jean broke into a laugh. He had to put his hands on his knees to keep from falling down. I started to get pissed off, but I had to keep cool. I got very uncomfortable as he regained his composure and looked at me. "I'm just messing around, man. I was only laughing because I went to band camp till I got thrown out! You're alright, bro! Come on in, enjoy the party!" I had been tested and passed. He threw his arm over my shoulder and escorted me in.

The walls were covered with carved wooden panels, and a deep fireplace sat at the end of the forty-foot living room. The English-style tufted leather couches lining the walls below the windows added startling contrast to the extraordinary modern art on the walls.

I saw some familiar faces, as well as Freddy standing in the corner, talking to some not-so-familiar ones. "Come on, I want you to meet some people," Jean said.

Mike was six-foot-four, with a childlike face. Rogen was right next to him, but in his own world. "What's up, man!" said the latter from out of nowhere, pumping my hand in an almost freaky way. He was a tall, slender kid with a bowl haircut and a huge grin on his face; he had pupils like basketballs as he leaned closer. "You a tripper, Davey boy? It couldn't be any better—clean, real clean." Arms flapping, he wandered off to the other side of the room.

"Isn't he a freak? Out of his fuck-ing-mind!" Mike exclaimed, trying to talk above the music, which was almost deafening.

Prince's "When Doves Cry" was blasting through speakers hidden in the walls. Mike had a calm about him that demanded respect even in such an environment. I nodded knowingly and went off to say hello to people I knew. Jane and Pamela were standing off to one side with a good-looking blonde guy dressed in a maroon Lacoste buttoned to the top, matching maroon Lee jeans, and white shell-top Adidas. They both threw their arms around me and gave me a kiss. Jane introduced the guy as Lloyd; I later found out he had been making it with most of the girls I knew.

"Whassup, man?" he asked in a very cool Brooklyn kind of way. "You had a good summer, bro?"

"Yeah, man, it was cool," I answered. I was distracted when Zed came running up.

"Yo, David," he whispered, speeding, tapping me on the shoulder, "we gotta go to the Gramercy Hotel, to hook. . . . What up, Lloyd?" Zed gave him a quick soul-brother shake and smiled at the girls.

He and I headed for the door. We were almost there when Jean came running over. "Hey, hey, where you guys going?"

"Gonna meet Kathy to grab some tabs. We were coming right back—if that's cool?" Zed said.

Jean walked us the rest of the way with his arms over our shoulders. "Yeah, it's cool. *You* guys can hang here, but I'm going to clear the place out a little." He glanced from side to side. "You mind grabbing me a hit?" he asked when we got to the door. He started pulling out cash.

"I got you, bro," I said, with a little wink and a smile, crossing to the door. "It's the least I can do."

"You're alright, man," Jean said, nodding.

"Yeah, no prob, man. We'll be back in a sec, okay?" Zed opened the door and rang for the elevator. "You ready, bro?" he asked me, nodding, doing push-ups against the wall, rolling his head from side to side, getting pumped.

I thought for a second and said, "Fuck, yeah, man, I'm ready!"

We strolled the half block to the hotel. It was a huge place. We went in through the revolving door. Kathy was expecting us in a room on the tenth floor. We passed the front desk feeling, not like the fourteen-year-olds we were, but like adults on a mission. The man at the newspaper stand stared at us as we waited to go up.

When we got to the floor, we looked around and, realizing the direction of the numbers, headed left to Room 1007 and knocked. Speaking through a crack in the chained door, a heavy-set girl with glasses gruffly asked, "Who the fuck are you two?"

I was familiar with drug dealers, but not female ones; this was new to me. "It's Zed and David, Jean's friends," he said. She unchained the door and let us in. There were a few people sitting around watching television. Everyone was older than us, but nobody seemed to care.

"So what do you guys want?" she asked in a businesslike manner. I hadn't realized there were choices to be made.

"Just some hits," Zed said.

"I got some really good coke too, if you want," she said, pulling out a sheet of paper from a book. It was perforated and covered with hundreds of individual musical notes. "How many you guys need?" She was waiting to pull them apart.

"Just three, if that's cool, Kathy, but maybe some blow next time," Zed said, having, apparently, learned the lingo. She tore off the three and handed them to him, who in turn tore off one and gave it to me.

"First time?" she asked, looking at me.

"Yeah, well, you know, always got to be a first time, right?" I said, knowing there was no turning back now.

"It's really clean and strong, like four hundred and fifty mics a hit, kinda like the stuff they used to take on sugar cubes. You're gonna love it. You'll be flying for like twelve hours or so," she said to me quite calmly. I took the hit and placed it on my tongue, letting it seep in as we'd been told. The two of us sat on the edge of the bed and waited for the acid to take effect.

CHAPTER 11

THE STEEP ROOFTOP I WAS WALKING ON *had an apex like a razor's edge; tiles loosened by my steps plummeted to an unfathomable place below. I lay down, balancing my weight as I stared up at the bluebirds circling overhead. I watched them swoop down and could see the ribs that made up each wing, the way they glided across the open sky.*

I was tracking their every move as I followed them with my eye, to my left and down. Turning my body, I lost my balance and started to roll faster and faster. Bang! Crack! My body pounded down the side of the slate roof. I was feeling every tile slam against my arms and legs, waiting for the final bit of air. The fear that came, slowly and then faster, wasn't as uneasy as I'd thought. All at once my arms and legs were weightless; I fell with fear and laughter.

I fell off the bed and hit the floor with a thud, the carpet beneath my hands feeling furry and good. I stretched my fingers deeper into it. I couldn't help but laugh as I slowly rose and looked at the T.V. everyone was staring at. I felt the air around my arms like thick water as I laid my head back.

I looked over and for the first time saw Zed, who had a look on his face similar to mine. We clung to each other's biceps and forearms like wrestlers, feeling the blood pumping inside them. We couldn't stop laughing. We went up to Kathy, who was seated on her chair by the door, and looked into her eyes.

"You're beautiful!" I said, my pupils as black as night and big as basketballs reflecting off her glasses. I couldn't get over how she stayed so calm in the middle of all the mayhem.

Zed stood by my side, feeling every breath he took, every muscle in his body working to expel the air.

I groped for his head. "Dude, don't stop! That feels *so* good!" Zed said, barely audible in his ecstasy. He grabbed me in the same fashion, and there we sat feeling each other's brains.

"You guys gotta split, okay?" Kathy said flatly, looking at beginners she didn't need screwing up her location.

We looked up at her and broke out in laughter once again but tried hard to compose ourselves. After regaining some kind of focus, Zed grabbed me by the arm, and with shit-eating grins we made our way out the door. In the hallway we started to run toward the elevator, not remembering where we needed to go.

I somehow managed to push the button for the elevator and we were lucky enough to have it empty on the way down.

"Everything is so fuckin' *funny!*" I got out between fits of laughter. We reached the lobby and passed the man at the newsstand, still sorting papers. I looked at him, rubbing my eyes and double-checking my vision, clearly noticing the trail that was following him. It duplicated his movements as he picked up stacks and laid them down on piles.

The lobby was vast nearly to the point of incomprehension as we watched the maroon carpet rolling in waves toward the front door.

"Do you *see* that?" I asked Zed, trying not to be too obvious. "The carpet, man—it's like *moving!*"

"Dude, that is so *insane!*" he replied, dumbfounded. We felt our steps for the first time, one after the other.

When we reached the outside, I first noticed the pattern. It was soft but growing stronger as I breathed. *It's fucking salamanders*, I realized, with their hands up like Egyptian hieroglyphics. They were connected to each other at the fingertips in a circular pattern, connected till every inch of space was taken up by one of them; it was so intense. I looked closely at the sidewalk covered with my newfound friends. The light from the street lamps had a yellow, murky glow as we made our way back to Jean's.

Once in the lobby, I could have sworn I heard a chair say something to me.

We got upstairs and rang the bell with arms over each other's shoulders. Jean opened the door.

"Oh, my god!" he said as he let go of the handle and took two steps back. He shook his head, looking at us tripping; the apartment was more cleared out by then. "Did you remember to get me one?" Jean asked, enunciating the words very clearly, unsure if he'd get an answer. He watched Zed fumble in his pocket and, with a smile of child-like success, pull out a cellophane cigarette box wrapper that he handed over, with a musical-note tab inside.

"I can't believe you actually remembered." Jean unwrapped the bundle and popped the tab on his tongue, but we were already off looking at things in the apartment. Jane was one of the only people left; she had full-blown basketballs as well. She came up to us and started to speak: "You guys are like totally trippin' too, huh? Isn't it crazy? All the colors—I'm totally trippin'! It's *sooo* cool!" She was going a mile a minute, but I could make out the words she was uttering.

Freddy came from what seemed like out of nowhere into the room with a look of shock on his face. "David, I don't know how to tell you this, but your mom's on the phone!"

I got totally paranoid. I felt the sweat drip from my forehead as I panicked. Why would she be calling? She *knew* I was tripping! That was it! I was condemned and totally busted. How had she found me? Had the salamanders told her? The paranoia that filled every pore of my body completely overtook me. I felt my heart race and started to sweat; my salamanders were everywhere. "My mom's on the phone?" I kept muttering to myself over and over again. I went into the closet in Jean's room and sat in the dark. I heard voices talking to me in the void. I felt out of control like a child, heard the heartbeat of the door breathing next to me.

"David, come out and *talk* to her!" I heard Freddy demanding from the other side.

With a choked-up voice on the verge of tears, I in a frenzy screamed, "I can't *talk* to her! *Please*, don't make me talk to her! Tell her I'm not here, okay? Just don't make me *talk!*" I started sobbing as I grabbed my hair and shook my head from side to side, entering a different domain altogether, one becoming more difficult to leave.

I suddenly felt a light fall on me as the door swung open and saw Freddy and Jean standing before me. I shielded my eyes from the dim light of the room.

"Your mom never *called*, man! It was all a big *joke!* Wow, man, you really freaked out, huh?" Freddy said as he looked at me; I could tell from the look in his eyes that he regretted fucking with my high, but it was way too late. "We were *kidding*, dude! It's okay, you're cool, man!" he added, looking into my eyes.

I remained on the floor with eyes wide open, blinking, letting my eyes adjust to the light, trying to come back, to understand the reality of the situation. I wiped my eyes and, staring at Freddy, said, "She *didn't* call? She really didn't?" Freddy's cheeks began to sink inward, and his mouth was sealing up with skin as he fought to speak. The floor began to roll, and I was finding it hard to focus.

"No one called, man. I *swear* no one called. I'm sorry for fucking with your trip." That said, Freddy, being the douche he was, grabbed his jacket and left. I went back into the foyer and sat down on the floor.

I began to relax, watching a painting of Catharine Deneuve melt before my eyes. I could *see* all the muscles as the skin seemed to fall away from that beautifully sculpted face. I was scrutinizing it when Zed sidled up beside me. "You cool, David? Isn't this *intense?*" He was watching the same picture. By then, Jean was tripping pretty hard himself, sitting cross-legged in front of a green candle burning in the middle of the living room, the flickering hall of forms and colors radiating in all directions. He called us over.

"This is Oliver," Jean said in a very calm way. "He is all-pow-erful and burns only to protect you and the others." This seemed very spiritual to me; I listened as if to a sermon.

Zed and Jean went to hang with Jane in the kitchen and make some food. I found myself alone, staring at the floor, watching an entire scene play out before my eyes. And things were really mov-ing. If I looked away, they didn't disappear but remained silent until I looked back. I was enjoying this on all fours.

"Jean, the *carpet* is moving. I see the dudes doing a *dance*—I *swear* it!" I laughed and looked up.

But I didn't see Jean. Instead, there was a middle-aged man in a bathrobe. Lazlo, Jean's stepfather, was Hungarian by descent and not amused at having been awakened by us. I didn't know who he was, or that he had come home during the jaunt to the Gramercy Hotel and been sleeping not twenty feet away.

"What does he mean, 'men are dancing'? Is he on something, some drugs, your friend?" he asked Jean in an irritated voice.

Jean, seeming completely composed, told me to go in the other room. "We're just sitting around burning a candle, enjoying some food, that's all." Jean and Lazlo continued to exchange words, the chicken potpie that had just come from the toaster oven steaming in his face. I tried to listen in the other room.

"Why didn't you tell us he was here?" I whispered to Jane, blaming her for my own carelessness.

"You can't blame *me*. *I* wasn't the one. . . . It's cool, man. Don't worry. His dad will be cool," she said, sitting down on the mattress and playing ping-pong with the trails her fingers were making.

Zed looked at us with excitement building in his eyes. "Let's go outside!" We waited for Jean to come back when he told us how he'd avoided a near-fatality. When we told him we wanted to leave for a while, Jean thought it was good idea. Zed, Jane, and I prepared for the great outdoors.

The patterns I saw, once we got there, were even more dramatic as I watched the others running ahead. I stared at a street lamp above looking as if it was bending over, coming closer. I skipped to catch up, enamored by the rolling sidewalk. We started to run loops around Gramercy Park; I ran my fingers along the spiked fence. The feeling of the wind on my face was incredible. We came across a couple in their twenties walking down the street.

"Have you ever done LSD?" Zed asked them, huffing, with basketball eyes and a wide smile. For some reason they weren't frightened by our motley crew. The man thought for a moment and shook his head from side to side. Zed looked at us and started to laugh as he replied, "It's amazing, really amazing!" They smiled and went along their way.

Zed and I wanted to climb over the fence to see first-hand what was inside—the park was stunning. I gave Zed a leg up so he could avoid the spikes and jump to the gravel on the other side.

Jane was next in line, but as she started to go over, something hit her inside. "I can't go in *there!*" she exclaimed when I already had her halfway up.

"It's *cool*, Jane. You *can*, and it'll be *awesome!*" I coaxed, to no avail. She came back down and pleaded with me, but Zed was saying the opposite from the other side. I, in something of a bind, trying to get over the high wrought-iron fence, found a section where the street was clear of cars in front of it and, with a running start, hit it like dynamite. My hands hooked the top of the spike, and I felt my body float over the precipice like an eagle in flight. I didn't climb it; I *vaulted* over it.

Zed looked bewildered, his mouth gaping, when he said, "*Wow*, that was so *cool*, man! You like were ten feet off the *ground!*" The two of us ran around, feeling the earth. We found benches and laydown to look at the bleak stars, trying to break through. We lay head to head as we spoke.

"I want to feel like this all the time!" he said to me; I was caught up watching a building crumble before my eyes.

"I can't believe how good this feels, you know, man? We're like acid brothers."

"Yeah, acid brothers!" Zed replied, and we sat up, grabbing hands, our fingers entwined in a monumental shake.

"*Forever!*" we said simultaneously.

WHEN WE GOT BACK UPSTAIRS, Jean answered the door in a hushed whisper. Jane was already sitting there, chewing her fingernails. Jean's father had been pretty pissed off and wanted someone to go. It was strange for us to comprehend in our drug-induced haze, but the realization that one of us would have to leave was frightening. I couldn't go home; God only knew what my mother would say if she saw me like that. And it was three in the morning. Zed might have an easier time, but the shit would hit the fan. Jane and her mother had a strained relationship to begin with, so it would not have been good.

Jean came back in the room and told Jane she was the one that was going to have to leave. She started to freak out, telling him it ought to be me who should go, not her, but the lack of solidarity seemed to agitate Jean even more.

"Look, you just have to *go! Alright?*" He didn't want to be argued with; it was his father, not him. She left soon after, and the three of us sat back around Oliver the candle.

We laughed and talked as the night wore on; before we knew it, the clock read 7:00. Because of the speed in the acid, sleeping was out of the question, so we watched T.V. I went into the bathroom for the first time and was appalled at what I saw: My skin was translucent, and I could see the veins flowing underneath. When I pushed my fingers into it, the elasticity seemed to be gone, and I watched the crater formed by my finger fill back at an alarmingly slow rate.

At last we started to come down, and when Jean's father awoke at 8:30, he told Jean to send us home. We collected our shit and slowly meandered downstairs into the world. The daylight was thrashing, and it was a Sunday to boot; the religious ramifications compounded the stillness in the air. Zed, feeling shaky, leaned up against a tree and vomited, flushing black gel from his insides just as a happy family of four was passing on the way to church. He looked up, wiping the black stain from his mouth as the father moved his children protectively to the other side of him.

We began the slow walk to my house, speaking of the strange events of the night. We still had the feeling of speed coursing through our veins. When we got there, it was a little after nine o'clock, and I felt safe enough to go up and face my parents. My mother hopefully wouldn't catch on—she was hip to things, but we needed to lie down and vegetate for a while. We looked at each other, laughing silently inside as we rode up, looking at Pete the elevator man's back.

When we got to my floor, I looked at Zed and sat him down on the staircase.

"Don't start laughing like a hyena, alright, man?" I warned him, trying not to laugh as well. Zed nodded, waiting for the bed he would receive. I put my key into the lock and opened the door as silently as I could. My sister didn't seem to be there, and my mother had a strange look on her face as well. Her eyes were a little baggy, and she was cleaning up wine glasses and bottles from what looked like a party. We said our hellos and made our way toward the bedrooms. My father lay on their bed, watching TV, fully dressed in what appeared to be the previous night's clothes. Could it be they'd had a drug-and-booze-induced frenzy themselves?

I went to my father and hugged him; he invited us in to watch the tube. I flopped down beside him, telling him about the movie we hadn't seen.

"That's nice, Dave. . .glad you had a good time," he mumbled, folding his arms behind his head. Zed reappeared from the bathroom and lay down on the other side of me. The three of us, totally relaxed and cut off from the blinding light of day by the inner courtyard, watched *Bonanza* on the tube; the lines running diagonally on the T.V. reminded me of Chardin's *Green-Necked Duck*.

CHAPTER 12

S INCE I NEVER SAW IT COMING, the look in my mother's eyes that night hit me in the face like a ton of bricks. I thought someone had died. My grandmother had gotten pretty sick that year. But she was tough, and I was her golden boy. I loved her, and the relationship we shared was like no other in my life.

My father's twin had died at birth, as well as his own father on his twenty-third birthday. I'd been told I had a lot of my grandfather's qualities, his way with people—Sam had been the kind that could wade into a party with a hundred strangers and get to know ninety of them but not quite make it to the last ten, the ones who turned out to be the assholes.

I thought that my grandmother made up for her failed relationship with my father *through* me. She had a great East Side apartment. The one thing that stuck in my mind about it as I stood there looking at my mother was the extraordinary disorder that created such a calm chaos. Grandma would periodically open bank accounts to get the free gifts that came with them that she never used, so toasters sat piled on top of one another, next to gift certificates and fans and jars full of candy.

But she had class—not the kind you're born with, the kind you hammer for yourself out of nothing. She operated on two principles: Don't deceive, and don't let anybody fuck with you. Orphaned at four, she'd reached these shores at fourteen and wound up owning an international business.

I had always been reminded of an expression growing up: "A good deal isn't a good deal unless *everybody's* happy." The moral values that she bequeathed to me stuck like sand to a wet body.

She smoked like a chimney—unfiltered Chesterfields—and when they found the spots on her lungs, it hadn't been all that surprising to my father or anyone else. I thought it would be one more thing in her life she'd shove aside. But cancer doesn't negotiate.

One time in particular when we were visiting her in the hospital after she received some radiation, the entire family walked into the private room and saw her lying there, her blonde hair fanned out and pressed against the pillow, her arms strapped to the bedrail in the hope of keeping her from ripping out her feeding tube. This wasn't my grandmother as I watched my sister take the brush that lay on the table and work on her hair. I was trying not to let the stench of the hospital filling my nose interfere with the love I so wanted to give to her.

"Barry, can we go and get something to eat?" she asked her son—in a voice dry from dehydration—who was trying to be a rock of his own, on the other side of the bed.

"Yeah, Ma, whatever you want," he managed to say.

We managed to get her home some weeks later, but she was

never the same again. She would hold my hand as she grew smaller before my eyes, her radiance always there to me, but I didn't want her to stay merely for my sake. I had the feeling my grandfather was waiting with open arms.

But the look on my mother's face that day wasn't the look of death, but of injustice. She had baggy eyes from crying for some time. I quickly asked if Grandma had died, but she shook her head.

"Your father is going away," she said, fighting the tears that had been flowing all night. Just then my father came in with a blank expression on his face.

A FEW HOURS EARLIER, I HAD BEEN MOVING through the subway cars, eating up the time till my stop. I'd passed a woman who was dressed pretty well for riding a train and who clenched her purse in her lap like a toy poodle as I walked by. Really, I'd thought. Do I look like that much of a hoodlum? I loved riding between cars or looking out the window of the first car: It was like mining gold.

I had gotten off at Fifty-Seventh Street and climbed out of the subway. I had a callback for a movie—one of my first, so I wanted to hit it out of the park. It was a really interesting script about a group of boys at boarding school. The working title was *Dead Poets' Society*.

I'd ambled into the casting office and seen a bunch of very familiar faces. I was nervous—and excited to see I was up against some good actors. "Ethan?" the woman had soon called out to a roomful of boys looking very similar in style. He'd gotten up, tall and gangly, but I'd seen his work, and even at our age he was pretty good. I had kept focusing on the script at hand, read it over and over again, trying to find the nuances, stood up and rolled my head, trying to loosen up. About ten minutes had gone by before Ethan walked out of the room, smiling. "David?" the assistant had called out, looking around the room.

"Yeah, that's me," I'd said, shrugging to loosen up even further.

"Are you ready?" she had asked with a smile.

"As ready as I'll ever be!" I'd said right back, with a smile.

She had led me into a conference room with three people standing huddled.

A salt-and-pepper haired guy with an English-style cardigan sweater had come over first. "I'm Peter. I saw your tape. Very nice work." He'd had no airs about him whatsoever. "You want to try this?" he'd asked, sitting down in a chair across from another.

"WHAT DO MEAN, 'GOING AWAY'? FOR HOW LONG?" I asked my father, whose head was bowed. A fourteen-year-old doesn't understand separation, and I wasn't an exception. My parents rarely fought, and the love seemed to be there, so I didn't get it.

"When are you coming back?" I demanded, since it was my life he was in the process of fucking up.

"I'm not *coming* back, David. It doesn't have anything to do with you or your sister, I love you with all my heart—but your mother and I can't live together anymore."

"This is *your* shit, Barry—don't put it on me!" my mother shouted as she walked into the kitchen.

My sister came out of the bedroom after hearing the commotion, looked at me with tear-stained eyes, and retreated again like a wounded creature. I ran in after her and saw her crying on her bed. I sat on the end of it. "What's the hell is going on?" I said, hope she would have some insight.

My sister sat up and looked at me. "I don't know. I came home, and Mom was sitting in the kitchen, crying. David, why does shit like this have to *happen?*" She leaned over and hugged me. I tried to calm her but felt tears of my own brewing. I picked up a doll she'd had since birth. It was ratty and old but reminded me of better times.

I put the doll on the bed next to her, went back to the living room accompanied by my anger, and stood next to the piano, not sure of what to say. My father sat across the room on the sofa. "You're a *sonofabitch*, you *know* that?" I screamed, choked by tears; I had never cursed at my father before. I walked my fingers over the keys of the piano, trying to ignore his presence. My family was being shattered like a mirror.

I HAD SAT DOWN ACROSS FROM PETER, and he'd picked up his script. "If you don't mind, I'd like to try something different," he had said as he stood up moved over to the conference table. "I'd like to have you sit under the table and imagine that you are in a cave." He had such fire in his eyes and was so into the work.

"Sure, I'm game for anything," I'd said, gotten up off my chair, and sat cross-legged under the table, unembarrassed by the other people, who I assumed were the producers, sitting on a couch about ten feet away. Peter had sat down cross-legged in front of me.

"I want you envision a fire in front of you. The glow shows the faces of your friends around you." He'd gotten very into the moment and helped me get to the place where I needed to be to start the scene.

MY FATHER LOOKED AT ME AS HE BREATHED in deeply and put his fingers beneath his chin where it was natural for it to rest. He pursed his lips as if he had something to say, but nothing came out. My sister came from her room with a face that she had tried to fix with make-up and, without a word, headed out of the house. I watched her leave as I slowly meandered over to the couch. I sat on the opposite side from my father. "Can't you go away for a while—see how you feel?" I said, not looking his way but trying my best to be diplomatic.

"I've felt this way for a long time, David, and I stayed till now for you and your sister, but I can't go on living like this anymore."

At that moment, I realized that the chain of events was genuine. I looked up for the first time and saw my mother's saddened face in the kitchen. I wanted to take away her pain and replace it with love. I went over and sat by her, holding her hand as she sobbed, mourning the loss of a husband who was now dead in her eyes.

Her marriage of eighteen years seemed a fraud. She gathered herself together, and I began to watch her morph back into the mother I knew. She walked into the living room, looked my father in the eyes, and said, "If you're going to go, just get your shit and go! Don't lose the backbone I *thought* you had now!"

I'D SEEN THE IMAGINARY FIRE and warmed my hands to it. "Good! Very good, feel the warmth of it, see the crackle, the way it lights up the walls of the cave!" Peter had gotten very excited, and as an actor it was an amazing thing to be taken into that world created by the script and brought in deeper by a man that cared so much for the work. "Now!" he had said. "Start your first line now!" I'd jumped into the dialogue and read with him. It was astonishing to feel so a part of the work and so in the moment. We had done it over and over again; he'd given me a critique and spoken to me as if I was a real professional and understood what he was saying, and I'd tried my best to give him what he wanted. After what seemed like an eternity, Peter had smiled and slapped his thighs. "Okay! That was really great, David. Thank you so much for humoring me." He had stood up, and I'd crawled out from under the table.

"That was one of the most amazing times I've had at an audition ever," I had said, feeling so comfortable in his presence. He'd put his arm over my shoulder and walked me to the door.

"I think you have amazing potential, my young friend. I hope this works out." I had walked out of that room understanding why Ethan had been smiling when he left. I think I'd had the same look as I left.

I LEFT MY HOUSE WITHOUT A SOUND and took the steps down two at a time as I sometimes did to clear my head. I saw no one I knew from the building as I headed to Positively's on Eight Street to quietly waste away, playing a game of Joust or Galaga. I fed in a few quarters but found concentrating on the game impossible. I didn't even notice when Patsy walked up to me.

In a white leather Le Tigre jacket and matching fingerless leather gloves, she was the toughest person I knew. She'd taken me under her wing at a young age, so it wasn't surprising that she could tell something was going on. "Whas' up, kid?" she asked as she messed with my hair, trying to get my attention.

I shrugged and turned away from her without saying a word.

Patsy was Irish; the fact that she was a lesbian wasn't an issue, since she was more man than most—but *nobody* ignored Patsy. She beat people senseless for less. "What the fuck is your *problem*, little man?" she said in an aggravated tone, saving face over a kid six years younger showing disrespect. She took about five steps from where I was standing; I could feel her stare burning the back of my neck. "Get the fuck over here!" she exclaimed, rubbing her fist into the opposing palm. I knew she would never hit me, but I wasn't stupid enough to chance it. I walked over to her as my eyes welled up with tears. She opened her arms and grabbed me, like a mother. "It's alright, Davey boy, I was kiddin'. C'man, you know that!" she declared to the crew that surrounded her. "What happened, kid?"

We sat down in a booth, and I told her everything. "Wow," she said, "that's a tough break." She spoke of the father *she* hardly knew and reminded me that parents were only human.

Her brother Doodles, as they called him in the neighborhood, was serving a ten-year stint in Attica for getting into a fair fight that had poured out into the streets from a bar on Third Avenue. After the cops broke it up, they separated the two guys into different squad cars, but Doodle's opponent leaned his head back as he passed out, choking to death on his own vomit. The Assault charge became Murder One, and Doodles got three hots and a cot, leaving his little sister to take care of their ailing mother.

"*You're* the man of the house now, David," she said to me, with a pointed finger. She was deadly serious as she looked into my eyes. "But I am *always* here for you, anything you need. Okay?" She walked me back to the game I had been playing and threw the kid who was on it physically to the side.

"Go an, finish your game," she said, dropping a few quarters on the screen. As she stomped out of the pizzeria, I felt—for the first time since I heard the news from my parents—things might be okay.

CHAPTER 13

T HINGS WERE DIFFICULT TO GET USED TO after my pop left. He'd found an apartment in Hoboken that was affordable and became the Monday–Thursday–Sunday guy. My mother was alone for the first time in a long time.

I was trying to take acting seriously and really learn the craft; it took my mind off the chaos that was my life. There was an acting school in the West Village with a well-known actor teaching in it— but, at my age, I had to get consent from the teacher himself. I learned that one of his classes met on Saturday, so I got up and trudged over in the cold.

When I got there, it had started to drizzle, and the place wasn't even open yet; I sat on a car and waited. An older gentleman came walking up a few minutes later, a slow limp in his step and an Eastern European way about him; he stopped and looked at me. I hopped off the car, but this wasn't the man I was waiting for; I smiled and leaned up against it instead.

"What are you doing here, young man?" he asked in a heavy accent, slapping the water from the newspaper he used to cover his head. When I explained whom I was waiting for, he replied with a nod. "Why don't you come inside and wait for him? I'm sure he'll be along shortly. He doesn't do well with schedules." We went into the building, and the man took off his coat and dropped the paper into the garbage by the door.

"This is a really cool place, huh?" I said, pulling off my hat. "I really like the vibe here. It'd be great to take a class." I looked all around the theater and sat on the edge of the stage. We talked for a little bit—I told him I hoped to get into the class and was honest about my age.

He looked at me. "Tell you what," he said, slapping his hand on his thighs and standing up to adjust his suspenders. "My name is Herbert. I teach a class here myself, and if he doesn't take you in his class, I'll take you in mine, okay?"

I didn't realize I was not only talking to a great actor, but to the owner of the school; I started classes with him the following day and never looked back.

Annabella had meanwhile been working hard, getting me some auditions—I really wanted it, the whole fucking enchilada, so I worked on the material I was given with a vengeance. She called me one afternoon with a big part on a soap opera. I hadn't been auditioning that long, so I wasn't very hopeful, but I figured it'd be good experience.

I dressed carefully, took the train uptown, got to the building, and waited in the lobby for my name to be called. There were quite a few guys sitting around on couches or the floor, reading their lines. I had memorized mine but had been told never to put down the pages—it gave the appearance that the scene was a work in progress.

When they finally called me and I got in the room, the casting director was looking at the newspaper. "Whenever you're ready," he said, not looking my way. I was a little taken back but went into the scene, reading opposite the *New York Post*. After I finished, the guy leaned around and told me I'd done a nice job.

When I got to the lobby, it had filled even more; I dumped the sides in the butt can by the elevators, left, and caught the train back downtown feeling pretty shitty. When I got home, there was a message on the machine to call Annabella. I hoped there hadn't been a problem reading against the newspaper. Maybe someone'd seen me throw the sides in the garbage? A million different scenarios ran through my head as I dialed her number. After getting a receptionist and then an assistant, Annabella came on.

"How'd it go today?" The tone in her voice suggested it hadn't.

"You know, it was fine. I did okay. He was reading a newspaper through most of it, though." Beat her to the punch, I figured.

"Ah, forget about the newspaper. He loved you! He thought you were very natural, and he loved your presence! Unfortunately, he thought you were too young for the role."

It wasn't my first rejection, but they never were easy.

"David? Are you still there?"

"Yeah, I'm here. Sorry—it just bums me out, you know? I really want to book something."

"Well, my little star, you *did*. You booked yourself a re-occurring part on the soap! You don't even have to *read* for it! It's a character in a different storyline than the one you went out on, but it's perfect! He's a bit of a bad boy, someone's boyfriend, and you start next Friday!"

I couldn't believe what I was hearing. A *job?* It was the best feeling I'd ever had! "You have to be fucking kidding me—I mean, after that audition, I figured, you know—"

"*Forget* about all that, kiddo—and watch your mouth! He loved you, and I am so proud! I'll have one of the girls call with the details."

I hung up the phone and sat on the arm of the couch in stunned shock. It was pretty damn cool to feel like a professional.

THE AGENCY TOLD ME TO BE DOWNSTAIRS AT SEVEN in the morning sharp. I couldn't sleep a wink the night before, and when I came down, there was a limo sitting out front. The driver stepped out in a black suit and said, "I'm a few minutes early, sir, but I have today's paper if you want to leaf through."

"I don't think you're here for me," I said to him with a bit of a laugh.

"Yes, I think I am. You're working at Fifty-seventh Street today? David, isn't that right?" He turned to the door of the stretch and opened it for me.

"Y-Yeah, that's right," I replied, climbing inside, taking notice of the thermos next to the paper.

The glass partition came down. Through the rear-view mirror, the driver said, "I picked up some coffee for you with cream and sugar—if you need anything on the way uptown, let me know. My name's Vincent." He started to raise the partition glass.

Utterly awestruck, I stopped him. "That's okay, Vincent—you can leave it open."

I'd passed the awning a hundred times, but it had never occurred to me I might be *working* there someday. When I entered the building, a short guy with a headset and a grin came up. "Hey, David!" he said, pumping my arm. "Name's Charlie. Glad to meet you! I'm the assistant stage manager, and I'm gonna show you to your dressing room and then take you through hair and make-up. Is there anything I can get you?" He spoke extremely fast but was clear as he led me through a long hallway.

"No, I'm fine." I was trying to play it cool—as much as I knew how, but I was pretty nervous. There were rooms on either side, and we entered one that seemed to have memorabilia all *over* it.

"I know it looks personalized, but don't hesitate to make yourself at home. I'll give you a minute to put your wardrobe on, and we can go to make-up." He left me alone in that weird soap opera shrine. The pictures were all of some guy I recognized from the show. It was pretty pitiful, right down to the *No Smoking* signs. I pulled out a cigarette and said to myself, "The man said to make myself at home," so I lit up and changed.

I followed Charlie to the make-up chair. "This is Charlene," he said.

The woman, with very done hair and cleavage for days, motioned for me to sit down and make myself comfortable. "Ah, so you're going to be the boyfriend. I see. . . ." She rubbed lotion on my face. She pursed her lips and started running her hands through my long hair.

"Oh, David," Charlie said, "I wanted to give you the pages for today." He handed over a packet.

I grabbed it and looked at him. "I worked on my script all night. I'm pretty good with them."

"Oh, no, David—these are *new* pages that came out this morning. I'm sure not *all* of your dialogue has changed, though. Take a look, and I'll come back for you in about thirty minutes." I watched him leave and started leafing through the pages. I saw my character's name a lot more heavily in the script. The thought of being on camera more was great, but trying to memorize all of it so quickly made me nervous. I kept on reading and started to get more panicky. Charlene just smiled and glanced at the pages over my shoulder. "Oo, look! You seem to be all over the place. You'll get it, sweetie—they always do."

When the stage manager returned, I figured I'd remember what I could and rely on the teleprompter for the rest. We walked down a long corridor to a door with a flashing red light above it. "That means they're rolling," Charlie said, finger to his lips. The light went off; he opened the door to let me in.

There were sets all over with bedrooms and offices, even a hospital. I saw a gorgeous brunette ahead of us, laughing with an older guy. Charlie led me over. "David, this is Emily. She plays Charlotte on the show. Emily, David. He's your Brad!" The girl looked me up and down without saying a word and returned to her conversation.

Awesome. First day, and I get a diva. "Hey, Charlie, where's the teleprompters?" I asked.

"Oh, we don't use those, haven't for years. That's why I gave you the *pages*, killer!" Charlie left, taking his irrepressible grin with him. I was getting anxious when I spotted a wooden box on the side by the craft service table, went over to it, and sat down to focus. I found it easiest to memorize lines by reading them with somebody—but not with *this* bitch.

My head was down when I first smelled her perfume. "Is this your first time?" a woman asked me. I was so pensive I didn't realize at first that she talking to me. At last I looked up: It was one of the stars of the show, an older woman, and she was gorgeous. She'd been nominated for an Emmy every year of her career and never won, but I'd always thought she was pretty good. "Yeah, I'm just starting today, and they gave me all these new pages—ah, just trying to memorize them," I said with a half-hearted smile.

"You never do get used to that, do you?" she said in a tone that spoke of understanding. She finished making herself a cup of tea and smiled at me. "You know, I'm not sure if you subscribe to this way of thinking, but I always found it much easier to learn it by reading it through with someone."

"Exactly!" I said, perked by the affirmation. "I really do, too! I can't *believe* you think the same way! I met Emily, but she seemed a little busy, so I don't really have anyone to read with."

"Nonsense. I'm here ahead of schedule, and I'd love to read with you. I have a little room on the set we can go to."

Flabbergasted, I followed her. "My name's Susan—and you are. . . ?"

"Uh, D—my name's David, and it's a real pleasure to meet you." I smiled a really big smile.

An hour later I was on set and going through the motions for real. Susan had really helped me out. I felt so good inside as the light shone on my face, the crowd standing around with grins on their faces—it was a world I wanted to be a part of. When I was doing my scene with Emily, Susan walked by, waved, and smiled to me. No one quite understood but her and me; it was obvious Emily didn't love that.

I GOT HOME PRETTY LATE THAT NIGHT, and the next morning my mother was sitting at the kitchen table when I woke up, coffee in hand, dressed in her usual flannel robe. I wanted to tell her all about my first day at work, but she seemed serious.

"Your grandmother died this morning, David. Your father called. He's at her house, waiting for you." She wasn't cold, but she and my grandmother had never gotten along. My mother'd never felt accepted, and that had not only frustrated but angered her. But she felt gratitude that at least her *children* were treated with respect.

My sister and I rode in a cab up to the apartment on the East Side as we had so many times before—but now I was going to say goodbye. When I entered the grand lobby of her building, heads bowed. I wasn't sure if they'd loved her or the huge tips they received at Christmas, but they gave respect, and that was all anyone could ask.

"Hey, buddy, I'm sorry about your granny," John the doorman said in a pretty thick Brooklyn accent as we came through the revolving door. He had known her for twenty years, so I believed him.

We waited at the bank of elevators. There were veined mirrors on both walls, so when you looked in, it went on forever. That always amused me: No matter how hard you tried, you could never look past yourself.

The elevator doors opened; I pushed 44. The familiar orange around the number lit up. When we got to the apartment, the door was open, and it seemed unchanged. Familiar smells hung like smoke in the air. My father was sitting in the kitchen, on the chair that she had sat in when we played rummy. He had an inconsolable look on his face. We went to him, and, from a seated position, he grabbed us, pulling us closer, and cried at our waists. It was wails and sobs, and was the first time I could recollect seeing my father cry. I felt his sense of abandonment. But his life was finally his now; the control his mother had over him died that day.

"Your grandmother loved the two of you so much," he said with deep feeling. There was a lot to be done that morning; Jews don't waste any time. No embalming, just a quick burial, and then the process of *shiva*. It's when the immediate family sits on boxes to feel the pain of loss and all the mirrors get draped because it is a time, not for vanity, but for remembrance.

He told us we could look at her if we wanted to—since it was customary not to have open casket, it might be the last time we saw her. The walk from the kitchen to the bedroom seemed an eternity. From the hall I caught my first glimpse of the white sheet that shielded her face from the world. The Haitian woman who had been her caregiver was sitting on a chair by the bed. I hadn't even known she was in the apartment, but it didn't seem as if any of it fazed her. I was sure she had been in that position more than once, and when we entered, she rose and calmly folded the sheet back.

"I was da one dat foun' her, children," she said, almost proudly. "I made sure to change de linen befo' yo fadda come ovah, put her teef in. I took care—don' you worry. You granny was nice to me."

Neither my sister nor I was sure what to say. I turned away but caught sight of her in the mirror that hung over the bureau. I turned back. The mouth was slightly ajar.

"She die real peaceful. No pain now, children," she said. I reached out and touched the cold hand, which lay composed at her side. Her flaxen hair was spread out on the pillow. She did look peaceful, even if only the shell of someone I had loved very much. I went to her and touched her cold hand and the reality set in.

We went back in the kitchen, where my father was already talking to Riverside Chapel about the service, and the *Times* for the obituary. Everything had its place, nice and neat, plenty to do, so those in mourning would keep their minds busy.

Since I had never been to a funeral, I didn't have the clothes for one. I asked my father what to do; without even thinking, he reached into his wallet, took out two hundred- dollar bills, and handed them to me. I normally would have been shocked at such a gesture but silently put them in my front pocket.

"What should I get, Pop?"

"A jacket and a tie. Slacks. Some shoes if you want," he mumbled almost inaudibly. My sister didn't even bitch that she didn't get to go shopping, since she had a lot of dresses, at least one to fit the occasion. But it would be one of my first such outings, and I wanted it to go smoothly.

When I got downstairs, I asked John where I might find a

jacket.

"Ah, I see," the man said, seriously pondering the situation. "Well, a young man can't really go wrong at Macy's or Alexander's for that. You want a cab, buddy?"

"No, John, I think I'll walk," I said, and headed out the door. Although Alexander's was on the East Side, I thought better of Macy's, since it was more on the way home. I walked down Second Avenue, thinking of Celia and the times we shared. As I headed west on Thirty-fourth Street, I recalled what had happened to me only months before in that same spot.

I was going to meet my friends at the theater there to see a movie about a guy who lived with apes. Sounded stupid, but I wanted to hang with my friends, so I went along. I was on my way when I realized I was a couple of bucks short and thought maybe I could go to my grandmother for them. She usually gave me stuff like that. I went to her house, where she lay in bed, the Haitian woman standing guard over her like a sentry. I went to my grandmother's side and said hello. "*Duvidel! Bubbaleh sheyna*, "she said, words I'd heard my whole life. But before she could say anything more, she passed out.

"She just took her sleepin' pill, boy. She can't talk now. Come back laytah, and you can talk to your granny, right?"

I nodded but noticed a roll of dimes sitting on the bureau in front of the bed. I took hold of it and made my way out the door.

"You bedda tell someone you took them, boy—don' wan' no-body blamin' me," the caregiver said with some unpleasantness in her voice. Which was strange, I thought in retrospect, since after my grandmother had died the expensively street-valued painkiller

Levodromoran had gone missing.

"No one's gonna blame you, alright? She wouldn't care, okay?" I added somewhat cockily, but I was fourteen, after all. Running late for the movie, I hurried down the eight blocks to Thirty-fourth, where I would make the right to the theater.

I saw the flashing *Walk* sign, which to any normal New Yorker meant *Run*, bolted across the street, and was nearing the other side when I felt a sudden pain on my hip and was thrown in the air. I felt weightless in the slow, unending motion of the moment and landed hard on the curb after being hit by a car that had jumped the light and sent me over the hood and across the roof.

"Don't move, kid," said a man who had bent down to help me. The car that struck me had tried to get away, but a semi-truck who had seen the whole thing had prevented that.

"Do me a favor," I asked the guy in a daze, "take my smokes, alright? I don't need hear it from my mother at the hospital." The guy laughed at the gesture, pulled the pack of Marlboro out of my front pocket, and put them in his own. He noticed dimes all over the street. "Those yours? I can pick em up if you want."

The paramedics had already pulled up and were already doing their job around us. I said, "Na, just leave 'em."

As the ambulance pulled away, I realized I'd been hit again by karmic rebound.

CHAPTER 14

LOOKED UP TO SEE THE MACY'S ENTRANCE staring me in the face, like the lions at the Public Library. When I entered, it felt different. I went up to the first guard I saw. "Excuse me?" I said. Though the man was standing and looking right at me, he was miles away. "Hello?" I said a little louder, which finally caught his attention, and he bent forward.

"You lost, kid? Just go to the lady at the desk in the front of the store," he said, pointing, "and she'll get on the loud speaker, okay?"

What a dick, I was thinking. "Actually," I said, "I wanted to ask you if you knew where I could find a jacket—for a funeral. Maybe a tie?"

"Oh," the guard said, feeling a little foolish. "Well, what do I look like, the directory for the store? I just make sure kids don't run out without paying."

I reached into my front pocket, pulled out the money my father had given me, and waved it in front of him. "You think you'll have that problem with me? *I* don't, but if you don't think the store needs my money, I can go somewhere else!" I realized my voice was raised. He walked around his podium, coming face to face with me. Who the fuck did he think he was?

Just as matters seemed to be escalating, an older man in a suit came over, causing the guard to come to attention. The newcomer was wearing a pressed shirt, a flawless tie, a perfectly folded kerchief. "What seems to be the problem here? Any way I can assist you, young man?" he asked, slipping between the guard and me.

I looked at him and froze, stopped in time. A situation had arisen quicker than I could have imagined; fighting the urge to cry, I said, "My grandmother died this morning. My father said I need to get some clothes, but this guy—" I couldn't hold back the tears any longer.

The man pulled the handkerchief out of his lapel pocket and handed it to me. "We at Macy's are terribly sorry for your loss. Horrible thing to have to go through. Please forgive me—my name is Robert. And you are. . . ?"

I rubbed my eyes, embarrassed to be causing a scene, but I missed my grandma, and it was slowly hitting me. I gave my name. "All I did was ask him. . . . I have money."

The man, who had bent closer, gave the guard a look that seemed to humble him before he said, "Please. Don't worry—I'm sure your father gave you ample money for your purchase. Is there anything specific you had in mind?"

I felt my grandmother beaming over my shoulder. "Well," I said, catching my breath and collecting myself, "I thought a jacket would be good. Not black, though—my grandmother thought that was a bad color for people to wear."

"Ah, yes, I see. Sounds like a very smart woman. Midnight blue, maybe. Why don't we take the elevator up to the third floor, and we can find something together? Would that be alright with you?"

We were already moving toward the lift. "That would be really cool, if you would help me. You know, my grandmother was in the garment business for a long time," I said proudly as we waited.

"That doesn't surprise me. She sounds like she understood style, from what you said about the color." He said, hands folded neatly in front of him as we waited.

The elevator doors opened, and the operator snapped to attention as we entered. "Three, please, Douglas."

When the doors reopened and we were standing in front of Young Men's Formal, the salespeople perked up and started to cross over, but Robert waved them away. "She was really tough," I said, "but classy—yeah, very classy." The man, busy pulling this and that from the rack, never lost track of the conversation.

"She has quite a grandson, and I consider myself a fairly good judge of people. You look like you're a. . .16 jacket, a fourteen-inch neck, twenty-five-inch waist."

I was impressed. "Wow! You've been doing this a long time?"

"My grandmother was also in the garment business, and my father, so clothes are what I know," said the man. "I picked a very simple assortment of white shirts that will be accented by a beautiful tie, pleated gray gabardine slacks, of course the blue jacket, and the shoes—do you prefer lace-up or loafers?"

I had never thought about lace-up shoes, I'd only worn penny loafer as my nicest, so this was new territory. "What do *you* think, Robert? You have style."

"Well, thank you very much, David—and if I may say so, you look like a size 8? There's a beautiful pair of lace-up wing tips that will work very well for the occasion; your grandmother would be very proud, David."

"Yeah, wing tips would be nice." We narrowed down my choices, picked a pair, and headed to the cashier.

"If you put on the pants, I'll personally get them hemmed immediately, and you can leave with them all pressed and ready to go for the day," he said solemnly.

"Thank you so much for everything. You're a really cool guy," I said. "My grandmother would have liked you. You're no bull-shit, if you know what I mean," I added sheepishly.

"I do know, and I appreciate the compliment, and I'm sure that I'd have liked her, too. David, I am truly very sorry. But she obviously instilled some wonderful things in you." We finished the measurement, and I gave him the pants back. He left to get them altered.

He came back in what seemed like an instant, handed me all my clothes neatly pressed and hung, shoes in a bag, and said, "Again I am sorry for any painful moment you had earlier, but it was a privilege helping you, and I wish you the best." We shook hands and parted.

I walked back to the elevator, pushed the button, and, waiting, felt eyes upon me—but in a good way—from the working girls. The elevator operator, hand on the brass throttle he was using to control the lift, like the kind in my own apartment building—also kept glancing at me. He finally cleared his throat and said, "Sorry to bother you, sir, but are you someone famous's son or. . . ?"

"No, I was just shopping for a funeral, and that man was nice enough to help me out."

"You know who he is?" the operator replied with a chuckle. "His grandfather built this store, and his family still owns the place. He is an extremely busy man, and in all the years I've been here, I've never seen him do that. I figured you must be one special kid."

On my way out of the store, I noticed a woman had replaced the bullish guard. I paused at the curb, looking for a cab home with the money I had left over.

It isn't exactly easy catching a cab when you're my age. They shoot by you unless they're really desperate. But a guy in a pin-striped suit, reading the *Times*, got the one in front of me, so I got the next, a Checker cab, my favorite because of the jump seats that pulled up off the floor for extra people; regardless of how many were in the cab, I always used them. "Eleventh and Fifth, please," I said, trying to sound like a grown-up. "And don't worry, I got money."

"I wasn't, or I wouldn't have picked you up, you know?" the guy said, looking back at me through the rear view. "I mean, I'm not really prejudiced or nothing, you know, for kids or coloreds." Had he just use the word "coloreds"? "I used to do a bit a' dine-and-dash when I was your age, so, you know, I know. The only thing I am sort of, you know, prejudiced about, I'll admit, is. . .ahh, most of the time, when I pick up colored people, they want to go back up to Harlem or something. And you know, it's not

them—I don't pick up people give me a bad feelin' or nothing anyway, but it's being a cabbie in the middle of Harlem after I drop
them off. That's kinda scary. You never know what's gonna
happen."

I leaned up to look at the hack license. Morton, his name read,
B6026, Morton, Gary. "Yeah, well, I don't know much about
being a cabbie, so I'm sure you got your reasons." I leaned back
against the jump seat, looking out the window at the cars on Fifth.

"Yeah, well, one day when you grow up, and you gotta fight
for a job that they give to a guy half as qualified as you, just 'cause
he's colored, you'll get the point. I mean, you must be doin' pretty
good, living where you do, huh? Shoppin' at Macy's an' all."

"Well, actually, it's a rent-stabilized apartment that we've been
living in for years now, and I was at the store picking up clothes
for my grandmother's funeral—since we're Jewish, I had to get
something quick, 'cause it all comes down real fast."

"Oh, yeah? I just woulda figured, you know, your people
woulda shopped somewhere more bargain-friendly," the driver said
with a humph.

"Since my grandmother came here with nothing, I think I owe
it her to look good, don't you?"

"Hey, look, I'm sorry she died and all. I didn't mean nothing
by it, you know. I was just sayin'."

I continued looking out the window as we neared my place.
"Left side, far corner," I said as the cab pulled up. I paid and got
out.

"Good luck and all," the cabbie said to me.

I replied, "I don't need luck. I'm only a kid. *You* need the luck, cause I doubt you'll ever change." I turned toward the building.

Eddy, who was as usual sitting in the lobby, slowly rose when I entered. "Hey, buddy, what you up to, making trouble like you do, huh?" He was sucking his teeth to finish the last of the lunch he'd picked out with his toothpick. I was silent. As we rode up, he must have felt the need to fill the void.

"What's the matter, cat got your tongue?"

"My grandmother died this morning, Eddy," I said, looking down.

"Aw, jeez. I'm sorry, buddy. That's a tough one, huh. Yeah, my momma die when I was fighting in the war, you know? Never got to say goodbye."

As I watched him replaying the events in his head, we rode up in silence. When he opened the gate, he said, "She was nice lady, your grandma. You're lucky. Be tough, okay?"

As he closed the door, I was numb.

CHAPTER 15

FELT SOMBER AS I GOT DRESSED. I knew my mother would have preferred not going, but my pop needed support regardless of what had been going on between them. I studied myself in the mirror as I put on my tie—I'd been able to knot it myself for a while. "You look nice, David," she said as she walked up from behind me to brush my shoulders.

"So do you, Ma." I grabbed my new jacket before leaving the room and gave her and my sister a moment. From my position on the couch, I had noticed Dana crying all over her blue dress when she entered the living room. We closed the front door and headed downstairs, where our father would be waiting; he was always prompt.

When we got to the street, we could see him staring off into space through the windows. He turned at our footsteps, opened the car door, and climbed out to hug us. I tried to ignore the formality as we loaded in and headed to the funeral home at Riverside.

When we got there, a man in a black suit approached my pop to offer condolences; looking around, I saw a sign with my grand-mother's name and headed toward it. I noticed the Star of David on the top of the casket and realized how small people looked in death. Even though she had been maybe five feet on a good day, I couldn't understand how she could fit into such a small box.

Dana came in and started crying—I watched our mother trying to comfort her; she fought it all the way to the chairs in front. I ran my fingers over the unstained oak. We had called as many guests as possible, but old people either have the gift of being one of the first to go or attend a funeral every week; my grandmother fell somewhere in between.

The first person I saw when I turned back was my uncle. It was tough to miss a guy six foot four, bald on top, with a beard sur-rounding his worried face. I didn't think the worry was for today; the past few years, he'd always had that look. I loved the man who, when he heard about the separation, had met me in the city to talk and give me a baseball glove.

My grandfather Poppy was tucked in behind the looming fig-ure, but I, spotting him, went up and hugged him especially hard, realizing his mortality. Poppy, a man of few words, had never been the same after his wife died eleven or so years before; death would only be a quiet end punctuation to the sentence of his life.

When it was over we headed back to my grandmother's apart-ment to begin the *shiva*. It felt empty without her. I was used to her standing in a housecoat by the kitchen when I entered the gen-erally unlocked door. I sat on the couch and stared at the T.V., waiting to hear her, as in a movie where someone speaks from an unknown, faraway place, but I didn't get my hopes up. Instead I took my shoes off, lay down on the Naugahyde sofa, and drifted in and out of sleep.

People came a few hours later. The hugging and crying persisted. I was hungry, so I went to the deli platter my father had ordered for the guests, made myself a sandwich, and quietly ate it. As I was finishing, I started to bawl uncontrollably, remembering the day in the hospital when she asked for something to eat from a good deli, and the fact that she would never be able to eat it again hit home. No more kisses, no more hugs; the glasses she wore still rested on top of the table, as if she had just gone out for a minute. It hit me like that: one moment, a sense of death, of never seeing her again.

I tried to compose myself and realized I was sitting in the same spot I had been when I'd learned of my father's dead twin; it was as if the two moments were linked now. I headed toward the balcony. Looking at the East River, it all sort of made sense: The universe unfolded as it should; everything happened for reasons.

I returned to the room and looked into the eyes of the people who had come together for support. I grabbed shoulders and squeezed as my father would do to me, and, inevitably, energy passed from one soul to another. My uncle was sitting on the couch, his long legs folded, trying to make room. "How you feeling, buddy?" He was good at being standoffish, a quality I had always appreciated.

"You know, Big Man, I'm okay, sad, but I understand, I'm not a kid anymore. Gotta be a man for the family." I stood a little straighter. He looked at me and smiled. On the other side of me,

Poppy sat eating a sesame bagel with a slice of Muenster cheese, and for a moment I watched the man bring the food up to his mouth as he struggled to take a bite. I looked at the signet ring he always wore; his late wife had given it to him on their engagement. But Poppy was staring into a void and something was speaking back as I watched the silent nods he gave. "Hey, Poppy," I said, startling him a bit.

He hadn't noticed I was there.

"Ah, David, come on now," he said, somewhat annoyed to be taken out of the place he was.

"I hope you know how much I love you, man," I said, taking the napkin off his lap and wiping food from the corner of his mouth. I put my arm over his shoulder.

Poppy patted me on the knee and said, "All right, all right now," having felt enough love for one afternoon.

I got up and kissed the stubble on his cheek. I walked up to my father, who was in mid-sentence, telling a story of how Celia had saved the life of a South American grandee who had later become his godfather. "Hey, Pop, if it's all right, I'm going to go downtown," I said, feeling my presence wasn't as needed, since the void was slowing filling.

"All right," he said, I hugged him tightly before I walked out the door.

When I got to the street, I realized it was spring and the smell in the air nostalgic. I walked slowly, enjoying the streets; I was walking for two. I spoke to my grandmother as I strolled. *Hey, Grandma, it was a little crazy this morning. Everyone cried for you. Not a dry eye in the place. I miss you a lot, but I feel you—*

honestly I do. I told this guy about you yesterday. Turned out to be an owner of Macy's. Liked your style from what I said. You with Grandpa? Tell him I wish I'd known him, will you? It was weird being in your apartment without you. Still smells like you, though. Dad is okay, but it's rough for him, you know that. He's not nearly as stoic as you. He cried a lot, which is perfectly understandable, don't you think? Please give him that, all right? Let him mourn the loss of you before he realizes you're really gone. I understand now, Grandma. I want you to know I'll never forget things you told me or showed me, and please try not to forget me, if they let you remember stuff like that where you are.

I feel like running all the time, wherever I go. Maybe it's to you, or maybe just to feel the wind. I love you, Grandma, I love you. I ended my silent conversation as my legs thrust me forward into a sprint. I didn't see the people looking at me running down the street in a jacket and tie. I felt the wind and knew I belonged.

FIFTEEN

(1985)

CHAPTER 16

I DIDN'T SET OUT TO MAKE MY MOTHER CRY, but it was working out that way more and more. I was standing in my room on a Saturday night, fixing my black leather tie and combing my pompadour with hair gel; it's not easy getting a perfect duck's ass when you only have the one mirror. I was going over to Jean's house for a bit of trouble, which was exactly what my mother didn't want.

"Where do you think *you're* going?" she said, coming through my open door, pushing it a little further ajar to establish her dominance.

"I already told you," I said, not even looking up from the mirror, my heart palpitating as it always did in those confrontations.

"Why do go to this Jean's house? You've known him for how long? And I haven't even *met* him! I *don't know what* you do there! Is his mother going to be home all night?" She knew full well a lie was coming but was giving me the benefit of the doubt.

"Mom, he doesn't *live* with his mother. God, how many times have I said that? His father will be there—all night. Why don't you ever trust me? Jesus Christ, I can't *stand* this shit!" I barked, feeling my blood racing. It was easier fighting with her than my father, since she carried the burden of being the disciplinarian in the house; and how could you fight with someone when you only saw them two or three hours a week?

"David," she said calmly, trying to defuse the escalating situation, "I don't want you going places where I don't know who is watching you, or what on God's green earth you're *doing!* Do you *understand* me?"

But I was off in my own world, trying to ignore the cries from the already beaten woman before me. She slammed the door, leaving me to brew. I turned to the half-open window, pulled out a smoke, and lit it as I exhaled, trying to make the smoke go out the window. She knew I smoked, but I tried not to be blatant about it. I sat on the radiator, smoking the cig, and checked my pockets for cash. She had gotten hip to my stealing and had taken to hiding her pocketbook in her closet when she came home from work, which didn't make it impossible but certainly less convenient.

My father threw me a twenty here and there—sort of guilt money, and I had a little savings from modeling and acting, which was quickly dwindling. My pot smoking was becoming more and more of a habit; I'd usually sneak out and hit the park on my way to Freddy's to share a dime bag I scored on the way almost every night, but fuck it. I was fifteen—I didn't have to answer to her anyway.

I felt completely stifled and suffocated by the only person in my life who was trying to keep me on the straight and narrow. I had about eighteen dollars, which I figured would suffice for whatever I was going to do that night. I checked the mirror one more time before leaving and headed to the living room.

She was sitting with tear-filled eyes on the couch, looking at me. It was always the hardest part of the leaving; I had to smooth it out so I wouldn't feel guilty all night long.

"I just don't know what to do with you, David," she said, trying to wipe the tears from her already swollen face. I looked at her and felt empty. "Would you pull this crap with your father? Why do you make it so difficult to have any inkling of a relationship with you? I am trying my best, David. Why can't you make it a little easier for me?"

"Why do you always turn it on him, huh?" I shouted back at her, feeling protective of the man, who wasn't there to defend himself. I rolled my eyes and, slowly turning the tables, said, "You never just trust me to go out and have a good time. Why don't you just trust me? I told you where I'm gonna be, and who I'm gonna be with. I mean, come on, Ma—it's Friday night, you know?"

"Fine, David, go out," she said, not looking back from the bamboo blind she seemed to have focused on. "You just do whatever you want. Are you coming back tonight?"

"I told you before that I was going to sleep over."

"You leave me Jean's number on that pad," she said, pointing to one of the many benefits she received from working at Bellevue Hospital—pads and paper clips were always at the ready in our house.

I went over to the walnut table against the wall in the foyer and grabbed the pad, along with a pen from a cup. The legend *Haldol: keeping psychotic symptoms in check* ran across the bottom of the pad. I contemplated giving her the number off by one digit—it was easy to make a nine look like a zero with my chicken-scratch handwriting. I looked at her, still sitting in the same position, and silently left.

"I love you, David," I heard as I was closing the door, which caused me to pause for a second. I listened to the familiar squeak the door made over the silence in the hallway.

Ralph was on duty when I got in the elevator; there was no conversation. We stopped on eight, and Murray got in, dressed in his usual herringbone jacket, beige shirt just slightly opened, beautifully creased pants, and the smell of Aqua da Silva cologne floating in the air. He slapped his thighs in the style of Bojangles, sticking his hand out for a shake as he spoke. "What's going on there, champ? Hey, say, you look pretty spiffy. You going out to paint the town red?" He pumped my hand and tried to elicit a smile.

"You know, Murr, just going out, hanging with some friends," I replied, trying not to look him dead in the eyes.

He let go of my hand and adjusted my tie ever so slightly. "You mind?" he said, pulling the knot a little further still to the right, making it loose but dead centered. I looked up as he was working on it, caught the man looking me in the eye, and darted away to the elevator ceiling.

In the lobby, instead of walking away with the familiar goodbyes, Murray kept to my side as we headed out into the autumn air. "Come on, David, let's walk for a sec," he said, putting his arm on my shoulder and strolling in stride like a true player. I was always cool with Murray—and knew I had been found out but accepted my fate.

"How you been handling the house, David?" Murray asked.

I looked up at the trees on the side of the block and at the shadows of the street lamps moving with us as we walked. "It ain't been easy, but I'm trying," I said.

"Your mother is one tough cookie, but I'm sure you're doing your best to make it easier on her." Murray stuck his hands deep in his pockets and took a heavy breath.

I thought of the scene that had played out upstairs only moments before as I searched my mind for an answer. "Well, Murray, it's just hard to—you know, be the man. She just wants to treat me like a kid."

He grabbed my shoulder as they ambled and patted it as he spoke. "I'm sorry you gotta take the brunt, kiddo. Just try and put your mom first—she just worries about you, I'm sure of that, but being the man is knowing when to say what, and when just *being* a certain way makes other people happy." He smiled and looked at me for a second as we turned the corner.

We reached the door of Bradley's, a jazz spot Murray often frequented. As he pulled on the wooden door, a crisp mixture of melody and smoke floated out onto the busy street. Looking as if he'd forgotten something, Murray reached into his front pocket and, grabbing his wad of cash, said, "You alright for dough, Champ? Need a couple of bucks?"

I shook my head from side to side. "I'm tight, Murray. Don't you worry about me."

The man looked at me as he put the cash back in his pocket

and raised both hands in surrender. "Of course you are. I should have known that."

"You're the man, Murray," I said, as I was turning away when Murray's reply.

"No, David, *you're* the man. I'm only the guy warming the seat till you get back."

I looked back and grinned.

University Place was alive that night as I made my way up it toward Gramercy Park. I loved the way the smell of the char-broiled burgers permeated the glass windows as I passed the Cedar Tavern—a hole in the wall really, but it had been around forever; writers and painters had hung out there. The smell made me think of past times when my family had been together in one of those worn and battered booths, discussing irrelevant things, laughing. . . .

I was moving quickly—not looking where I was going, but for-ward. I loved the sushi place that was a little too expensive for me, but my pop and I frequented it often during our visits. He felt he needed to work hard for my love and understanding, he needed a friend, while I just wanted a father; at times, we were like passing ships.

In front of Bowlmore Lanes, out of nowhere, a bum was nearly in my face. "You got a dollar?" he said, his breath like a sewer mixed with scotch. He looked old, probably twenty years beyond his age, in the worn and tattered coat that matched his short, chopped white hair. I was almost nose-to-nose. The griminess of the hand that he stuck out in my direction seemed to float in the air.

"Jesus, I don't have *shit* for you," I said, moving backwards, feeling violated. The one thing you learn growing up in the city is personal space; this guy had practically invaded mine.

"Come on, kid, just a buck," said the bum, keeping his distance but closing in. "You gotta have *something* to spare."

"Look, I'm sorry, but I got nothing for you."

"I'm just so *hungry*," the old man explained, turning away to look for another victim. I marched into Stromboli's Pizza—a good joint, though the sauce was always a little sweet for me—headed for the counter, and ordered a slice from the sweaty- looking guy who ran the place, framed by tattered posters of Italy and Sicily.

"You want it piping or just hot?" the guy asked.

"Doesn't matter, just give it to me as is." The guy plated it up and asked me if I wanted it bagged. I shook my head, paid, and left. I surprised the bum, still harassing passers-by.

"Jesus! You could kill a guy by doing that!"

I chuckled at the twist of the turns. "Here," I said, handing over the slice.

"What, no pepperoni?"

I laughed as I took two steps back and replied, "Just eat the fucking slice, alright? Jesus Christ," I said, before rolling on.

"Thanks, kid! I was just teasing," I heard in the distance from a chuckling bum with a mouthful of pizza.

I read in the *Post* about a bum being murdered in the bathroom of Bowlmore Lanes not two months later; I've always wondered if it was him.

CHAPTER 17

WHEN I GOT TO GRAMERCY PLACE, IT WAS LIKE a different world. I passed the hotel where I had taken my first steps, so to speak, got to Jean's door, and rang up.

"Hello?" came the usual voice from the other side.

"Hey, man, let me up," I said, waiting to hear the buzz. It came.

I was surprised to see so many faces at Jean's—none of my usual crew, but in the past few months I had seen quite a bit of Jean, and it suited me fine.

Star was a friend of Jean's from one of the many schools *he* had gone to, and was always sweet to me when I was in her company. She had an Irish look, with feathered hair that drove me crazy. I saw her sitting on the couch when I walked in and nonchalantly waved hello. She was a few years older, but that didn't scare me— just had to play it cool. I peeked around the corner to take her in.

What a body—perfect tits, and a round ass that filled her skin-tight Sassoon jeans just right.

I found Lloyd in the bedroom, in his Adidas get-up, this time all black. Lloyd had a joint, so we lit up and had started to smoke it when Star came in. "You boys got a hit for me?" she asked, like a Southern belle waiting for chivalry to step in. I passed the joint her way before taking a hit.

"Oh, no, I couldn't smoke it like that—I'd smudge my lipstick. Come 'ere," she said, pulling me to her with a smile. Lloyd glanced my way enviously and stepped back to let it happen. She placed the joint backwards in my mouth, grabbed the back of my head, and pulled me close so I could exhale the smoke into her mouth. All I could think of was the sensual touch. I was pretty sure she didn't need to rub against me while she did it, but I wasn't going to fight. Her cheeks had a velvety texture I could only compare to fresh snow when I put my hands on them; I almost forgot I had a burning joint in my mouth.

She took as much as she could and held it in her lungs as she stamped her feet, pulling back, holding her nose with one hand and waving furiously with the other. I took the joint out of my mouth, but before I could take a hit myself, she grabbed me again and pressed her lips against mine, blew the hit back, and gave me a kiss. "Now that's a true shotgun," she said, and sauntered off, leaving us stunned. I looked in the familiar bathroom mirror and saw bright red lipstick all over my mouth.

In a moment, Lloyd was chuckling behind me. "You alright, bro?" He patted me on the back as he studied me in the mirror. We had gotten close in the past few months, but Lloyd was Brooklyn and I was Village, so there was only so close you could get.

"Yeah, man, I'm cool—ain't my first time, you know," I replied as indifferently as possible. Lloyd shook his head and sidled out of the bathroom.

I gravitated to the couch to listen to the new Yes album on 97.1 FM and saw a box of Whippets just sitting there for the taking. I looked from side to side. They were most likely a leftover from the past party but, checking the box, I found not only quite a few unused, but an unbroken balloon as well.

I liked to take two canisters' worth and inhale deeply. Usually that caused me to pass out, blue-lipped and smiling as I slid deeper and deeper into a void. I set up a hit, careful to wipe the connection of the balloon to the discharger with spit so as not to let the freezing-cold air break it. I sat back to breathe in that sweet air deeply and blow it right back into the balloon. After four or five of these breaths, I slowly felt myself lose consciousness and fell back into the cushions with the balloon at my side.

I was dreaming of running through some forest with branches brushing my face. I watched myself from above and laughed uncontrollably. I felt a hand sliding around on my leg but wasn't sure I had the energy to move it. Star had crept into the room. As I came to, I felt her tongue in my mouth and her legs wrapping around mine. The music was blasting from the speakers; I lifted her shirt over her head to admire her breasts. I was getting hard as she stroked me, running her tongue over my neck and her hand between my legs.

Having a connection in that state, I just wanted to fuck her brains out. I didn't know if it was going to happen, but I was satisfied with the groping I was giving and receiving for now. "Where the fuck *is* she!" I heard someone scream from the other room.

"Oh, *shit*," Star said, gathering her clothes and pulling herself back together.

"What do you mean, 'Oh, shit'?" I asked as I sat up on the couch.

"I've been fucking around with Rogen for the past few weeks, and he gets jealous, okay?" she replied very matter-of-factly.

"You're getting it on with Rogen—he once ate like thirty hits of fucking acid, and you screw around behind his back with *me?*" I replied in a loud whisper, realizing the gravity of the predicament I was in. Rogen wasn't the thickest guy in the world, but he was six-two and had become pretty nuts. He'd recently cut all his hair off with a butcher knife in a drug-fueled rage.

"Don't yell at *me!*" She said it so sanctimoniously that it baffled me. "First of all, I didn't even know he was showing up, okay? And second, I didn't exactly pull your lips onto mine, sport!"

The condescending tone made me fucking reel. "What-the-fuck-ever," I replied, trying to figure out what I was going to do as I buttoned my shirt up. The door flew open, with Jean trying to block Rogen's way as he barged into the room.

"What the fuck is going on?" he barked, and then, *"You!"* he said, pointing straight at me, looking through tweaked eyes. I had the sense that he'd snorted an entire eight ball himself, was really pissed, and was *really* out of his mind. Jean and a couple of people were trying to hold him at bay while onlookers peeked over shoulders.

"Rogen! Just cool out, alright, man? Nothing is going *on!*"

Jean screamed, trying to calm him down.

"Star, what the fuck happened here?" Rogen spit through Jean's arms, inching closer and closer into the room.

"Nothing," she said, looking over at me. "I was trying to get to the bathroom, and David sort of, you know, grabbed me and kissed me, pulled me on the couch. . . ." I heard my death sentence being read before a now-crowded room.

"Rogen," I insisted, "that's fucking *bullshit*, man. I didn't do *anything*, I *swear* it!"

"What, are you calling her a liar? Is that what the fuck you're doing, you fucking piece of shit? Calling my girlfriend a *liar?*" He practically climbed over the three guys holding him back.

Understanding what was about to take place, I wasn't sure which way to turn. A fucking psycho ready to kill me was blocking the door. There was a window, but it was thirteen flights up. And then there was the bathroom.

"I wasn't calling anyone a liar, man, I just—" I was trying to slowly back my way toward the john. "I just didn't know what the fuck was *up*, man. I swear it." Just one more step, and I was in.

"So you *did* fuck around with her, you little cocksucker!" Rogen threw his defenders aside, jumped the couch that separated us, and lunged for me. I felt him tear at my shirt, but I pulled myself away with all my might and slammed the bathroom door.

I felt all the energy of a drug-induced freak on the other side. My heart was going a mile a minute. I didn't know what the fuck to do. I heard voices trying to calm him down and defuse the situation, but he wasn't having any of it. I felt the pounding on the door like a battering ram, knowing it would eventually give way. I braced myself against the toilet, jamming in my body like a wedge.

"Rogen! Jesus fucking *Christ*, man! I don't want *any* of this!" I screamed, the thought of bloodshed choking my voice.

"You shoulda thought of that *before*, you piece of shit! Nobody does that to me, man! Nobody, you little fuck!" he screamed back, slamming all his weight into the door, finally breaking it off its hinges and landing right on top of me. I didn't know what had happened, as I lay there half unconscious, crumpled on the tile like a wet towel.

"What the fuck did you *do*, you fucking psycho?" I heard Jean say from a distant place. As I came to, all I saw was feet, and the door that was now on top of me being thrown aside. I felt myself being stood up and thrown out of the bathroom ten feet into the other room. I landed on my head. It was a blur after that. Kicks and shoves I tried fending off what I could—I couldn't comprehend why it wasn't being stopped. I tried to crawl away but felt my feet being grabbed. I gave one good kick, and the grabbing ceased; I felt as if I had connected with bone. I turned and saw an unconscious figure, with Jean and two others lying on top of him.

"Jesus, you knocked him out cold! Dave, get your shit and get the fuck out of here!" Jean said as he felt Rogen coming to.

"I swear, man, I didn't start *anything*," I said, trying hard to fend off tears mixed with anger in the now-emptying room.

"I know, man, but he's gonna kill you when he gets up, so just *leave*, okay?"

I grabbed a shoe on the ground that matched the one on my other foot and high-tailed it out of there. I felt hands grabbing my shoulders and looking. Everywhere I turned, not sure what I looked like, I saw hands over mouths. I made a beeline for the front door but saw Lloyd give me a quick nod from the other room as I was walking out; I guess that's how Brooklyn handled things— they let you fend for yourself.

When I reached the street, I pulled my Converse back on and ran for a few blocks, zigzagging just in case I was being followed. I leaned against a parked car, got my breath, and looked at myself in the window. I wasn't bleeding too badly: a little from my lip as well as my head, but it seemed mostly to have stopped. One shirt sleeve was conveniently ripped at the seam, so I went to work on the other and had to admit it didn't look all that bad. It was the tie; it gave me that Sting look.

I grabbed a comb from my back pocket, which I had miraculously managed to hold onto, and went about fixing my hair. Since I was sweating a storm, I rubbed the mixture of sweat and blood into my hair to re-activate the gel. I spit on the torn-off sleeves and went to work on my mouth. The cut wasn't too bad; it was inside, so it didn't show, although I had a feeling a rib or two were bruised. I was shaking but very much alive.

I couldn't exactly go home in the state I was in—my mother would freak. I figured I'd hang out all night instead, till it was time to go home the next day. I was just a few blocks away from Danceteria; I'd gotten a job through a friend's uncle as a bar back at Palladium a few months before, and I was hoping they'd give me reciprocity. I checked myself once more in the car window, had a quick look around, lit a crushed smoke, and headed to the club.

CHAPTER 18

I GOT MORE AMPED AS I CLOSED IN on the place; I'd been walking quickly until I saw a line that stretched for half a block.
The scene wasn't unfamiliar to me—the same thing happened
at Palladium, but I'd always used the side entrance there.

I was amazed by the array of people in the line; since Danceteria
was a massive club with different vibes, it attracted all sorts. When
Studio 54 closed its doors in 1980, this place had taken over. Everyone who was anyone had played there—from R.E.M. to the Ra-
mones, Madonna, Iggy Pop, it was *the* place.

I strolled up the line looking for an entrance I could maybe
sneak into but couldn't find one. I finally succumbed to the fact I'd
actually have to go through the front door. People were looking
me up and down as I passed them on my way to the doorman in
the familiar yellow light of the streetlamps interrupted by the flare
of cigarettes from the line.

I approached a massive figure behind the velvet ropes at the top of the steps. He looked Puerto Rican, I was pretty sure, and was dressed in black, a good six-five, with a demeanor like that of a prize fighter's bodyguard. There, he was king.

He didn't look *at* the people coming up to him; he looked over and through, so as not to miss a beat of anything going on. I joined a small list line to his left.

After a moment or two, I got to the step and looked the looming figure in the eyes, he was sort of looking down at me, but that was more height than attitude. "You on the list?" he asked, scoping five moves ahead.

"I'm from Palladium," I told him. "They said to talk to the man when I got here." I knew the guy was watching for a flinch.

"*Who* did they tell you to talk to?" The guy was giving me one look for every five across the sea of heads.

"Some big cat named Luis, supposed to run things," I said, knowing I was pretty safe with that name, since half the Puerto Ricans in New York were named Luis.

"Yeah, well, you got the right man, but I don't know about any deal with your joint," he said without moving a muscle.

"Dennis, from *my* door, had it set up with your people," I replied, knowing that, as long as you kept them talking, you were in.

"*Who* do you work for? What did you say your name was?" the big guy asked, trying to make sense of the yarn but being careful, 'cause you never knew who was who.

"I didn't, but my name's David. Rubell hired me, but Schrager relies on me. I usually work by his table. You can check it with Dennis if you want—I've got a number right here." I reached for an imaginary piece of paper in my pocket, my blood pumping fast;

I lived for that shit.

Luis shifted his attitude, looked me up and down, and reached for the velvet rope. "That won't be necessary, David. I like to go to Palladium every once and a while myself. Tell Dennis to get it cleared up for next time, okay? And no jeans in the future. You have a good time, and here—" he added, handing me drink tickets, for which I thanked him as the rope slid aside. The big man smiled back, nodding for a comp.

Through the double-door entrance, after my eyes got adjusted to the subtle lighting, I laid eyes on a drop-dead beautiful cashier. I enjoyed her smile as walked up to her; she reached for my hand to stamp it. "You must have a great rap," she said to me; I was admiring the cleavage she wasn't ashamed to show. She had glitter on her eyelashes that reminded me of falling rain. "He hasn't let a guy in for two hours, let alone on the house. By the way, how old are you?" she asked, batting those lashes and smiling.

"Old enough to get in for free. I guess I just have one of those faces," I said, putting my best grin forward. She stamped my wrist, letting her hand linger on mine for what seemed like an eternity; I enjoyed every minute of it before thanking her and heading in.

The huge room was stark white, with neon strips adorning every wall that gave the place an unnatural glow. Chicks in miniskirts and feathered hair were lined up at the absolutely black bar. There was a stage built into a wall on the right and open spaces everywhere just waiting for people to fill them. The club didn't seem half as full as Luis would have led people to believe, but that was the mystique—making those who got in feel like stars.

I sauntered up and waited till the bartender was in screaming distance. The music was pumping, something I was quite used to.

"Long Island, please," I said above the noise as I handed a drink ticket to the guy. The bartender had a punk rock look, which was becoming more and more common. I loved Long Island ice teas; they packed a hell of a punch. The guy came back, his jet-black hair covering his eyes as he placed the drink in front of me, and walked away. "Hey!" I yelled, catching his attention.

"You don't like your drink or something?" he asked, a little taken back: He wasn't used to being called anytime twice.

"No," I said, pulling a five out of my pocket and laying it on the bar in front of him. "I just didn't think you worked for free," I added as I took the first sip of the cedar-colored drink.

"Thanks, man, I appreciate. You need anything, I'm Scotty, all right?" He was checking the bar for bullshit as he headed over to a couple of honeys on the other side. I had learned, *even* when the house was treating, to take care. Most bartenders live on tips alone, and even though I'd just blown almost a third of my wad, I knew Scotty would take care of me if I needed him to. I was trying to numb the pain in my ribs, fumbling in my front pocket for smokes. I grabbed a Marlboro and lit up, instantly soothed.

I couldn't have had three or four pulls before someone came up behind me and a pair of hands closed over my eyes. I would have freaked but smelled familiar perfume. I pulled the hands off and, turning around, saw Theresa standing there with a smile from ear to ear.

I'd met her a few years before, playing guitar in Washington Square Park. She was a few years older than me. She was cute— not a model or anything, but extremely sweet, and all of five feet one. She had on a striped halter-top and, because her breasts were big, she kept pulling it up during our conversation. The black vinyl pants made her auburn hair even darker.

"Where have you been? I haven't seen you in *months!*" she exclaimed, putting her hands on her hips and giving me the once-over. I caught her up on the superficial and shifted the convo into her world. She was a pretty good girl, although she hung around with an older crowd that she found exciting.

"Patty is just the *coolest!*" she said, speaking of the friend who had obviously given her the coke that was practically falling out of her nose. "You have to come back to the room and do a few lines!" she added with an upward inflection, amped out of her mind, and practically dragged me toward the dance floor. We walked across—doing a few moves to a new Madonna song, heading in the direction of a hallway that contained a few rooms with drapery for doors.

The artwork on the walls, under the black light, made crazy visions—just like salamanders. I looked up—the narrow hallway and the ceilings seemed infinite. I was trying not to spill my drink while looking around as she pulled me still further into the belly of the beast. A moment later, she opened one of the draped doorways and led me in. "Everybody, this is my friend David. David, this is everybody!"

Heads turned briefly; we moved further into a room with people in mid-conversation. Some were lying across couches, sitting on the floor; the party had real love-in atmosphere. The friend, Patty, was beautiful but not a day under forty. She was sitting next to a man in a suit and turtleneck, with piles of cocaine on either side. He had white hair in a blunt cut sneaking over one eye and a demeanor that screeched eccentricity and made me realize who he was.

"Hey, David," Patty called out with a smile sexy at any age, "this is Randy." She draped her arm over the man's shoulder and leaned against him for support. She had long red wavy hair and was wearing a full-length dress without a pair of panties in sight. *Jesus*, was she gorgeous. "You want some coke, David?" she asked, using a credit card to cut up one of the longest lines I'd ever seen. She handed me a rolled-up fifty, and off I went like a champ. I took half of the line in one nostril and half in the other, came up for air, and sniffed in.

"That's pretty good," Randy said to me; my eyes were still closed, waiting out the stinging pain in my septum.

"Now, what do you do for an encore after a performance like that?" He laughed. I had walked into a very different circle. "You're very handsome, do you know that?" he added, plucking the fifty out of my grasp.

"Thanks," I said, and wiped the excess from my nostrils as I shook my head. Randy took a bump himself, as he lay back enjoying the moment. I watched this, hammered my drink, and noticed a fresh one was within reach before I even finished.

"We'll take care of you here," Patty said. She was running her fingers through my hair. I stared at Randy, a mystical figure I had always heard so much about.

"What do you think art is, David?" he asked as he leaned over on his hand and gazed at me.

"I don't know—creativity, maybe?" I offered, coked out of my head already, not trying to sound profound, but was already getting wired.

"I paint when something is beautiful," he said, as he looked me in the eyes. "Art is the state of mind from which that comes."

Theresa came back and handed me a joint that I gladly smoked. It was pretty good weed and instantly cut the edge. She sat down with us, and we smoked it all. Everyone seemed to be grooving, it was as if they weren't in a club at all but some magic place far away from anything *this* city could offer. I was soon talking to all kinds of people, some famous, some stoned—no pretentious attitudes or phony bullshit, just people having a good time, partying.

I started spinning as I stood up looking for the bathroom, the hardwood floor playing tricks with my eyes, and I stumbled into the wall. I pushed past the drapery and saw a lockable door to my right. There were two, unmarked, side by side; one could only assume. I entered and, locking the door behind me, took a piss. I had to lean against the wall, having had at least three of those teas plus all the rest of it. But coke was funny that way; it sobered you up from the drink, but when it started wearing off, you suddenly became aware you were really fucked up. I looked in the mirror and ran some water over my face, which was a bit swollen by then, and could see where the blood in my hair had come from but felt no pain.

I made my way out of the bathroom and, having stumbled through a few of the wrong draped doorways, managed to find my way back. I looked around at the crowd, which had suddenly thinned. Theresa was sitting on the floor, talking to another beautiful girl I had noticed before.

"Where's everyone going?" I said, leaning over her shoulders with slurred speech.

She and the other girl laughed; looking up at me, she exclaimed,

"It's almost four-thirty, and the place is getting ready to close!"

I couldn't believe the time had slipped away so effortlessly. "But you can come back to Patty's with us. . . ." Her friend was also eyeing me.

We got ourselves together and headed out of the twisting maze, reaching the street through a door that I hadn't seen coming in. So there *was* a side entrance after all.

CHAPTER 19

P ATTY'S APARTMENT WAS ONLY A FEW BLOCKS away from the club—fantastic luck, since I couldn't have stumbled much further. We entered a very posh doorman building complete with mirrors and leather couches in the white marble lobby. Andy and his entourage had gone off on a different route to see a late-night performance artist, leaving me mostly with women.

Crossing the lobby and getting to the elevators was a feat in itself—everyone was hammered, and I nestled between Theresa and my new friend, Scarlet, about five-seven, who had a mane of dirty-blonde hair that went down to the middle of her back. She was wearing white terrycloth hot shorts and Dr. Scholl's, which leant a hint of schoolgirl—but, having met her in the club, I knew different. What tits; god, did I love her tits. They were at least a C-cup, and the skin-tight wife-beater tee showed their every curve. Bra? What bra? Perfectly centered nipples. When the elevator arrived, we huddled in and rode up with the whoop of a high school cheerleading squad; it was already five in the morning, but Patty didn't seem to be worried about the neighbors.

At her floor we stumbled down a hall carpeted in black-and-gray checks, past walls covered in flocked silver wallpaper, to a doorway at the end. The light was murky, and Patty fumbled with her keys until the door swung open, revealing a spacious, modern-looking apartment. The wooden floors, in wide oak strips, were bleached, anchoring black leather Barcelona chairs and a tufted Nelson couch that looked extremely unlived-in.

Patty threw her keys down by the door, dropping her purse in the center of the living room, and headed straight for the kitchen. She pulled out a bottle of Absolute vodka from the freezer that she immediately began to consume. I, seated on the couch, began making out with Theresa. My tongue went into her mouth as I grabbed her hair; her hand went onto my crotch.

Completely consumed with groping, I felt a tug at my other side and, looking up, saw Scarlet was smiling at me with sex written on her face. She pulled me to her and kissed me while she spat ice-cold vodka down my throat. I grabbed her ass as she was straddling my lap and explored her mouth. The girls seemed to have done this before, which became apparent when I caught them looking at one another and smiling. Then they started to make out over my lap, and I was finally able to grab Scarlet's breasts. I coddled them in one hand and seized Theresa's ass with the other.

I looked at Patty cutting up lines as she watched the three of us going at it. She looked really turned on at the sight, but there was more fucking around in the room than I realized. Carlos was fondling Patty. He had been quiet the whole night, smiling and running with the music; his girlfriend, Simone, was passed out on the floor.

I started tonguing the two girls and felt a multitude of hands on my body, which made the bulge in my pants grow faster. The dim lighting only added to the allure, turning the whole scene even more primal. I seemed to be spinning in a dreamlike, drunken state; my heavy breathing was like climaxing itself. We broke apart only long enough to snort lines off the table. I had my shirt pulled off as I retreated to the coffee table for another long one. I stood up, feeling the coke hit my brain as it pounded. I watched Scarlet pull off her tee shirt, revealing her supple breasts, put coke on her nipples, and wait for me to come lick it off. I wasn't spinning anymore, just coked out of my brain. Theresa came over and snorted a line. She pulled off her top as well but, after placing the coke on her nipples, the two took turns licking it off. I loved watching their party.

Patty came back from the other room with a freebase pipe and a few rocks, and started to smoke. I hadn't smoked coke before, but I was game. Topless and fucked up, I went over to her, got handed the pipe and fondled while I smoked. The flamethrower I was using to light it almost singed my eyebrows off, but I realized if I turned my head to the side I could manage. The first hit was astonishing.

I didn't feel as if I'd taken much smoke in—I was used to smoking pot from a bong and knowing when I'd choke. Coke, on the other hand, seemed to dissipate in my lungs, but when I exhaled I saw a huge cloud of smoke appear before me. I spotted a guitar in the corner and picked it up. I wasn't making much music, but it felt tangible in my hands as I gritted my teeth; it was almost a relief to squeeze something. The ladies started to dance in circles; they followed me, making moves like gypsies or belly dancers. I was whisked to an awaiting bed that seemed to come from nowhere. I dropped the guitar and we all lay down. I took off their panties and began to orally please them both at the same time. It was absolute heaven. *Boom, boom, boom* my heart beat over the screaming passion before me. I was sweating and couldn't focus.

I straddled them with one of my legs between the two and was grinding them when I discovered my hard-on was quickly dwindling. What a bitch. It seemed almost impossible, so I went back sucking tits and face. Sweating profusely, I came up for air and tried to reach for a glass of water next to the bed. I got hold of it as Scarlet was grabbing my leg and took a long swallow, realizing only afterwards that it was straight vodka. It wasn't very refreshing, but I managed to keep it down, feeling the need to retreat into the bathroom for a moment of reconciliation.

In the mirror, I saw a version of myself that scared the shit out of me. My face was pulsing, and my heart felt like it was going to burst out of my chest. I splashed cold water on my face and ran it through my hair. I sat down on the toilet and tried to get a grip. It was difficult not letting my sudden paranoia run away with me, but I'd never felt like that before. I opened the medicine chest and looked for anything that could help me escape the state I was in. I found a bottle of Valium; remembering my grandmother taking it in the past, I figured it couldn't hurt. I put one of the blue pills in the back of my throat and stuck my mouth under the faucet for a drink. My heart was still racing. I hoped it would stop soon, before I really freaked.

I came out of the bathroom after what seemed an eternity and found Scarlet passed out on the bed with Theresa smoking a cigarette on the end. She turned and looked at me as I re-entered the room and, sensing I was unsettled, came over, threw her arm around my waist, leaned her head against me and gave me the cigarette.

"You okay, baby?" she asked with so much compassion it made me quiet. I looked at her and immediately felt calm. Maybe it was the Valium or maybe her voice, but I was good.

Day had started to break as we looked out the window over the buildings that made up the city. The clouds seemed to whirl around as we watched with sleepy eyes. "Some night," I said to her as I looked back at Scarlet's beautiful naked body lying there like an angel's.

"Yeah," Theresa replied, giving me a quick kiss on the cheek, which caused me to blush. "We should do this more often." She laid her hand across my chest and squeezed. The draft from the window raised goose bumps up and down her arm, or maybe it was me.

WHEN I AWOKE I FELT LIKE A PLANE HAD CRASHED into my head. I studied the girls lying huddled under the covers as the light danced on the dresser in front of the window. My mouth was so dry I needed to quench my thirst before I thought could speak. I ambled naked into the kitchen, where I grabbed a Perrier bottle out of the fridge and started chugging it. It hurt going down, the carbonation stinging my throat, but it satisfied.

My head still throbbed. My hangover was compounded by the

ache I felt all over my body. The clock read 1:30. *Shit.* I had to call my house. I looked for my pants and found them on an abandoned chair in the room. I pulled them on and grabbed my smokes from my pocket, the whole time hunting for a phone. I found one by the sofa in the living room and contemplated it. Finally, I sat down, picked up the receiver and dialed my number.

"Hello?" I heard a voice say on the other end. It was my sister, which was funny for a Sunday, since she rarely slept at home.

"Hey," I replied. Taking a drag from my cigarette and blew smoke rings at the light beaming in.

"David?" she said, a bit more energetically than usual. She had something strange in her voice. "Where the fuck are you?" she asked.

"I'm at Jean's house. Why?" I didn't understand her concern or tone; it wasn't like she gave a shit. It was just another Sunday morning.

"No, you're not! Mommy called his house this morning, and you weren't there! *He* said you left last night! She's with the *police!*"

"*What?*" I bellowed back, utterly dumbfounded. Could this be true, or was she just fucking with me? I thought the former, since she didn't seem to be in the mood.

"Alright, wait a minute—what's going on?" I asked, getting scared, hoping she would change the words that came out of her mouth.

"Here," she said, a little indignantly but calming. "Take this number down. It's for the Sixth Precinct. They told me to stay here and wait, and if you called to tell you to contact them *immedi-*

ately!" She rattled off a number, and was through being the big sister yet again—but I was glad it was her on the line and not my mother.

"Yeah, I got it," I replied, shaken.

"You're lucky you called when you did. I was supposed to stay home all day and wait!" *There* was the guilt; I'd known it would come.

"Sorry for fucking up your day," I said with my mind running, consumed by what the outcome could be.

"Are you sure you're all right?" I knew she cared. It wasn't like she had that much to do.

"Yeah, I was just partying all night, and I'm kinda hung over, but I'm not *dead* or anything."

"Well, obviously! You better take some aspirin and call that number. I have a feeling you're gonna need it. Bye." She hung up, leaving me to my problems.

I started to freak out, trying to figure out the situation. I knew I had to call Jean's house—if my mother had called, I wanted the stories to be straight when I finally saw her. I wasn't sure how much trouble I was actually in.

After a few rings, Jean answered, "Hullo?" he said, drone as usual.

"It's David,"

"Dude, where *are* you? Do you know your mom has the police looking for you? Where did you go?"

"I went to Danceteria and then slept at this chick's house I met!" My voice was elevating unconsciously as I puffed away on my cigarette.

"David, your mom was *here*, with some *detectives*, this morning!"

"What did you tell them?"

"I told them you were here, but that you got into a fight and left. I thought you went home. They wanted to know who the fight was with, so I told them it was some guy who was a friend of a friend, so Rogen wouldn't get in trouble. They figured the worst—whoever you were fighting with followed you out, stabbed you a few times and put you in a dumpster or something."

"Did you *forget*? Rogen *did* almost fucking kill me!" I screamed. "And now *my* mom is with the fucking police? They should lock *his* dumb-ass up. He's fucking *nuts!*"

"I know, man, but he calmed down after you left. He even wanted to find you, to apologize. I'm sorry I couldn't do a better job of helping, but it was a bitch. Good kick, though," Jean added with a chuckle. "Where's your mom now? Have you talked to her?"

I remembered I had to call her and couldn't put it off any longer. "I called my house. My sister gave me some number to call. I guess she's at some precinct or some shit. Sorry for the trouble at your pad, and the door. I'm sure it was a freak session this morning," I said with a laugh. "I gotta go. Be cool, man. I'll see you soon."

"Yeah, no sweat, David. Good luck."

I looked at the piece of paper I'd scribbled the number on but, as I was about to call, Theresa came in.

"I overheard your conversation. Your mom called the *cops?*" She seemed worried.

"I wasn't where I was supposed to be this morning, so she

freaked," I said, quieted by the lucid pain in my head. "I gotta call them." I reached for the receiver again.

"You can't tell them you're *here!* Patty will get in trouble! Just tell them you're on the street!" Theresa exclaimed.

"All right—let me just call, okay?"

I dialed the number and waited, looking out the window.

"Sixth Precinct," came a woman's voice on the other end said.

"My name is David," I said. "I guess my mother called you guys. Is she there? I was told to call this number. . . ."

"David. . . . Uh, just one moment while I transfer you to the detectives' office."

I chewed my nails and hoped for the best.

"Sergeant Davis."

"Sergeant, my name is David? I guess my mom—"

"You know we got guys looking for you right now? I can't begin to tell you how many kids go missing everyday. You really scared your mom something bad, you know that?"

"Is she there?" I asked quietly, hoping she was already home.

"No, she's out with a detective in a car, looking for *you!*" the cop replied in a flat, hard voice. "What's your location? We'll send a car right over."

I wasn't sure; I looked out the window and spotted the back of Barney's, so I was around Eighteenth.

"I'm on Seventh Avenue, right by Seventeenth Street. I'll go downstairs and wait, okay?"

"You go downstairs, and you sit there," said the sergeant.

I hung up the phone and looked for my sneakers. Patty came out in a kimono, holding a cup of coffee with both hands.

"You all right? What did you tell them? Theresa said your mother called the *police?* How old *are* you?"

"Yes, I'm fine, they're picking me up down the street, my mother is with them, and I'm. . .fifteen," I said sheepishly.

"You're *what?* Oh, my god! I'm going to *jail!* You cannot let them know you were here, okay? Oh, my god! You're so *young!* I can't believe this is *happening! . . .* You gotta go, okay?"

She started getting panicky, wiping the table and flushing shit down the toilet. I tried to calm her, to make her understand I wasn't going to tell anybody anything, but she wasn't buying it.

"You never know. Cops can be tough, and I don't want to go to jail for contributing!" She started to pour the vodka down the sink.

I got dressed and said goodbye to a smiling Theresa, who told me it was cool, that she would try to straighten it out. I repeated I would never say a word and thanked her for letting me stay the night. Ambling out the door, I caught a last glance of Scarlet, who was still crashed on the bed by the window.

I got downstairs and hurried a block to Seventeenth. I'd been right, the apartment building *was* on the corner, but I didn't even remember what floor it was on anyway.

No sooner did I hit the far corner of Seventeenth and Seventh than an unmarked police car pulled up. I saw my mother and father in the backseat. An Italian-looking cop in a cheap sports coat rolled down his window to speak. "We've been looking all over for you, David. Get in." He leaned over and opened the passenger side door. I caught a glimpse of my mother, who had a look of anger mixed with tears. My father was in a silent rage, sitting next to her in the back seat, looking out the window, but I felt stares on the back of my neck.

"You really gave your mother some scare, you know that?" my father said. "Do you have any idea what you *do?* Your mother calls me this morning beside herself with grief, and you have nothing to *say?* You could have been killed for all we knew, but that doesn't seem to matter to you, does it? What's gotten into you? *Say* something!" I felt the weight of predicament that I had put myself in. My father, more angered than I had seen him in years, breathed heavily through his teeth, and my mother was trying to halt the tears that had, I suddenly realized, been flowing for hours.

I was fixated by the piece of paper stuck to the dashboard with a piece of tape. It was Jean's number I'd written the night before for my mother before leaving the house. If only I'd *been* off by one digit.

SIXTEEN

(1986)

CHAPTER 20

I WAS IN DISBELIEF WHEN SHE CALLED. I hadn't booked much since the soap—and that'd only lasted a few months. They'd gotten rid of the diva—which meant her boyfriend got the ax as well. So I'd gone out on a shitload of auditions and finally landed another gig. It was a just a commercial, but a national campaign; I would, hopefully, make some cash.

The morning of the shoot I had to get up early. To be on the Upper East Side by eight o'clock meant getting up at seven, and although I was a pretty solid sleeper by then—the insomnia had left when puberty walked in the door, you had to *be* in bed to sleep, and I wasn't usually there for too many hours in a row. My problem was, I'd been having a really good time.

I was mostly just hanging out, ogling girls and smoking cigarettes. For years it seemed like thousands of kids would hang out on Eighth Street between Fifth and Sixth Avenue, at night and on the weekends—the *Rocky Horror Picture Show* played a midnight show every Friday and Saturday night at the Eighth Street Playhouse, across from Positively's; that brought out a really interesting crowd.

The streets were packed fifteen deep off the sidewalk with people my own age and a bit older. It was crazy, but it wasn't as if they all knew each other from school or something. Everyone was from different neighborhoods, walks of life. People drank and partied hard—after the weekend, the streets would be littered with nitrous canisters from people doing whippets all night long. There would always be a few fights, cops rolling up and down; it was quite a scene.

I think I'd crawled in the door at 3:00 a.m. that morning. I had been doing well at sneaking past my mother's bedroom door and out of the house without notice. The tricky part was the coming back through the front door; it had a serious squeak. The secret was opening and closing it really fast so you got past the noisy part. My heart was always racing when I snuck through, sneakers in hand. The guys working the elevator late didn't care what I did; they were just irritated that I woke them from their sleep in the basement, ringing the bell to get back inside. I went right to sleep but only got about four hours or so before the alarm started ringing like a banshee. I needed a seriously loud one, and found just the watch on Fourteenth Street. It had twenty different ring sounds, including my favorite, "La Cucaracha." I took a brief shower and ran a brush through my hair before leaving the house; god, I was fucking tired.

I got downstairs and blew into my hands. It never seemed to matter what time of year it was, at 7:30 in the morning it was cold.

I had few options to get there. Either I ran to Union Square, got the 4, 5, 6 Lex line uptown train to Seventy-seventh and walked the rest or, grabbed a cab. I stuck my hand in my pocket and fished out the crumpled bills that were shoved in there; I had a grand total of eight bucks. I knew they'd feed me lunch, and I had a school pass for the train back down, so I hailed a Checker cab, and my nostalgia and me drove uptown.

I was at that time going to an "alternative" high school where students worked in the real world at real jobs but, instead of getting paid, got school credit. It was actually a lovely system for me; I worked in a photography studio, where I got an education in taking pictures and an appreciation for classical music—all while avoiding English and science. The nicest part was being able to split for an audition when I needed to; it was a win-win.

I'D GOTTEN TO THE PHOTOGRAPHER'S the day before on time and been sent down to the fancy market on the corner of Greene and Prince Streets to get food for the clients coming in that day. I'd taken a hundred out of the petty cash box, put on my army jacket, and gone out into the cold wearing my Walkman and listening to Vivaldi's *Concerto in G for Double Mandolins*. It had been a cold December—the frost on the ground looked like white spray paint on the cobblestones, but it was always busy in Soho, even at 9:00 in the morning.

I'd known what to get, but when the advertising agency is involved *anything* wrong could be devastating, right down to the muffins. Everyone dressed a little nicer, kind of walked on eggshells. As I hustled over, I thought about New Year's. I was looking forward to a good time with my friends—my parents hadn't forgotten about the day the police were called the previous spring, but were loosening the shackles occasionally. My friends and I managed to get pretty fucked up on the occasion, and it was becoming tradition.

When I had returned to the studio, the man I worked for was busying himself getting the camera and lights ready with one of his assistants for the day's work. He was an easy-going enough guy. Forty-five, he not only walked confidently in cowboy boots and flannel shirts in Soho but had a huge mustache a la Freddie Mercury that reminded me more of a rancher than a famous photographer.

I'd taken all the stuff to the kitchen and started brewing a fresh pot. I hadn't been a coffee connoisseur when I got there; now I couldn't stop.

I was just finishing when Bruce came up to me. "I want to tell you, David, that I really value your efforts here, and I like what I see," he'd said. I'd finished arranging all the food, realizing that what I had been doing was appreciated. The shoot day had gone off without a hitch—the clients couldn't stop talking about the muffins—and I was cleaning up the shop before leaving for the night. I'd spoken to the guys that afternoon, and the plan was solid. Freddy's folks were supposed to be out for the evening, so the plan was at least to start there. I would tell my mother I was crashing at Freddy's—which I probably would—and party hard till the sun came up.

As I was leaving, Bruce had ambled over. "Good day today, David. When you finish school I think we can talk about something permanent," he'd said.

"I really like it here, man. You guys actually make it enjoyable to come to work," I'd replied, and we laughed a bit.

"I wanted to give you a little something for New Year's. I hope you have fun, and be cool, alright?" he had said, handing me an envelope. Knowing how to be classy, I had put it in my pocket without looking and thanked him.

I GOT TO THE ADDRESS ANNABELLA'S ASSISTANT had given me paid the cabbie, and went to the door. I buzzed the second floor and walked inside. "I don't care what the hell his agent said, I don't want him here!" I heard someone scream to someone else in the other room. Could he be talking about me? "Who else do we have this morning?"

I stood motionless by the door, not wanting to move further into the room. After a moment I listened to what sounded like papers being shuffled and then, "Fine, he'll do. Let me know when he gets here." I heard footsteps go off in another direction and entered the room. I walked to an open office to my left and introduced myself.

"Ahh, David! I was just talking about you!" Shit! I thought. I hadn't even started, and I was done. "Here, sit down," she said, pulling a chair out for me. Her name was Diane, and I guess she was one of the producers for the spot.

I took my off my jacket and sat down. "Is everything okay?" I asked, not really wanting to know the answer.

"Oh! More than okay! You were originally going to be one of two guys being bullies to the boy that grows up, remember?" The commercial was for milk, the National Dairy Boards. It was a cool idea. A kid of about fourteen stands there and grows up to be a guy of twenty before your very eyes. You know "Milk, it does a body good" kind of thing? "Well, now," she said, "you are going to be the focus in the other spot, with the girl growing up as you play it cool! You are going to be Michael Martin!" She seemed very excited about it, so I smiled and thanked her. I wasn't sure why it was so cool, or who Michael Martin was, but a commercial is a commercial. She ushered me to a place to change and get some breakfast. Not as nice as the Dean & Deluca stuff I got for the studio, but nice.

WHEN I GOT DOWNSTAIRS FROM BRUCE'S STUDIO, it was already hitting twilight. It got dark at around five o'clock, which gave the whole city a calm over-layer. I headed north toward the park. The streets, even in the chill, were lovely. The girls getting out of work—still wearing high heels from the day—made me drool, watching them take step after meaningful step toward their own goals and homes. Greene Street ended at Houston, so I hung a left and headed toward Thompson Street, which suited me just fine. I loved the smell as I past Arturo's Pizza—an original joint from way back that had its own following. I'd never eaten there.

When I got to the park it was desolate as winter, but the thrill of the New Year was an interesting contradiction to that as I walked along, feeling it beneath my feet. I was about to head into the park when, from a church stoop on the other side of the street, I heard, "Yo, little man, where you going in such a hurry?"

Tony had grown up with Patsy and was about her age. He was sitting there in his blue janitorial outfit, with a joint in his mouth.

He and his brother Rocco were a couple of years apart, and all Italian. His hair was quaffed perfectly, with a Travolta vibe to it and the comb in his back pocket at the ready. He was at least six-foot five, skinny as a rail but never, ever, fucked with. He did these karate kicks over people's heads, like Bruce Lee, that freaked them out. He and his brothers were infamous all over the city. Which was sort of how we'd met.

I had seen this gorgeous girl at school—whom I had found out through different people was named Adrian. One day I saw her outside of the building and contemplated talking with her, but I'd been told by one of my friends that she had a crazy family and brothers who would kill me. I had thanked him for the info and thought nothing more of it.

A couple of months later I'd been hanging with Patsy, who introduced me to a couple of guys she knew. We all smoked together, and after a while this one guy, Rocco, looked at his brother and said, "Yo, Tony, I like this kid. He's about our sister's age. Maybe he should, like, take her out or something?" He'd picked a piece of weed off the tip of his tongue, looking at his big brother for approval.

"Yeah. Sure, why not? David, you know our sister?" Tony had asked me, nodding, trying to avoid getting the smoke from the joint in his eye.

"Nah, I don't think so," I'd said, thinking it would be a little weird to get hooked up with their sister.

"Yeah, you must know her—she goes to I.S. 70. Real looker. her name is Adrian, Adrian Vitello." I had been in shock for a second and glanced at Patsy, who didn't understand.

"David, you all right?" she'd asked, shaking my shoulder a bit, as she looked at the brothers. "You look like you seen a ghost or something." She had chuckled, fixing the zipper on her white leather jacket. Could life be that simple and so small?

UP ON THE EAST SIDE, I WAITED FOR HOURS. They set up lights; the director Steve, had this thing for smoke, loved it, asked people to smoke on set, so I did. I must have hung around for four hours, eating bagels, drinking coffee, and smoking cigarettes. That was what amazed me most about the business; it's always hurry up and wait. So I waited—fuck it, I was getting paid. I had by then figured out what was going on: The guy who was supposed to be Michael Martin had gotten attitudy with the stylist, who'd gotten back to the director—who happened to be the stylist's father, and that had been that. I was a good replacement. The girls started showing up at noon. I was introduced to the first, very sweet about eleven or so; the next size up was around my age. Then, vavoom! Salene was about twenty-one, and was she gorgeous. I couldn't take my eyes off her. She had one green eye and one blue, a body that wouldn't quit, and a smile that could kill. I knew I was way too young for her, but what the hell. I still made eyes at her all day. I got called by the A.D. to get into position on my mark. I saw Steve standing by the camera, with a bunch of people dressed in black; I assumed they were the ad agency people.

"Fine!" he said, threw his arms in the air, and walked away from them. I just stood there waiting to find out what to do. It a little weird when you have all eyes on you and everyone is just waiting around. Steve came back to camera. "I need more smoke!" he said, moving the air around with his hands. He came toward me but went right past, looking up at the light from my point of view. He moved around me like I was a manikin standing waiting to be dressed.

A guy I assumed was the prop master started running around with a black contraption that emitted smoke. "No! No! I don't want mole smoke! That shit will stick to the walls and make a mess! I need *cigarette* smoke, goddamit!"

Everyone on set immediately pulled out their pack and started puffing away; I think even a few who didn't smoke grabbed one and lit up.

After ten minutes or so, he looked around again and was finally content. "You ready to do this, David?" he asked from his position next to camera. "I want you to stand there and look cool, you know? Run your hands through your hair, cross you arms in front of you, you get it?"

"I think I know exactly what you want," I said, getting into character and feeling my space already.

"Perfect! That's the attitude I want!" He added, "Don't worry about moving around. I put some marks on the floor. I'm shooting the girls in a separate shot, so just don't cross too far to your left. Other than that, just have a good time with it."

I started nodding in a cool way and shrugged my shoulders a bit.

"Perfect! *Annnndddd, action!*" The camera started rolling, and he just kept egging me on with what to do. Since I didn't have lines, I had to show it all in my face. I crossed my arms, and uncrossed them, for ten minutes straight. The whole time he was happy, and the clients were nodding in affirmation as well. He got the shot of me and thought it would be a good idea if I stood in for eye lines for the girls. Why not? I did my thing as they spoke their lines about how I only cared about girls' outsides, and not her insides, but she was drinking her milk. . . .

"YOU GUYS ARE THE *VITELLO* BROTHERS?" I'D SAID, flabbergasted. "Jesus H. Christ! I had no fuckin idea! I heard you're fucking crazy!" We'd all started cracking up at my breakthrough. I'd realized that day that crazy is only a problem when it doesn't like you, but I'd never dated Adrian anyway.

I looked back at the stoop that Tony was sitting on outside of the park, saw a space for me by his side, sat down, said hello, and was handed the joint.

"So what's goin an? Staying out of trouble?" Tony asked in a big-brother kind of way.

"I've been working at this studio, getting school credit. It's kinda cool. Been laying low for a bit," I replied, taking a big hit off the joint before returning it. I remembered the envelope in my pocket that Bruce had given me. I reached for it, pulled it out, looked it over.

"What's that?" Tony asked, choking off his hit and blowing out smoke rings that were exaggerated by the frost in the air.

"It's something my boss gave me today as I was leaving— maybe a card, some bullshit, who knows?"

"So open it up, I'm dying over here!" he said in his best Ratso Rizzo impression. I fumbled with the envelope and tore open the top, revealing a card made up of one of Bruce's photographs—a woman standing it the middle of a cobble-stoned street, completely naked, shot from the back, with a white dove over her head. There was huge blow-up of it in the studio, which I had commented on. I opened the card and read the inscription first: *To David, one of the team. Have an incredible New Year, Bruce.* And I found two hundred-dollar bills! I couldn't believe it! Tony looked at me a little strangely before replying, "I don't to have kick this guy's ass, do I? He's not some kind of a fag, is he?"

I laughed at his machismo. "Tony, he's married, got a couple kids, I don't get paid, so he throws me a coupla bucks every now and then—but never this much."

"Hey, I've seen fags that were married! . . . All right, all right, I'm just making sure. Gotta take care of my little brother, right?" he reminded me, fucking with my hair and putting up his fist, dodging the imaginary blows that I wouldn't throw. "C'mere. I wanna show you some kicks," he said, hiking his pants up to get a bit more flexibility.

"Come on, Tony, we're in the fuckin' street, for Chrissake! Plus, you're stoned. You're liable to *hit* me," I said, trying to reason with the figure before me that was already throwing roundhouse kicks.

BY THE END OF THE SHOOT DAY, I WAS IN LOVE with Salene but never going to get anywhere with it. Steve was very happy with the day. We got out at about eight. We were milling around as you do after a job, when Salene came up to me. "You were really great, David!" she said, putting her arm over my shoulder, and flashed me an incredible smile. She was by then in flat shoes and only a little bit taller than me.

"You really think so? You were fantastic!" I said, giving her a squeeze around her waist. Was something happening here?

"Where are you headed?" she asked with another smile.

"Just going to grab a cab and head downtown." As I said this, the realization I had no cash left came over me.

"Really? I'm going downtown, too. You want to split it?" she asked with interest. I couldn't exactly bail: I was kind of committed. I walked out with her as the crew looked on and wondered, *Is she into me?* I didn't know but was willing to find out. We got downstairs and turned toward the Avenue. At least we were on a downtown street. I wasn't sure how I was going to get out of it. At that point in my life cabs would stop for me, no problem—and it didn't hurt that I had a beautiful blonde at my side. We pulled one over and I, gentleman that I had been taught to be, opened the door so she could get in.

"Well, thank you!" she said, moving over and curling up against the door. "I wish my boyfriend had your kind of manners," she remarked and moved her eyes to the ongoing scene out the window. Shit! She had dropped the boyfriend bomb, so not only was I going to be incredibly embarrassed by lack of funds, but there wasn't a chance in hell I was getting anywhere with her.

"Oh," I said grimly. "Maybe you should reconsider who you're with then," I said, and smiled. She looked over and smiled back.

"I'm going to get off at Thirty-sixth Street," she said to the cabbie.

"I'll just take it the rest of the way downtown," I said matter-of-factly. We drove down in silence; I watched people on the street zooming by as we headed down. When we got to her stop, the meter read six bucks. She searched in her wallet for a minute. "Don't worry, I got it," I said.

"That's crazy," she said pulling out a ten from her wallet. "Here. Just give him a good tip." I couldn't fight with her, considering my position. We exchanged numbers and goodbyes, and she walked out of my life. I was incredibly relieved that I wasn't going to have to ride and dash. I rode for a few more blocks and told the cabbie to pull over.

"I thought you wanted to go downtown, no?" the guy said, turning around and looking at me.

"You know, I think I'll walk. Do me some good." The fact that it was twenty degrees out didn't change my mind. I gave the guy the ten, and it wound up being a nice tip. He shrugged and thanked me.

I got out of the cab and started to walk—it *was* pretty cold, I must say, but it didn't bother me, I was still high from the day's work. I walked a few more blocks and found an entrance to the 4, 5, 6 train. I went down and knew I'd be back in my hood soon enough.

"YOU'RE SHORT—I WON'T TOUCH YOU," Tony had replied but, seeing my face, felt a little bad for his choice of words. "Come on, I didn't mean nothing. You're gonna get bigger. Besides, everyone is shorter than me! Come *on*." He had stood me in front of him. "Now, look, if you get into a fight, right, and the guy's no matter how big, just remember what your pal Tony told you. The weakest place on the body is the knee. You give it a good kick from the side and it'll pop right out—fight over, only takes twenty pounds of pressure." He'd bent down, grabbing my knee, as he showed me the sweet spot. I'd started to giggle like a little girl.

"What the fuck you laughing at?" he had asked, standing back up and taking the joint from me.

"That tickled, alright? I got sensitive knees!" I'd said, sitting back down and looking at the bills again.

"You just remember what I told you, okay? Give a good kick, a stomp, right on the side," Tony had repeated, demonstrating the kick blow without moving from the step, motioning like Bruce Lee with his hands. "And put that money away! Jesus, you want it to get snatched?" He'd zipped up his jacket, facing the cold.

"How you think I'm gonna lose it? Get mugged? I got you right here," I had pointed out as I handed the joint back to him.

"Yeah, you do. I'll always look out for you," he'd replied, trotting down the steps and turning to leave. I had tried to pass the joint back, but Tony had said, "Nah, you keep it, I gotta get home—my mother's making some food. You wanna eat over? I think Adrian is gonna be there." He'd had a smart-ass look on his face.

I'd looked at him for a second before saying anything. There were a lot of pretty girls in the world who didn't have crazy brothers. I'd looked back at Tony, who was waiting for an answer, and said, "I gotta get home too—my mother ordered some Chinese. But you tell that gorgeous sister of your that I said hello. Can you remember that?" I had told him sarcastically, walking down the steps back to the street.

"Yeah, I'll tell her. You be good, Davey boy, and have a great

New Year's, okay? Be safe, little man."

"Tony, you wanna show me that roundhouse kick again?" I'd asked, knowing he would.

"Yeah, sure buddy," he'd said, cinching up his pant legs, prepping. I had stood right in front of him, watching his every move. Tony had thrown the kick high over my head, and as it passed I'd grabbed his ankle and dropped him on his ass.

"That's for the short-guy comment!" I'd said with a huge grin on my face, sticking my hand out to help him up. Tony had smiled at me; we were even. And with that he had taken the biggest steps I had ever seen toward his house on West Fourth.

I'd put the cash in my sock before leaving the stoop and, with the card in my pocket, crossed the park to my house on the other side; it seemed like a different world from where I'd stood. My mother probably wasn't home, so I was looking forward to the quiet time and figuring out how to spend the cash; but it would mostly get spent on the drugs and alcohol I would consume the next night. Maybe I'd buy myself a new shirt or a pair of jeans before that. As I walked up Fifth and looked around, it suddenly started feeling like something big was going to happen; I couldn't wait.

CHAPTER 21

THE WHOLE THING SEEMED TO FIT TOGETHER like a puzzle. You told one story—and as long as everyone else told the same one, it all held together. That's the way it was for my friends and me; our lies were the glue that bound.

I got the call from Freddy about 6:30. "Yo, what's up?" I asked.

"You know, this, that," Freddy replied, in an extremely round-about way. It wasn't exactly shocking.

"So? Is it all worked out?" I asked, fumbling with the lighter I was flicking, making the flint spark, my urge to get a nicotine fix building. I wasn't all that concerned—I knew I'd have a good time regardless—but I wanted to make sure it wouldn't get sticky later on.

"Yeah. I *told* you it would be cool, man. Chill!" Freddy had a lovely patronizing quality about him that made phone conver-sations sound like a favor. I heard a bong hit being exhaled on the other end.

"All right, all right, I just want to, you know, make sure, that's all. I'm gonna tell my mother, and I wanted to make sure, that's all. Later."

I hung up, thinking about the shit I put her through. I wanted to make things different in the New Year. I thought about it as I sat on the heater cover by the window and smoked my cigarette at last. She was gone for a while, so I only aimed the smoke at the window.

I heard the front door open. My sister was home remarkably early—she was going to a private school on the Upper West Side, so it wasn't terribly odd. She walked into the room and immediately gave me a disapproving look. "Why do you smoke in the house?" she asked, with a tone in her voice that sounded like a squeaking door, throwing her bag down on the desk across from me. I looked at her without replying and exhaled. "I hope you know that Mommy knows you smoke. And stop doing it in *my* fucking room! At least I do it outside," she added, turning to the closet to pick out her clothes for the night; she wasn't all goody-two-shoes, I guess. There were a few moments of silence, which wasn't uncommon between us, before she made a stab at light conversation. "How've you been liking your job? Mommy said you were working for a photographer or something? Sounded cool. I'm glad you're not flunking out—it means a lot to her."

I pushed out my cigarette butt on a familiar spot on the ledge and flicked it to the street below, my hand feeling the icy wind as it worked.

"Yeah, it's pretty cool," I replied, re-adjusting my posture and letting my guard down a notch. "I'm thinking, maybe, I don't know, I'll become a photographer, too. I work in a nice studio down in Soho, learning stuff. He treats me pretty good. . .look at this," I said, pulling the card from my back pocket and the cash from my sock handing it to her.

"Wow, he *pays* you? You got to be kidding me! No real school, and *money?*" she asked with a sarcastic edge, and continued looking through her array of oversized leather belts. She did not approve of the way I scammed my way through life.

"He doesn't *pay* me. It was like, you know, a tip or something. Read the card." She did and handed it back, happy I was finding something to connect with.

"What are you up to tonight?" I figured it would be boring.

"Well, first I'm going to a dinner party at my friend Sacha's. Then, afterwards, we're all going to see Urban Blight play; it should be really cool. I'm spending the night at her house. What about you?" she asked, unconcerned.

I looked at her. It was arresting to see the differences between us. We'd been brought up in the same house, had gone to mostly the same schools—till I got kicked out—but were really different people. She was a scholar. I'd become street; she'd become straight.

"I'm going to Freddy's meet up with some of my people. Then who knows? Hang out and get stoned, watch the ball drop." As I said it, the words falling out of my mouth like drool almost made me feel like a loser, but then I remembered the drugs and felt cool again.

"Well, I hope you're careful. Mommy gets really worried, you know." She held up a skirt in front of her waist in the mirror. I got up off the radiator cover I was sitting on and started for the living room. As I was passing her, a feeling of pride in her came over me. I reached into my pocket, and pulled out the card, grabbed a bill, and handed it to her.

"Here, have a good time tonight," I said sheepishly. She looked at me and smiled.

"Are you kidding? Wow, I can't believe it! Thanks, Dave. Are you sure?" She couldn't take her eyes off the bill.

"Yeah, I'm sure. This is plenty," I replied as I stuck the other hundred in my front pocket. "You know me—if I have too much, I'd just get into trouble anyway." She hugged me. Though she was older, I still towered over her by a good six or eight inches; but the hug was good and well felt. I left her stunned.

I turned on the set and started watching a rerun of *Gilligan's Island*. I thought it was funny that they never got off, but I really like Ginger's tits. Man, what a rack. I was caught up in the show when my mother came through the door, bags of groceries in hand. She put the bags in the foyer and heaved a big sigh. She looked tired in general. It had been a few years since my dad left, and the transition hadn't been easy for her. I felt her pain that was only masked by the daily grind of life.

"Come here," she asked with a slight hint of a smile on her face. I got off the couch and meandered over. She leaned in to kiss my cheek, the familiar smell of Chanel No. 5 permeating the air between us. "You mind putting these—" she asked, not realizing I had already grabbed the bags and was in the process of carrying them to the kitchen. I was a good kid at heart, but I didn't think it was cool to be one all the time. I put the last of the bags on the dining table and looked at her sitting on the chair next to me.

"So what are you doing tonight, Mom?" I asked, hoping it would last at least till 12:30.

"Going out with some friends to a party. Nothing big, really, just some champagne at midnight sort of thing. I probably won't even make it till midnight. I'm tired already. What about you?" she added, easily, trying to be non-confrontational, which was a strange move for such an important question.

"Going over to Freddy's with a couple of the guys, watch the ball drop, nothing major." I spoke softly, not trying to arouse attention.

"Is his mother going to be there?" she asked, rubbing her face with her hands, wiping away the dregs of the day. Here it was.

"Yeah, she'll be there. She doesn't trust Freddy," I replied, shifting focus. It seemed to work; she headed into the kitchen to get something from the refrigerator.

"Well, *please* be safe tonight, all right? I should be home when the ball drops. I doubt I'll make it at the party, if you feel like calling."

"All right, Ma. If I remember." I left the room thinking how easy it had been.

I looked at myself in the mirror. White Converse high-tops, rugby shirt, and my favorite pair of Pepe jeans: Had that not-put-together look. It was pretty cold outside, but I figured, if I wore the concert jacket I had, it'd be warm enough. It wasn't as if we were going to the fucking Arctic or anything. My hair, getting long in the back, didn't lie exactly as I'd planned. I strolled out of the house unnoticed at 8:30.

When I hit the street, it had an extra buzz—and brisk for the last night of '86. I took the familiar path through the park and hit Freddy's in ten minutes flat. When I got to the door, I heard the guys downstairs. I knocked and waited. I heard someone making their way up the staircase. When it opened, Remy was standing there with a Budweiser in each hand. He immediately handed one to me through glazed eyes. We climbed down the staircase together. The others were waiting. Freddy and Marlon were seated close to one another, huddling over the table that had a rock of coke on it, loading bong hits with that and weed as well as a bit of hash. They handed one to me; I lit up and inhaled the smoke. I went over to the table and did a small line of coke and ecstasy. It gave me quite a buzz as I looked around the room at the others.

"Thanks, man. I needed that," I said, handing the bong back to Freddy, who took a hit himself. "So what's what? You guys get enough to go around?" I asked, looking at the blank face in front of me.

"I thought you were hooking up," Freddy replied as he blew the smoke out of his lungs that hung in the air above us. I *had* thought I was going to hook up some Ex for myself, but I'd figured there would be an extra hit to buy, assumption being the mother of all fuck-ups. I quickly got the gist of the situation. Freddy and Marlon were doing blow all night, and Gerard and Remy were tripping on Ex. There wasn't enough of either to get one more guy high. The bong hits were good, but I wanted to get really fucked up. My watch read 9:30—plenty of time to run to the park and grab something. I finished another bong hit and told the others.

"Don't get burned," was all Freddy had to say. I headed up

the stairs and out the door.

I walked up West Fourth and entered the park on the west side. I headed over to the Garibaldi statue, where I knew there would be guys hanging out. I was hoping to see Hash Paul or one of my regular dealers but didn't see any. I caught a glance of a cat I'd seen around. I strolled over to him and sat down. The guy was short, with curly hair and glasses, real nerdy- looking. If I hadn't seen him make sales with my own eyes, I would have taken him for an undercover cop.

"What's up, man? You holding?" I asked nonchalantly blowing into my hands. It was cold. The guy looked me over as he put his hands in his bag.

"I got some tabs of candy cane, some weed."

I didn't really want acid, but if it was the only thing. . . . "You got any Ex?" The guy looked at me and shook his head. "How much for the tabs then?"

"Five apiece, or two for eight. They're really good, too. You only need like half or maybe one," the dealer replied, already looking for the next.

I shrugged, reached into my pocket and palmed the cash. I slipped it carefully to him and got the acid; the last thing I needed was to spend New Year's in jail. I got up and left the park fast. I hadn't done two tabs before, but I figured it wouldn't be that good anyway—maybe even bullshit—so I put the two on my tongue and headed back to Freddy's.

When I got there, the door was cracked open and I heard the guys ripping it up downstairs. I grabbed another beer from the fridge as I made my way into the room. They were doing bong hits and laughing hysterically.

"So what'd you get?" Freddy asked, jaw grinding from all the coke that wasn't on the table anymore.

"Coupla hits of Candy Cane. Nothing much, most likely bunk crap anyway." I reached for the bong and loaded myself a hit, scraping some coke off the table and some weed from a baggy. I lit up and felt the effect immediately; the expansion in my lungs and the taste of the coke in the back of my throat was numbing. I blew out and started coughing wildly, looked at my friends, and began to laugh. I was practically rolling on the floor.

I sat back on the couch and felt my heart racing. Remy began to dance around the room as the T.V., which was tuned to Dick Clark bringing in the New Year, began to throw off wild lights as it glowed. I watched him dance around, a twenty-foot trail behind him mimicking his every move. I rubbed my eyes and blinked a few times, but everything stayed that way. When I looked at the floor, a pattern of lizards appeared before my eyes. It couldn't have been more than twenty or thirty minutes since I'd taken the acid, but as Remy passed me again and the trails continued, I knew something was wrong.

CHAPTER 22

I SAT STARING AT THE CEILING; my legs were fully extended, but they seemed farther away than usual and not at all part of my body. My hands, weightless, were floating upward, and I was unable to bring them back down. I heard voices in my head, screaming and taunting me relentlessly. The background reverberation of my pounding heart—as constant as the ever-flowing sweat running down my face and welling in the nape of my neck—freaked me out, practically to the point of incapacitation. I had never gotten that high that fast.

I felt pain in my head, as if I was being beaten with an aluminum bat I couldn't fend off. The air around me got thicker in the dim light. I saw a muddy, impenetrable haze floating around me as the confusion of the moment left me speechless.

I needed *air*: That was it. Air would cleanse my body and clear my mind. I broke away from the couch. In one movement I threw my shaky body onto the small winding staircase that led upstairs.

I got to the top and opened the door to the outside and breathed in deeply for life, as though I had been held underwater by a stumbling, drunken uncle.

The yellow cast over the entire scene before me was surreal. I sat on the stoop, breathed in and out, almost hyperventilating— hearing the salamander men that were everywhere laughing at me, the pattern growing as strong as the wind that quickly began to freeze my face. I looked at people passing me on the street, unable to utter a word or respond to the gazes I felt. The street lamp above, falling down in slow motion, crashing before my feet, and then suddenly upright again, boggled my mind. *Boom, boom, boom, boom*: I could *see* my heart pound out of my chest, faster and faster, causing pain in my head. I needed to go somewhere, to escape. I considered running down the street and attracting the attention that only a crazy man would provoke, but I knew that wasn't the right thing to do—not yet.

I stood up—leaning against the black wrought-iron railing that was like an exposed bone of the stoop—and felt tears welling up in my eyes. I didn't want to die, but I knew I was on a road that I hadn't traveled before, and wanted off. *That* was it, I thought as a clear moment burst upon me; I needed to rid myself of the toxins I had ingested. I clambered back through the open doorway, almost falling down—the sweat that was now soaking my clothes and running down my failing arms made gripping anything an impossibility.

I fell in one movement to the bottom of the stairs and stumbled to the bathroom. As I was closing the folding wooden door, the smell of the litter box sickened me. I sank to the ground, lifted the wooden lid of the toilet, and, like some bulimic prom queen, forced my fingers down my throat; the tears started streaming down my cheeks.

I gagged—the taste reminiscent of gasoline in my mouth—as the sweat from every pore in my face hit the water in the bowl and mixed with the saliva that was streaming out of my mouth. I sensed the veins popping out of my head; the pain was excruciating. I sat up, realizing I couldn't throw up anything and terrified of what that meant. My head throbbed and rang like sirens in my ears. I needed to go to the hospital, but I didn't feel I could make the trip. I came to a conclusion as I stared at my shaking hands with tears in my eyes: This is what it felt like right before you die. I staggered out of the bathroom and over to Freddy. "Hey, man, I don't feel too good. I think I have to go to the hospital," I said, ghostlike and absent, the words curling from my mouth as the actuality of the situation rushed toward a culmination. At that moment, I didn't care who knew what I had done. I needed help and couldn't make it alone. Freddy, who was higher than a kite, looked at me with a freakish grin as he spoke.

"Come on, man, you're all right! Just go upstairs and lay on the couch for a minute. It'll be cool. Trust me."

"When's your mother gonna be home? Maybe I can talk to her—"

Freddy looked at me and screamed in frustration, "What are you, *crazy*? You want to tell my *mother*? No way, man, she'll totally freak and realize I'm fucked up beyond belief. Just go lay *down*." He sent all my fears and me upstairs like a misbehaving child.

On hands and knees I stumbled up the same staircase again and crawled left into Freddy's room. It was candle-lit and shadowy, with a presence all its own, like that of a beast burning in a fire. I went over to the table and saw all the things Freddy held precious. The gnome on a hill, looking at me, started to speak.

"You really looked fucked *up*, kid! You might want to get yourself some help. You don't want to die, do you? But who am I to say? I'm just a fucking little gnome sitting on a fake hill in some asshole's bedroom!"

I turned away, rubbing my eyes to refocus, and turned back again. The gnome stood still. I was losing my mind. The dragon that had a crystal in its mouth was breathing fire; the cobwebs in the corner were dancing in the light. *Boom, boom, boom,* my heart pounded; I was overdosing, and no one gave a shit.

I heard a rustling of keys in the door. If it was his mother, I would be found out for sure; I was a fucking mess. But it wouldn't be my fault if she just *saw* me. I couldn't be blamed for ruining everything for just *sitting* there. I heard the front door open and steps in the hall, looked up, and saw a figure looming in the doorway. Jimmy was Freddy's older brother by ten months. He looked at me with a half smile that quickly turned somber. Jimmy was a pretty big guy, six-two, two hundred, with a head of hair the color of a carrot. We'd always gotten along, and I didn't understand why Freddy treated him the way he did. He came over to me; I was sitting on the sofa with eyes like basketballs and sweating as if I had a fever.

"What's up? You all right?" He assessed the situation rapidly as I clung to his sleeve.

"Please don't leave me, Jim. I don't think I'm gonna make it. . . ."

Jimmy sat down next to me and called out, *"Freddy!* Get your *ass* up here *now!"* loudly enough to be heard throughout the house. Freddy meandered up the stairs and looked in. He broke out in laughter at the sight of me sitting there motionless. "Don't fucking laugh, you idiot! What the fuck are you gonna *do* with him? Mom's coming home any minute, and she'll find him for sure, you *schmuck.*" The New Year's chime had come and gone, unaware of my misfortune.

"We *can't* tell Mom, you fucking moron! *Look* at me!" Freddy screamed back, grinding his jaw, fists clenched.

"Well? What the fuck do you want to *do?*" Jimmy replied, rubbing my back.

"We'll take him to Zed's house," Freddy said. "That'll be cool. Don't worry, David, you'll be okay." But no sooner had the words left his mouth than the door opened and his mother walked in.

"Hello? Where the hell *are* you, guys? Why is the *hall* light out?" she yelled as Freddy motioned to his brother to move me into his own room, which couldn't be entered except through Freddy's. With his finger to his lips, Jimmy motioned for me to follow him a few feet in silence. We heard Freddy talking to his mother as the screaming about beer and cigarettes proceeded downstairs; he was always good for a diversion. I fell back on a bean bag chair in the corner of Jimmy's room, and the looming figure asked me to close my eyes and try to relax.

"What did you take?" Jimmy asked, rubbing my arm. With my eyes closed, I told him. He kept reassuring me in a hushed whisper that things would be okay. "Just think of yourself floating down a river, both sides covered in sand. You feel calm and easy."

But I felt my heart race faster and faster as I fell back into the abyss. And it wasn't a sandy beach but a black hole in space sucking the life out of me as I fell deeper and deeper into unconsciousness.

"David. Wake up, David! Wake *up!*" I felt Jimmy shaking me and smacking my cheeks. I was falling into unconscious, and he knew that I might not return in the current state I was in. "You can't fall asleep, man, okay? You've gotta stay up! Come *on,* Dave."

But, heart pounding or not, I just wanted to sleep and make it all go away. Freddy and the rest made it up the stairs, dressed for the outdoors. They looked me over and got me dressed. Remy smiled with a tripper's eye as he held my arm at the top of the stoop.

"What do you want to do with him?" Marlon asked Freddy through clenched teeth.

Gerard was already down the steps, amazed by what he was seeing through Ecstasy eyes. "We'll give Eddy a call from the pay phone on the corner. Anyone got a quarter? He'll know what to do, David," he said to me. "He used to be one of those acid guys or some shit in the sixties."

Freddy grabbed a coin from Gerard and dialed the number. The four stood motionless; I was shivering in the cold and woozy. "Come on, come on, pick up the goddamn phone! Hello, Eddy? It's Freddy. . . . Yeah, yeah, and Happy New Year to you, too. Listen, I'm sorry to bother you, but we have a little problem. I'm here with—" I saw him look around at the crew, choosing whom to bring into the mess with him. He decided Marlon was the only one who could've managed with us. "I'm here with Marlon and David, and we have a little problem. David took a bunch of acid and shit, and we think he might be overdosing."

When I heard the words, they really rang. Everyone was scared; I was fucking petrified, the streets blinding, cars moving like lightning, the trail that was following them as long as a speeding train. "...Yeah, all right. We'll be right over." He hung up. I barely understood what he was saying; as he spoke, the words trailed out of his mouth, sprouted wings, and flew away. He and Marlon were going to take me over and deal; the coke they were on would eventually wear off, but the Ex that Remy and Gerard were on would last for hours. We all headed down Bleecker to Westbeth, side by side. I was having problems walking; my speech was slurred when I tried to talk. "I'll be okay. Don' you wirry bout me."

Remy grabbed my arm, and Gerard propped me up the other side as we neared the building. Gerard smiled at me and patted me on the back, which made me feel better, but I was in a dreamlike state. Nothing was real, not even the concrete beneath my feet.

Then, all of a sudden, it came full circle. I looked at the others and broke off in a run. I went ten feet in front of them, spun around and realized the situation: I was tripping my face off. It was like a light had suddenly come on. I didn't feel my heart racing or the cold air that was frosty to the touch. I looked at my friends and screamed, "I'm just *tripping! I* get it!" They looked at me in silence; no one wanted to be responsible.

"We're still going to Eddy's. We have to!" Freddy said angrily. Maybe it was the walk or the coke wearing off; who knew? I was just glad I didn't feel like I was going to die any more. We said goodbye to Remy and Gerard, who headed off to some party uptown, while we went up the stairs to Westbeth and to the elevator.

When it reached Eddy's floor, I looked at Freddy. I started to crack up, which made him laugh, too.

"You look like you're tripping your face off—how many hits did you take?" I raised two fingers. He pushed me out of the elevator, and I stumbled down the brightly lit hall. The light danced in my eyes as we moved. I saw the walls breathe, and lizards all around me.

CHAPTER 23

WATCHED THE LIGHTS TRIPPING against the walls of the apartment, consumed by an aura I couldn't comprehend. Everything was linked, the energy rolling from one form into another with the grace of water. Eddy was at the kitchen table, flanked on both sides by beautiful women. Freddy and Marlon were making tea at the stove, a lucky thing considering their own state. I remained on a chair by the doorway and stared at the floor.

"What do see, Duvey?" Eddy asked me like a doctor trying to feel out his patient.

I had the most elaborate scene being played out in front of me, a living cartoon, and couldn't understand why everyone else couldn't see it. "It's wild, man! I see this crazy cartoon in the floor! It's like some desert island, people running around waving their arms—so *wild!*"

Eddy suddenly grasped how much acid I'd consumed. I was turning my head this way and that to take in the apartment. The shafts of wheat hanging on the walls made sense. The pedestrian way the masks had been hung seemed to have been devised by a skilled hand. "It's like totally intense, your place, man. I can't describe it, it's like flowing everywhere!"

Eddy looked in my basketball eyes and laid his hand on my shoulder. "I know, David." He had a smile on his face as he spoke. "Everything has energy, when it's right. It has the perfect place to go, to move. . .I'm glad you see it." The two women sitting at his side weren't concerned. God, they were beautiful. One looked like an American Indian, the other a blonde goddess. I took the few steps toward the kitchen with a huge smile on my face to oversee Freddy finishing the tea, his jaw clenched, hands braced against the age-worn butcher-block counter.

"Stop smiling at me, you freak. I can't believe you're just tripping your face off!" Freddy was by then in no mood to play, his evening slowly slipping away, but he took care of me. I glanced from the fluorescent-lit kitchen to the cabinets, to the worn parquet floor that could have told stories. The peeling paint on the walls winced at my gaze. Everything was getting better and better as I felt the acid really kick in; every movement I made was as if I were a marionette being pulled by a knowing puppeteer. The floor had really begun to roll, as constant as the air I breathed. I looked down at my naked arm and saw the skin crawl, the blood pump through it. I wandered around, feeling everything, feeling safe. Marlon was milling about, finding something to do, not looking Eddy in the face.

"Hey, man. You good? I feel amazing!" I said, feeling Marlon's arm as if for the first time. I got him to smile, which wasn't that hard, Marlon being an easygoing guy.

"Dude, I'm grinding my teeth so hard they *hurt!*" he said.

I went through the apartment to the living room and opened a window to feel the cold air on my face. I closed it and headed back to the kitchen. Freddy and Marlon were putting their coats on.

"Where you going, man?" I asked, my heart starting to pump, feeling suddenly alone.

"Going to meet Remy and Gerard. . .you better stay here," Freddy said.

"I think that's a good idea, David," Eddy added. "You can hang here and go home in the morning."

"Yeah, okay, I'm cool." I felt strange being left but knew my friends needed to get out and party. Freddy half-heartedly hugged me, Marlon nodded with a smile, and then they were gone.

I went to the bathroom after they left and closed the door. The light still felt lifeless as I extended my arm to the mirror. My whole face seemed to be alive and moving. I looked deeply into it, at the capillaries running with the blood in my face that gave me life. I opened and closed my mouth to feel the motion, turned my head this way and that. I began to stretch in the little space, knocking into the walls, truly peaceful in my own world and wishing someone could identify with me.

I heard the familiar clang of the doorbell that sounded when the door slammed shut, and left the bathroom to see Zed standing there with a girl, Ally. I had fooled around with her a couple of years before. Her long dark hair, with almost Egyptian features, finished off a smile that could cause a train wreck, but it definitely took Zed by surprise seeing me there. His eyes grew wide.

"You came *here?*" was all he said after a brief synopsis from Eddy. All of a sudden the air seemed to change. A feeling came over my body that was only silenced by the pounding of my heart, and I realized: I wanted her. She sauntered up to us, the slung-shouldered shirt she was wearing half falling off when she hugged me. I felt her breasts through her embrace and her silent whisper of longing. She wanted me too; this I was sure of. I inhaled her scent as she went back to the T.V. room.

"Dude," I said, "she wants come home with me." I felt the testosterone boiling inside.

". . .She never said that," Zed replied, watching my pupils enlarge and dilate with every breath I took. Before he could say anything else, I had turned to the other room. I saw her sitting on the sofa and looking at me invitingly. I sat beside her and started making my moves, the acid fueling my fire like an avalanche. I felt her lips on mine, and her breasts with my hands. She put her arms up against me, but I knew she wanted it.

"Wow, you're hungry, aren't you?" she remarked, looking in my eyes, which were dancing like fireballs.

Zed entered the room, looked at me, and made eyes for me to follow him into the kitchen. Once we got there I said, "*What?*" Feeling the sparks myself now, I was twitching, my insides exploding.

"What the fuck are you *doing?* I brought her *home!* I've been working it all *night,* you schmuck!" Zed said it in a soft whisper, so as not to alert Alley in the next room. He wasn't sure what was going on, but he didn't like it.

"Don't talk to *me* like that—and I don't give a fuck *how* long you were working it, I'm taking her home!" I shoved him back, causing him to stumble, feeling my power now.

I saw her rise in the other room, went over, and wrapped my arms around her. "You want to leave?" I said as I pulled her to me and started to kiss her again. She tensed up—a game, I told myself, and she was just doing it to make Zed feel better.

"I don't know—maybe you should just stay here, chill out." Her smile was fading, the T.V. behind her flickering scenes of joy and drunkenness from a distant and more enchanting place. She turned toward the door; I, smiling, blocked her way.

"Where you going?" I asked, feeling now complete with the darkness.

"To the bathroom," she said, sliding by me. I watched her trail move after her as I blinked my eyes and first heard the voices.

"What?" I looked up at where I thought the sound was coming from in the wall. I saw nothing. My head was spinning; the room having adapted a life of its own was laughing at me.

You can't even get the girl, can you? I spun around to catch the moving lips of the demon that spoke. *You're useless! All that power, and you're alone again, you little piece of nothing. You're fucking pitiful! . . . You should go now.*

The demon fell silent as I turned around to see my coat being thrown at me.

"I said you should go *now!*" Zed said with fists clenched.

I let the coat hit the floor as I shoved past him out of the room. Eddy was there, with Ally under his arm. I felt the words fall from his lips, but it wasn't clear what he was saying. The people standing before him were like a stone-faced jury sentencing me to exile.

"You should go home, David." I saw the words come out of

his mouth but couldn't grasp them. I saw Ally, and the other women standing there scared. What are they scared of? I thought. A shove in my back put me at the door. A hand reached around me and opened it. I glimpsed faces nodding side to side as I left.

The hallway was gloomy in its embrace, and voices echoed in the distance. I felt another shove at my back. I turned to catch Zed behind me. "Stop *pushing* me!" I screamed at him, flailing my arms, covering my face from the voices.

"Shut the fuck up!" I felt Zed's arm wrap around my neck and my feet come off the ground. I rammed my elbow into his stomach and felt the sudden sense of release. My heart was the only sound I heard as I hit the staircase running, past the smell of urine hanging in the air, two steps at a time. Feet were pounded behind me; I fought to focus down to the stairs moving in front of me. I heard laughter from everywhere. I slipped on the last few stairs and fell, feeling the cold concrete against my cheek. I picked myself up for what seemed only an instant before a force was upon me. I struggled to get up and kicked the safety release bar on the door, shoving it open, and ran.

The streets were silent, my confusion collected in an abyss. My heart was leaping out of my chest. I couldn't remember where I needed to go. The yellowing haloes above seemed to move with me in a rhythmic way. It was freezing, but I didn't feel the cold that clung like monkeys to the sweat on my back and face. I blinked, trying to keep my eyes open since I was seeing everything blurry. *Ba-boom, ba-boom, ba-boom*, my heart kept screaming.

I raced down the block, begging for clarity and understanding, and turned the corner to feel the rush of wind on my face and the darkness fall over. I saw a glass door—the only place I needed to go. I launched my body through after clamoring at the handle. I fell back into a corner of the vestibule and felt tears streaming down my face. My body was shaking. The sweat poured off me. I couldn't catch my breath, but I looked at the door closing and the realization came over me: If it shut, I would die. I clumsily rose, fighting my legs that did not want to move, and slid my hand into the opening just in the nick of time.

Terrified of the demon that was laughing and pushing me, I sank onto the concrete and felt my legs burning. My head pounded; the ground swelled. The voices told me to strip. It was the only way to stop my legs from burning off. I fumbled with the zipper of my pants and cried to God. I turned my head to catch a couple walking past, shaking their heads, and I screamed, *"Zeeed!"*

I couldn't stop the voices: I needed peace. *Ba-boom, ba-boom, ba-boom, ba-boom.* I felt my body fall inside. My pants, tangled around my ankles, made me stumble as my naked form felt the whipping of the wind. I saw an iron fence rising stories above me. I heard the voice speaking, luring me, telling me what I needed to do. I began my ascent screaming in pain, just screaming. I looked at the other side and saw an immense fall. I felt the iron bars against my groin, and the cold on my legs was a relief from the heat I felt, but I had to get to the top. I looked around and saw light coming toward me, then darting past. I heard laughter. I felt the sorrow of my own demise and knew the end was imminent. The city seemed to grow smaller and go out of focus. I was higher than I'd ever been and felt I was going to God. The demons poking at me made the climb harder, but I knew I had to reach the top to make it all stop. I was truly alone as I felt the spikes in my frozen hands. I tried to focus only to see blurry forms far below. I looked out, the wind calling me to jump, the lights of the city beckoning me to kiss them good night as I screamed in a primal tongue and the darkness descended upon me. *"Zeeed!"* I felt the pain from the spikes stab into my abdomen. I waited for the peace I'd been promised—I needed it, wanted it.

CHAPTER 24

WHEN I OPENED MY EYES, I saw him sitting in a chair next to my bed, looking as if he could have been there motionless for days. His white hair was reminiscent of snowfall against the blue madras shirt he was wearing. His eyes danced. I had been told Sam could walk into a room and make everyone feel at ease. The white walls of the room seemed clean but not barren. I felt a tugging at my arms when I tried to sit up to look at my surroundings. My throat was dry. I couldn't tell where I was, but for some reason didn't care. I looked Sam in the eyes. Yeah, I did look like him. I stepped onto the ground and again felt the tugging at my arms. I crossed out of the room, following my grandfather in that impeccably pressed madras shirt; I would never have guessed that I was taller then he was, though our builds were remarkably similar. We were suddenly walking side by side. The hallway walls were covered with tiles in a brickwork pattern that reminded me of salamanders. He didn't speak, and my mind was blank, although I had thoughts racing through my head. There was a feeling between us that couldn't be explained.

He's not responding.

It felt as if we had walked for days, but Sam never said a word. When I looked at the light, it was intense but not blinding in the halls that led nowhere. He was looking down at his shoes as he walked, hands in his pockets; he briefly looked at me. Yeah, I thought again, I did have his eyes; it was comforting. We took a series of lefts and rights.

There's no pulse .

We reached a doorway; I turned to look at the man, but it was already open for me. I turned and stepped through but was again momentarily stopped by the feeling of being pulled at my wrists, and then my shoulders.

Pupils fixed and dilated.

We were approaching a stainless steel wall punctuated by many small doors. I suddenly felt cold, unprotected from the elements that were moving right through my bones, into my very being. Sam walked ahead of me; for the first time, I noticed the floor was shiny, covered with constant running water.

Sam pulled a handle on the wall to expose a white sheet against the stainless background and turned to me, as if I was supposed to know what to do. I felt tears in my eyes, and touching the sheet felt so strange.

Clear for paddles.

I pulled back the sheet and was awestruck by what I saw. I looked peaceful lying there naked. My body wasn't strained at all. It seemed calm and unmovable. I glanced at my grandfather and saw a single tear roll from an undisturbed eye. He was shaking his head. I turned to look back at myself lying there but instead saw Sam. For the first time I reached out to touch him; the flesh was cold and still.

I felt a million volts run through me as I came out of the tunnel into the light. I bolted upright, the current moving through my body and along my veins. I felt my heart pound, gasped for air, and opened my eyes, feeling a mask on my face; my arms were restrained with sheepskin ties.

"Did you have a good time last night?" the cop asked loudly in a tone that fit the moment as he lightly slapped my face.

I looked to my left and saw him sitting there. The nametag read *Santoro*. He was shaking his head, looking at me in disgust. "You know where you live?" the cop asked, tapping his pen against the pad he was holding. I tasted blood in my mouth as I moved my head to the side. Every part of me hurt. My legs, which were also restrained, felt bruised and beaten. I wasn't sure if I had any teeth left in my head.

I tried to speak but only mumbled a telephone number before I put my head back down and cried. I tried to turn away, to hide my face from the onlookers, but pain shot out of every orifice. I was alive now, that much I knew, but badly damaged and torn. The light in the ambulance was murky, caused by the fluorescent fixtures on the roof of the ambulance, the only thing I noticed before passing out.

I woke up again when I felt it shaking to a stop. I heard rumbling from the outside and saw the faces at work. They opened the back door and pulled on the gurney to begin my descent. The cold was biting in the early morning hours, the gray sky ahead slipping into the clear white light of morning. I didn't remember anything. I felt a draft against my naked flesh. They pulled me off the ambulance and picked up the gurney, fully extended the legs, and rolled me to the doors. The guy in the front stamped on the pad for the electric door, which wasn't opening.

"Well, now you know you're in a city hospital," he said, as he shook his head and physically forced it ajar until some machine memory took over and both doors slid open. I was rolled down a hall. I saw more eyes on me, the gasps and shaking heads; what did I look like? Stopping at a doorway, they backed the gurney up and rolled it through. They left me parked in the middle of the room as I came back into reality. I stared at the person coming at me, followed by a heavy trail.

The guy was smiling as he lifted the mask from my face. He had pins from various ski resorts on the lapel of his white smock.

"You probably don't need that anymore," he said to me. "Here, drink this. It'll make you feel better." He moved his hand to my back to help me sit up and take the straw. I screamed as the pain of the move shot through me. Lifting my head as far as I could, I suddenly remembered the restraints. I looked at the guy with tear-filled eyes, I was like a puppy that been beaten. "Sorry, man," the orderly continued. "I can't take those off. You gotta wait for the doc to come, okay?" I drank from the plastic bottle and felt a chalky taste in my mouth. It wasn't pleasant but better than the blood. I drank hard to quench the thirst in my throat that was so dry.

I had nearly finished the pint container when a queasy sensation came over me. My mouth was watering, and I needed to throw up. I turned my head to see a yellow pail sitting there that the guy grabbed and put in front of me. I wretched from deep in my belly five or six times and, when I caught my breath, looked up and saw a mirror. It couldn't have been more than ten feet away on a column. In horror, I saw what I looked like.

My face was completely raw and bloody, like an Abraham Lincoln beard except where it was black and blue. My naked chest and arms were badly bruised, my hair caked with a thick, jellylike substance. The only piece of clothing it seemed I had on were the cuffs of my long-sleeve shirt. I was a fucking mess and prayed my manhood was still there.

I put my head back down and was sobbing when the doctor came in. He was sober-looking South Asian, and he adjusted the glasses on his face; I noticed the grave look in his eyes. He wasn't very tall next to my gurney. "You are very lucky. You nearly didn't make it, you know? How are you feeling?" I noticed his accent was thick when I stared at him; he looked at me intently. He then told the orderly who had fed me the Epicac to loosen the restraints. "You won't hurt yourself if I take these off, will you?" I shook my head in affirmation; they came off.

The doctor felt my arm and moved to my wrists. Again, a jolt of pain rang through my body. "I think it is broken, but we need to take X-rays, to make sure of what is wrong. As soon as the results from your blood test come back, I'll come and talk to you." He patted the arm of the gurney and walked out.

I heard her before actually seeing her face. "I don't care *who* you are. I was told he's *in* there!" My mother marched into the room and put her hand over her mouth to hide the screams of shock she obviously felt inside. She worked on a different floor of Bellevue and had seen people in my state, but not her own flesh and blood. My father followed in, sighed heavily and took a breath as he turned away. She rushed to the gurney but didn't know where she could possibly touch me. It seemed every spot on my body was bloody, or bruised. I tried to play it off, as if nothing was *really* wrong, and I forced a small smile in the corner of my mouth: I'd just fallen down, hit my face on the concrete fifty or sixty times. But for the first time in my life, the hustle wouldn't work.

It hadn't been easy for her to find me. I hadn't had any ID when they scraped my naked body off the sidewalk after dragging me off the fence. The phone had rung on my sister's and my line at 4:30 in the morning, which seemed odd, but she had run to pick it up. She'd adamantly said her son was at a friend's house to the cop on the other end—but she was never sure.

They'd told her it had taken six officers to subdue me, that I'd fought them all the way. I, out of my mind, had thought they were trying to hurt me. I'd put one of them in the hospital, so it wasn't at all odd they'd ground my face into the concrete as they fought to hogtie me. I remember the feeling of suffocation as they were trying to subdue me fighting for my life. I'd broken free from a pair of handcuffs as they were shooting me up with a hundred cc's of Thorazine; it was all in the report. What they hadn't known was that I was a minor, only sixteen—and don't think my mother hadn't reminded them after it was over.

So there I was, her very own John Doe, the first to arrive in the emergency ward in the new year of 1987. But I was alive, and for that she thanked God. She looked in my eyes, which were the only recognizable feature about me. "David, I. . . ." Her tears were falling like rain.

"Mom, I was only—" I began instinctively to lie, but before I could finish my bullshit the same doctor had stepped into the room with the toxicology report; it read like a fucking grocery list.

"There was alcohol, marijuana, cocaine, MDMA, lysergic acid, hashish, and methamphetamine in his system, and it is very surprising to me that he's alive at all," he said matter-of-factly, and left the room, leaving my mother and me alone. I had done the speed a few days before but didn't see the need to bring it up just then. She was dumbstruck. I couldn't deny anything; it was all in black and white.

Before she could get a thought out, the orderlies came in to take me to X-ray as my father returned. He was quiet as he put his hand tenderly on my chest.

"I love you, David," was all he could say. They wheeled me down the hallway to another room that had a large X-ray machine in it. With help they slid me onto the steel table in the room. I again wanted to scream, but I was trying to fight the urge, so I closed my eyes in pain. When I opened them again, I saw my sister in tears in the doorway.

"Hey, Sue, did you blow all the cash?" I asked, faking a smile, grimacing in agony. Her face registered the horror that I had come to expect as she waved meekly at me, turning away to receive comfort from her father.

After the procedure was complete, they moved me onto the ward for minors. The kid lying in the bed next to me had been shot in Times Square as the bell rang on New Year's Eve and was pretty bad off. My reports came back with a fractured wrist and ankle as well as bruising of the jaw and kidneys, along with a slight concussion. They needed to put a catheter in me to see if I was passing blood. I'd asked if they could just check my urine, but it wasn't good enough. The nurse was rough when she pushed the tube into my urethra.

All grew mellow for the moment. Then I heard a knock at the door. A black woman was standing there looking in. I thought maybe she was a relative of the kid in the other bed, but she asked, "Are you David?" reading my name off a report.

"Yeah, that's me, I think." I still had my sarcasm.

"You mind if we talk for a minute?" She had a pleasant demeanor about her.

"No, I don't mind." I moved the blanket over so as not to show the embarrassing tube hanging down the side of the bed which ran into a bag of piss.

"Are you feeling okay?" she asked somberly.

"Well," I replied with embarrassment, "considering the stupidity of the evening, as well as can be expected."

"Why do you say stupidity? So you didn't mean to do what you did?"

I took a breath. "You must be the shrink, huh?" I replied with a wink.

"I am a psychotherapist. Do you want to talk about anything?" She was calm, nice.

"I can tell you this much—I didn't mean for what happened to happen. I'm in a lot of physical and mental pain, and I can tell you I will never, *ever*, do that again," I said, as honestly as I have ever said anything.

She looked into my eyes and must have sensed my remorse and disdain for my situation as well as, possibly, my sincerity. She said her good-byes, and that was it. I never saw her again. Nor did I need to go to therapy for the episode. I knew I was lucky to be alive. If it's the wise man who learns from others' mistakes, and an average one who learns from his own, it's the fool who doesn't learn at all. I had a hell of a lot to learn.

EIGHTEEN

(1988)

CHAPTER 25

SOMEHOW MANAGED TO SQUEAK through high school. I used my own money to go to Europe with my friends. It was a completely unreal summer filled with playing guitar on beaches in the south of France. And the women; man, oh, man, an American in Europe is a hot commodity. I'd taken more than one thing away from what I'd gone through that New Year's Eve: I would never do hard drugs again.

My sister was happy at college, where she had been for a year by then. Dana needed the freedom of being away while I was holding the city close. My mom longed for change and had left for her new home in San Francisco.

My mom had left for her new home in San Francisco. It was melancholic when we rode together in the cab to Kennedy Airport. In the loud silence, I stared out the window, suddenly realizing what it meant for her to be gone. I'd boasted to my friends how I had my own pad now at last and all I could think about was how cool the parties would be; I was eighteen, had crossed the line in Amsterdam. But not *seeing* my mother every day was something I hadn't fully comprehended, having her grab my face, even her bitching. In that moment, I wanted to be a kid again—put away all the experiences that I'd been through, and laugh through the eyes of a boy.

I remember that I observed my mother with a matching gaze and wondered what was going through her mind. She had her hand partially covering her mouth—the rays of sunlight just catching her lashes as the girders of the bridge, which crossed through her field of vision, gave them momentary shelter. I saw images of her own youth running through her head. She was returning to a place she cherished, and I knew it was tough for her to leave.

"Do you have enough money?" she asked quietly, not looking over, trying to make small talk.

"Yeah, Ma, I'm fine," I replied with a smile, not even calculating. I'd made real money from the milk commercial; it had been running already for two years, and the residuals were astounding; I was Michael Martin. I was also taking acting a lot more seriously—landing a few soap operas, something maybe worthy of a future. My father being only twenty minutes away in Jersey, where he lived with his fiancée, made sure we still maintained our ritual Mondays, Thursdays, and Sunday dinners.

I detected a clean, fresh stillness in the air. I saw the city clear as a bell from the BQE off in the distance. I looked around the cab—the Naugahyde seats had an age-worn look that provoked memories, as did the music I heard from an old tape player I saw strapped to the dashboard.

"You know you can always come out to visit me."

The sound of her voice had startled me out of reflection.

"I will, Ma, I promise I will," I said, knowing very little of California—having gone there only once, and never to San Francisco. California was a place of movie stars, constant sunshine, and blonde girls.

We had reached Terminal C at least three hours early for her flight—at her insistence. The cabbie brought the bags out of the trunk and set them on the curb. I paid the man. I stared down at her feet. It was hard for both of us to look each other in the eye. I grabbed as many of the bags as I could manage and headed inside—it was a machismo thing, the need to carry as much as humanly possible—but I enjoyed doing it for her. She glanced down and picked up the only thing left—a small sack that contained my most prized possession, my teddy bear. I'd gotten him at the age of two or so—on our family trip to England—but I didn't need Charlie anymore. It was my mother who needed him; he was an extension of me. She reached for the bag with the bear's head popping out, and the tears fell like rain.

"Mom, it's okay, don't cry," I replied, dropping the bags and rushing to her side. I did this, not only for her sake, but for my own. I'd start crying too if this kept up.

"Maybe I'm making a big mistake," she blurted through her sobs. "I don't think I can do it, David—"

"Come on, Ma, you're the strongest person I know. We both knew you'd go back there eventually—I mean, you love it so much, you know? You never stop talking about it." I held her hands and, trying my best to give some levity to the moment, smiled. She sniffed the snot that was running out of her nose, looking in her bag for a Kleenex; I was always her strength.

We went to the counter and checked in her bags as I looked at the monitor for the flight status: on time. We meandered to the security check point, where a dopey-looking kid with a excessively big shirt and a clip-on tie informed me that only ticketed passengers were allowed past that point. What did they think I was, a terrorist from the Village?

"Look, man, my mother is moving to California, and I'd really appreciate if you'd see your way to letting me, this once, go through *with* her." I used my best smile and kept the charm easy but flowing. I respected the kid's position, but I had learned you caught a lot more bees with honey than vinegar. Stroking his half-assed goatee with his hand, he looked at us and, without making eye contact, flagged us through with his arm. I nodded thanks, letting my mother walk in front of me, and followed quickly, making it to her in two strides.

It was a long way to the gate from the checkpoint. The red carpet on the floor was constant as I, without prodding, held her hand. We sat in front of the glass window overlooking the tarmac and smiled at each other. She looked at me and patted my hand as it rested on the arm of the institutional chairs we were sitting on; she even faked a smile.

Flight 301 to San Francisco now boarding rows 29 and higher, I heard over the loudspeaker, and people around us started muddling their belongings together like sheep. She stood up, grabbed her purse, and reached in. She pulled out a hundred-dollar bill and handed it to me.

"I told you I don't need it, Ma," I said, pushing the money back toward her purse.

"I know you don't need it, but I'm your mother and I want to give it to you, okay?" It was rare for her to insist, so I gave in with a grin.

"Thanks, Ma, I'll take some chick out to dinner," I replied.

She smoothed out her clothes and fixed her hair in an invisible mirror. "How do I look?" she asked, giving her best model turn. I looked at her; I knew the people around us were staring at this odd couple. We didn't look anything alike, so I played the part.

"You look like a million bucks." I moved to hug her as she sank into my arms and enjoyed the embrace. I fought the tears that were breaching my eyes and stared at the dropped tile ceiling of the terminal.

"I love you, David," I heard her whisper in my ear.

I smiled and whispered back, "I love you too, Ma. You're my hero, you know?" We moved apart. She looked back as she handed the stewardess her ticket to take one last glance at me.

I waved and started back toward the entrance, went outside, and hailed a cab rolling past. "Manhattan—the Village, please," I said, and the taxi began to move. I almost made it a full ten feet before I started to sob; I was proud I'd made it that far. I realized I'd never again be where I was before.

MARLON HAD BEEN PRACTICALLY LIVING at my apartment for a while. There were always people crashed out on the couch, the living room scattered with empty containers from Charlie Mom's Chinese restaurant or pizza boxes. The kitchen sink was filled with dishes, and the thought of cleaning out whatever had found a home there unthinkable. Marlon and I now looked similar, with hair well past our shoulders and a constant stoned expression on our faces.

Ruby had always been one of the boys, so I didn't mind her hanging out for the long haul; she also managed to clean up every once in a while. Plus, in the past few years, puberty had hit her—and had it ever. She'd turned from a mousy-faced little thing to a curvaceous woman who could really hold her own. But we were like siblings, so the thought of acting on instinct rarely crossed my mind.

Archer came from Jersey to hang out, too. I'd met him at camp four or five years earlier and had maintained a great friendship. Although Arch was bipolar, he was a hell of a musician. It helped, though, if acid didn't enter into the mix. I caught the smell of patchouli oil as he approached the door. There he was, all hippied-out, standing at my door, waiting for someone to answer. His hair was nearly down to his ass, and he was a big boy, at least two-fifty.

"What's up, dude! Party on, brother of mine, shamalama ding-dong, Spank!" Arch was a couple of years older than me but rarely showed it.

We slapped hands; I opened the door and let him in. There were people lying around in the living room, high on some pot butter that had been left in my freezer by a good friend for safe keeping in fear of his mother finding it; I personally got heartburn from the stuff. He stretched out on the floor and listened to the conversation already in progress.

"It's just getting worse and worse, dude. I can't believe how shitty the city always looks now. It's a cesspool," Ruby was saying passionately to Marlon, who was hardly listening.

"I've been looking at that school again. I gotta get the fuck outta here. My mother is driving me crazy, dude! My father's nagging me about getting a job. I don't know." Marlon exhaled, the cigarette smoke punctuating his words. He had been taking the bass pretty seriously after joining a band with Freddy and Remy, but the band hadn't lasted long, and only the love of the music remained.

"What about you? You want to go to L.A. with me?" Marlon asked me. I was staring at the ceiling. The idea had never even entered my head. I could use a change of pace, I told myself—but what a move that would be.

"I don't know, man. Maybe," I said casually. I couldn't imagine leaving New York, but you never knew where life lead, did you?

"I was going to go to the Shoreline Dead shows. I'll be in Cali, too!" Archer blurted out as he danced around the living room. Good-hearted freak, he picked up an umbrella and started twirling it like Mary Poppins. As I ambled to the fridge to get something to drink, I looked down at my stomach, which was still pretty lean despite all the beer I'd been drinking. There was very little, other than beer, in the fridge, so I grabbed one. I glanced at the courtyard through the kitchen window, the sun climbing the wall on the other building, gleaming as it hit some of the hand-blown panes of glass.

I cracked my beer and walked back to the living room, trying to contain the foam oozing out of the can. Archer was still dancing around to the constant song in his head. The carpet actually looked clean compared to the filth of his feet. He was opening and closing the umbrella. I shouted to him, "Hey, schmuck, can you not do that inside? It's bad luck."

No sooner had the words left my mouth than Archer opened the umbrella once again as he stepped backward—right onto the neck of my guitar. There was a sharp crack, and the room fell silent as I looked on in horror. I bent down to pick up my instrument, which was now in two pieces. The headstock was dangling from the steel strings. I didn't know what to say. Archer looked on with a half-stupid grin on his face that only irritated me more.

"You *see*, you fucking asshole? You see what you *did?* This guitar cost me four hundred and fifty bucks! You gonna buy me another one?" But I knew Archer didn't even have the money to fix it. Anger was raging inside me. I screamed, "Get the fuck out of my *house!* Get *out!*

If it was any indication of what California would be like, I was going to die a New York rat.

CHAPTER 26

Pretty thought-provoking, though, the California idea: I couldn't get it out of my head. When I reached the park— I could have walked to it in my sleep—I looked around, angling toward a hot dog vendor. The business was being taken over by people from Bangladesh, which was fine with me as long as they weren't stingy with the condiments. The guy was parked right under a tree that cast a shadow over his entire operation.

"Yes, sir, can I help you?"

I had to look around and do a double take. *Sir?* Was I actually . . . ? I had a sudden sense of adulthood as I perused the menu. "Ah, yeah, sure, I'll take a dog, mustard, kraut, little bit of onions, and a grape soda, if you don't mind."

"Absolutely. I will fix it for you right away." The man really looked like he was enjoying what he was doing; maybe where he came from it was the way you treated people. He handed me the dog two-handed, with a smile and the nod of a geisha. I didn't know what else to do but hand him the money and smile back; he just kept thanking me.

I sat on a concrete ledge overlooking the fountain, with the sun on my face. The fountain rarely worked, but it was a nice place to sit. I had started eating my dog when I felt a gust of wind move over my head and caught an object out of the corner of my eye. I turned around to see Tony just finishing a roundhouse kick, with a cigarette dangling out of his mouth and a joint behind his ear, standing there in a Bruce Lee stance. "Glad you didn't move—I woulda taken your head off with that one!" he said affably. The concrete railing I was sitting on was an easy three feet off the ground already, so I was extremely glad my head was where it ought to be. "What the fuck're you eating that shit for? It'll kill ya." Tony took a deep drag off his cigarette and tucked the cross that was dangling on his chest back into his wife beater, kissing it first of course. He was dressed in the usual janitor's uniform—he could've been a garbage man—but he loved a uniform.

"I was hungry. What's it to *you?*" I asked with a smirk; you had to give it back. Tony laughed and threw his arm over me as he sat down to watch the chicks drift by. He spit a piece of tobacco off his tongue, kicked back with his legs crossed at the ankles, and ran his comb through his hair; he was such a fucking mook. I finished the dog, wadded up the napkin, and shoved it inside the can, sucking my teeth to loosen the last bit of kraut.

"When are you gonna marry my sister, Davey boy? Huh? You could be family," he said, slapping me on the back and shaking a finger. He hadn't stopped asking for years. Not that Adrian wasn't a nice girl, but one wrong word from her, and I'd be dead; dead wasn't what I needed.

"She's too good for me, Tony. Adrian needs a nice accountant or a cop or something, you know?" I thought for a second. "Hey Tony, what do you know about California?"

"California? I don't know. Sunny? Heard the chicks are into guys with cash. I wanted to go there when I was a kid, but you know, things change." He sat up, looking down at the inoperable waterspouts for a second, and I saw a glimmer of regret in his eyes. The cross he was wearing popped out of his shirt again; this time he kissed it and looked up to the sky.

"You can always go, Tony," I replied like a motivational speaker. Tony gave me a 'what, are you stupid?' look.

"Sometimes life makes decisions *for* you, kid." Tony had knocked up some girl a couple of years before. Nice Catholic chicks don't get abortions; even not-so-nice ones don't. "Why, you thinking of going out there? Making some moves?" Tony egged me on with a smile, throwing a little punch at my ribs.

I tried to block the punch. "Yeah. I don't know. Maybe."

"What the fuck are you waitin' for? You gotta do shit before you can't, before you *won't*." He tousled my hair, heckling a passing chick at the same time. "Hey, sweetheart, I think my friend here is in love with you!" He pointed at me, which made the girl smile a little as she flipped her hair and kept on walking. I shook my head.

"Don't worry, Davey, I'll take care of the Village for you. You heard from Patsy?" She had joined the army about six months earlier, and I hadn't heard from her. I shook my head. Tony continued, "I got wind that her mother died. Figure she woulda been around by now for the funeral or something."

I thought of when my grandfather Poppy died. It'd been a few years. Patsy had sat up till four in the morning helping me write a eulogy for him as she spit-shined my shoes for the funeral; I wished I could be there for her. I said my good-byes to Tony, not knowing if we would see each other again.

I walked down West Third and took a quick look at the crappy rings the Nigerian were selling before turning left on Sixth Avenue and rolling into Joe's Pizza.

"What's up, Sal?" I screamed over the radio that was blasting Sinatra in the background. He turned around and came out of the makeshift prep room off the side.

"David! You want a nice slice?" He smiled as he picked a fresh piece of dough off the counter and started to stretch it for a pie. Before I knew it the dough was three feet wide, spinning in the air.

"Nah, Sal, but I'll take one of those Italian ices when you finish."

"I'm always finished for you, Davey boy." He let the dough float down to the counter and fall perfectly onto a pan, ready for coating.

"Gimme a chocolate lemon number, okay?" Sal practically submerged his entire body in the freezer and came up with the goods, which he slammed on the glass counter like a bartender. I started to slurp up the lemon as I stared off into the Miller High Life clock that had such a hypnotic effect.

"You all right, Davey boy?" he asked, throwing his foot up on something behind the counter and leaning his elbow on his knee.

"Yeah Sal, I'm okay. You ever been to California? I'm thinking of going out there, and I was just wondering."

He sucked his teeth and squinted as he patted his lips with his forefinger and thought. "I gotta brother, okay? He went out to California in, let me think, maybe, '75? I don't remember. Anyway, he stopped smoking and didn't eat pizza anymore. You know, Davey boy, gotta real healthy."

I smiled at the picture. "Yeah? So how does he like it now?" I asked, fighting the juice of the icy from melting down my arm.

"He moved back a few years ago, got a cancer. They said maybe from the smog they got out there, I don't know. You go if you got to, Davey boy, okay? You just don't breath in too deep, okay?" And as Sal started to laugh, I kind of half-heartedly laughed with him, but I'd lost my appetite. I waved at Sal as I said my goodbyes and threw the icy in the garbage on the way out.

Sixth Avenue had become a bazaar, with people selling books and crap on every corner north of Bleeker. I glanced at some of the stuff as I made my way up the avenue. I turned on Ninth Street and went toward Fifth. I liked Ninth—it had nice brownstones—and I was constantly reminded by that voice to keep life interesting.

I was strolling at a nice pace, looking at the leaves floating above my head, nearing the corner of Fifth when I heard my name echo from the buildings as if through a ravine. I looked around and, across the street, saw Murray waving his arms. I smiled and crossed to say hello. "Hey, Murray, how's it going?" I asked the man, who was practically tap dancing in front of me.

"Not too bad, David, you know? Every day above ground is a good day! How 'bout you? You doing good, champ?" He asked it as if he cared. I had always respected that about him, sincerity.

"Well, Murr, I'm thinking of maybe going out West, make a change." I nodded as I heard the words coming out of my mouth; it gave the thought some validity.

"Yeah?" Murray replied, eyebrows dancing in affirmation. "Change is good, David. Got to shake up the nest every so often. Good for the circulation. You do what you got to do, all right? Whether you become a movie star or a beach bum, just live." We stood there appreciating the pretty girls going by. I said goodbye, and we shook hands like the friends we were.

I made it to my building unscathed and rang for the elevator. Ralph, strangely enough, was on duty. It was Petey's shift, so I was a bit surprised.

"Hey, where's Pete?" I asked, knowing the answer coming would be short and to the point.

Ralph was as usual looking down as he spoke, running a thumb over his pinky ring. "He is a sick man, David. Petey, he made a heart attack. He's in the 'ospital. He's not so good, so I cover his shifts for 'im."

I was stunned. Pete never took care of himself that well, but I'd never thought of him as a guy who'd be sick. I wondered if you could have a heart attack from anger. I knew it wasn't my fault, I really did love the old guy.

"You know where he is, Ralph? What hospital?" I asked.

"He's in a 'ospital in Queens named St. Anne's or Jude or somesing like that."

I felt stupid but had to ask, "What's his last name, Ralph?"

"Callahan. His last name, Davey, is Callahan."

I got to my floor, thanked him for the information, and headed to my apartment.

I immediately went to the phone and dialed information. A woman answered—it seemed like they were always women.

"Directory assistance. What listing, please?"

"In Queens, the number for St. Jude or Anne's Hospital, please."

"Well, sir, which one is it?"

"I'm not sure. Can you check both, please?" I was amazed at the stupidity of people some times.

"Which one would you like me to check first?" she replied.

"Jude, please. Check for St. Jude." I was getting exasperated but maintaining.

"What is the address?" She said it in so monotone a voice that I wasn't sure if she was even alive.

"I don't have an address. If I knew the address, I'd probably know the name, don't you think?" The sarcasm was tough to hold in.

"Checking in Queens, I have no listing."

"Can you check for St. Anne's please?"

There was silence on the line. "How are you spelling, please?"

"I don't know—A-N-N-E?"

"I do not have a listing with that spelling. I'm sorry." She wasn't sorry.

"Do you have any listing *close* to that spelling?" I asked in a last-ditch effort. Just hoping.

Checking in Queens, I have a St. Ann Hospital on 76th Avenue, spelled A-N-N. Would you like the number?"

"Yes, I'll take the number," I replied, glad to have something to go on.

"Thank you. Here is the number you requested."

"Yeah. Okay—and by the way, have a nice day." Silence. She ran off the number as I—not having a pencil—tried my best to remember it. I dialed. The rotary phone had a familiar and comforting clicking sound to it as it ran around. I sat at the kitchen table.

"St. Ann's. How may I direct your call?" The operator on the other end was a bit happier, most likely better pay.

"Ah, where would you send someone with a heart attack? Ah, intensive care, I guess?" I said as I heard a pause then a ringing on the line.

"ICU, Givonne speaking." I was momentarily stupefied at my accomplishment.

"Ah, I'm looking for Pete—I mean, Peter Callahan. I think he had a heart attack?"

"Are you family?" the nurse asked as she flipped through papers and charts.

"Well, yeah, I'm a cousin, by marriage." Bullshit flowing, check.

"Well. . .unfortunately, he's not with us anymore," the nurse said in a hesitant voice.

"I don't understand. If he's not with you, where did he go? Did he just walk out? He gets kind of grumpy sometimes, real crotchety, so I'd under—"

"I'm sorry if you misunderstood me, but Mr. Callahan is gone. He died this morning. I'm very sorry." There was a long pause before I hung up the phone, stunned. I sat for a moment staring out the same kitchen window I had for years. The phone rang.

"Hello? Hey, Annabella. . . . Yeah? They want to see me for a lead? Okay. Sure. . . . By the way, I've been doing some thinking. I made a decision. I'm moving to California." After I hung up the phone I thought of Pete and how much I'd miss him. That's when I knew in my heart that change *was* in the air.

CHAPTER 27

I HAD BEEN ON THE PHONE FOR HOURS trying to get a few things straight before even considering the move as something realistic. Marlon was going to live with an uncle in the valley. His school was in Hollywood—right in the heart of it, and although the city sounded great, I had hopes of living by the water. I'd heard that a friend of Ruby's from high school was living in California, too—he'd also been the drummer in a band Marlon and Freddy played in, I'd known him as well for a few years, nice guy. I got his number and gave him a call. As the phone rang, I had visions of beaches and beautiful California girls; I was stoked just dialing a new area code.

"Hello?" The voice on the other end was mellow. I could swear I heard a seagull.

"Is Chase there?" I asked, looking around my room nervously as I bit my fingernails, praying it was the right number.

"*Chase!* Phone!" the guy screamed into my ear. The anticipation built inside me as I heard rumblings in the background and, after a few moments,

"Hello?" The voice sounded groggy and about half there. I looked at my watch, knowing there was a time difference—but it was three o'clock in California.

"Hey, what's up, Chase? Hope I didn't call at a bad time? It's David. Friend of Ruby and Marlon. . .and Freddy?" There was no reply. I tried again. "You remember, we all smoked a joint in the studio just before you left for the coast?"

I heard a deep breath. "Yeah, yeah! *David*, right! Sorry, man, I partied really hard with these chicks from Sweden or some shit till five in the morning. Yeah, man, right—how are you? You out here?"

He had a nice tone to his voice, and I was glad to be remembered in a positive light. "Actually, bro, I'm in New York, but I'm thinking of coming out West. I was wondering if you might know of any places, maybe I could rent?"

"That's so *crazy*, man! I mean, my roommate is moving out in a couple of months! You could totally take his room! We have an apartment, there are three of us, and it's right across the street from the beach in Venice. But it's four hundred a month. You think you can hang with it?" Chase was so casual, he didn't realize how much life change he was throwing my way.

"Yeah, man! That sounds dope! I can totally swing that!" I said my goodbyes—telling him I'd call in a few weeks when I knew a bit more about my move.

I hung up the phone; the B-side of Van Morrison's *Moondance* was flipping on. It was one of my favorite albums of all time; it just set the mood for greatness. I felt it coming in the wind and was happy about it. The conversation had inexplicably lifted a weight off my shoulders.

I needed to call my agent. We'd been working together for a long time—she'd launched my career at Ford eight years before. I wasn't sure how she was gonna take it, but I thought she would understand my desire for change. I grabbed the jeans that were lying on the floor and fished a crumpled pack of Marlboros out of the pocket. There were still three left—a stroke of luck; I didn't have to go downstairs for at least an hour.

I sat on the familiar heater cover by the window and looked out over the city. I'd miss it, but I needed change, yearned to look out at something different. I was in the middle of a drag on my smoke when the phone rang. I went over to the cluttered desk and grabbed it on the third ring.

"Yeah, hello?"

"Hey, what's up, buddy? It's Luke." The voice sounded a little anxious, not surprising for Luke. We'd met at an audition for some Western movie a couple of years back. I'd arrived late at the makeshift trailer that I'd been told to wait in when I saw a James Dean-looking character sitting in the corner with his feet up on the desk.

"I can roll a cigarette with one hand," the guy'd said to me cockily, and proved his point. I had nodded, taken the cigarette from his hand, and checked it out, laying my bag down on the chair in front of him. I'd sat down and, smiling at him, handed it back.

"Yeah?" I'd said, reached into my bag, pulled out a pack of Bamboo papers, and, waving them in front of him, said, "I can roll the tightest joint you ever smoked. . .with *two*." As we laughed at our common sundry talents, I realized we would be friends for a long time.

But the tone in his voice wasn't playful at the moment. He was a couple of years older than me and was living with a girl on the Upper West Side, an actress as well, which seemed to bring him down.

"You want to shoot some pool? I've gotta get outta here. I got some good smoke, too." There was a real need in his voice. I told him to come down, and we could hang out. I finished my cigarette and ran my hands through my long hair. I hadn't showered in a couple of days, and it looked pretty greasy, but it was way cool. I tied it up in a ponytail as I grabbed the phone to make the other call. I was rolling the stray hairs that couldn't quite make the ponytail behind my ears. It was raining pretty hard. The water bounced off the ledge outside my window, which was fogged up in a way that put me at ease.

I dialed my agent's number and waited for her to answer. The receptionist who picked up was a real cutie; I had always hit on her when I went over to pick up scripts.

"Is Annabella there, you beautiful woman?" I could *hear* her blush on the other end. She transferred the call.

"David! What can I do for you, sweetheart?" Annabella asked in a very motherly way that I had always valued.

"Hey, Annabella, I wanted to talk to you about the Coast. I'm making my plans to move out there, and I just, you know, wanted your support."

There was a bit of silence but a general sense of calm.

"David. . .when you told me the other week," she finally said, "I wasn't sure if you were serious, but I guess you are. I'll give them a call on the Coast to see if they'll support the move."

I hadn't really thought about that. I was signed bi-coastally, and the possibility of rejection had never entered my thinking. "Well," I said, taken back, "I thought that since, you know, I was signed in both offices, it wouldn't be a big deal."

"David," she replied, trying her best to calm me, "do you know how many people are moving out there? Business is business. Look, I'll give them a call and refresh them about you. I'm sure it will all work out."

I thanked her in advance and hung up the phone.

I wanted to shower and hunted around for some clean clothes. I managed to find a halfway clean shirt and some jeans that didn't stink as I stripped down and went into the bathroom. I stood in front of the mirror for a minute, flexing and being generally stupid. It amazed me that the face looking back at was the same as when I was a child, only now I was eighteen; same shit-eating grin, just longer hair.

I reached over the tub to the faucets and turned on the hot water. It always took a couple of minutes to heat up, so I sat on the hamper and waited. It was on that very spot I'd masturbated for the first time. Admittedly, I had been completely awestruck when I saw that monumental squirt of white goop; I'd thought it was a catastrophe.

After what seemed like enough time, I moved my hand under the running water to check it. Satisfied, I stepped over the edge of the tub to the awaiting spray. I looked up, feeling the hot water cleanse my very being. I loved showers, though I didn't take them that often. I grabbed my hands behind my back and stretched my chest upward, feeling my pectorals expand; I was in pretty good shape for a smoker.

I finished up and reached out for a towel. Fuck! I thought to myself. I realized I'd forgotten to grab one off the floor of my room. I hemmed and hawed but, knowing that one wasn't going to just appear, stepped out of the shower and ran dripping to my room. I nearly killed myself slipping on the hardwood floors before regaining my balance and cursing the apartment.

I dried off and had finished dressing just as I heard the buzzer. I walked barefoot to the front door and swung it open. Luke was standing there dripping wet in his overcoat and baseball hat, his pool cue slung over his shoulder but under his jacket; got to keep it dry. He furrowed his brow and, shaking his head, sighed heavily as I invited him in. He made his way into the living room, laid his drenched jacket on the chair, and leaned his cue against the wall. He sat on the couch and threw a bag of dope on the carpet before putting his head in his hands. I reached over and started the ritual of breaking up the weed and rolling.

"Roll a massive one, Davey, I got a lot to forget," he said ominously from between his fingers. I complied; in moments we were lighting up and smoking away.

After a while Luke seemed to chill out, and we started to rap about his situation at home. The girl was driving him crazy about work and the like. She had a picture-perfect idea of how their life was supposed to be, only she'd never asked *him*. He loved her but was tiring of it. Her mother had been diagnosed with terminal cancer, forcing him to stick around for support.

We finished the joint as I went into the closet for my cue. I strapped it over my shoulder and threw on a baseball cap. We made our way downstairs and into a cab.

It was still pouring as Luke told the driver to head down Eleventh to Sixth Avenue and make a right. We were pretty stoned, and the conversation came to a halt. That was the great thing about sitting with friends; you didn't feel the need to talk through the companionable silence.

We reached the front door of Chelsea Billiards and got out. Breaking into a run for the door to avoid getting totally drenched, we made our way to the front desk and got a table in the back, where we set up the rack. I could rack in my sleep—I'd become a player in the past few years and hustled pool to make some extra money, following in my father's footsteps, I liked to think. I racked up for nine ball, lit a smoke, and signaled for Luke to break as I leaned against the wall.

"I'm thinking of moving out West, man. I need some new scenery," I said candidly.

Luke shifted his gaze from the table to me for a second before executing a perfect bank shot with a half-assed leave. "Yeah? Can I live in your closet?" he asked jokingly. "That's great, Davey, you'll like it out there." He missed his next shot and leaned on his cue. He'd had a short-lived stint on the West Coast trying to make a life of acting but had wound up spreading asphalt in the city of Diamond Bar. It wasn't till he moved to New York that things had picked up for him.

"Thanks, man, I hope so. Marlon is going too, so at least I'll know someone there," I replied, looking the table over like a hawk, seeing three shots ahead. That was how you won pool; it wasn't the shots you made but the ones you left. Shooting with precision, I ran the table; it was easy. Luke laughed as I finished off the nine ball with a three-bank shot.

"I got some numbers for you, bro, some cool people, some ex-honeys," he said with a smile, trying to avoid smoke in his eyes as he hunched over the table, racking the balls. "You'll do well, Davey. By the way, what did your agent say?" Luke was always one step ahead; it was always about consent. As I told him about the conversation I'd had that afternoon, he just sighed. "Isn't it just like a fucking agent to expel happiness? You just get the fuck out there, *then* worry about it." I answered with a hard break and sank two balls. I looked up and smiled in appreciation of Luke's support. We kept on playing all afternoon, talking and winning, even hustling a couple of pigeons with fancy cues we could've beat with house sticks. If making it in California was gonna be as easy as hustling pool, I'd be running Cali like Minnesota Fats.

CHAPTER 28

I T ISN'T EASY PACKING YOUR LIFE UP, especially when you're not sure where you'll land. I was swimming among bags of old clothes and childhood memories that I'd somehow became the keeper of. My sister was studying abroad in Italy and didn't care what happened to the stuff as long as she didn't have to deal with it, and it wasn't in my mother's plans. Luke was sitting on my bed playing with an old tilting labyrinth game I had gotten when I was ten; the steel ball had become pretty rusty, but the game still worked.

After numerous phone calls, tapes of my work being sent, and what felt like something just short of the Inquisition, I was being given my shot. It'd been decided a few weeks before that the agency I'd been with for five years would represent me on the West Coast. I wasn't going to California with the intent of pursuing an acting career, but a man's got to have choices.

"What the *fuck* am I going to do with all this crap?" I said to

Luke, who was using body English to get that little fucking ball around the maze. I was leaving town in less than a week and needed to get my shit sorted.

"Don't *think* about it," he said without looking up from his game. "If you haven't looked at it, worn it, or touched it in two years, trash it." I thought about that, and I had to say it made sense. I'd talked with Chase about his roommate moving out and when I could move in, so things there were looking good. Marlon wasn't ecstatic about moving in with his uncle, but since I had *lent* him the five grand needed for school and no more cash was readily available, it was his only option.

Luke lit up a joint he'd tucked behind his ear as I picked up this, or threw away that. "Don't forget to call J.B. He's been out there for a while, and he'll help out if you need. And get a reliable car man, all right? Don't skimp on it! You're gonna do a lot of driving out there, and your car will become your best friend." He said all this with the smoke retained in his lungs. He passed the joint and leaned back on his elbows blowing smoke rings that hung in the air like cotton balls.

I toked at the joint and laughed, " You think I should maybe get a license first?" Luke cracked up. "I can't believe I'm getting out of here, you know? It just doesn't seem real. I don't really have any people out there, but it doesn't bother me—with any luck I'll get some job in a restaurant or something." I'd been working at a fancy restaurant uptown for the past few months and had gotten a few of my friends jobs there. All that shit was charm and a good smile, just smoke and mirrors. It was Luke who wasn't one for people skills, so that kind of work was out of the question. He'd been brought up to appreciate working with his hands or driving sorts of jobs that he'd been forced to take many times over the years.

"Yeah, if you can handle it, I'm sure you can waiter somewhere," Luke said in tone. "Isn't that what an actor really does for a living, anyway?" We laughed and polished off the rest of the joint, enjoying the stoned state we were in. I heard a muffled ring under a pile of clothes on the radiator and, grabbing for the phone, knocked it over in the process. It fell to the floor with a crash. I picked up the receiver.

"Yeah?" I said out of breath and still laughing.

"David, sweetie, it's Annabella. I've got to talk to you for a minute." I was hoping it was a last-minute audition that might keep me in the big apple for a few more years.

"What's shakin'?" I said, but she was different, not her usual self.

"David, I've got something that I need to talk with you about."

". . .The West Coast didn't *sink*, did it?" I was laughing at my own joke, but she was silent on the other end.

"No, David, but there *is* a problem out there." She hesitated.

"What do mean, 'problem'? Is the office still running out there or what?" I was getting dry mouth.

"Yes, sweetie, the office is still there, but unfortunately, since talking with me last, they decided the West Coast wouldn't have enough enthusiasm for your coming out there. . .they're not going to represent you, David."

I needed a moment to let the words sink in, and then I just got pissed. "What the *fuck!* All that bullshit, and fucking phone calls, sending tapes, for nothing? What kind of fucking agency are they running anyway? Bunch of assholes! They're all just fucking assholes." I was practically in tears of rage. Luke was sitting in the corner, shaking his head, getting the gist of it. But the worst was yet to come.

"David, I fought for you," Annabella continued. "You've got to understand that I really believe in you, which makes what I have to say even harder."

I was confused—I didn't understand what more there was to say—but you never really know do you? Annabella sighed as she continued, "The higher-ups here thought that, since you were leaving New York anyway, thought it would be best to severe ties with you on *both* coasts, David."

I was dumbstruck and felt completely betrayed. I'd been with Annabella for eight years and couldn't believe it was this easy for her. It's not that I wanted to stay in New York. I didn't—but I didn't like decisions being made for me. I breathed heavily into the phone and clenched the receiver in my hand like a bat; abandonment was washing over me like a cold shower. "That's just great, Annabella. It's been swell. I guess I'll talk to you later," I said, as I moved to sit on the heater to avoid falling over.

"David, I didn't want it to be like this, but I'm only one person. *Please* understand." There was compassion in her voice, but I knew it was all business.

"Yeah, I understand. Tell the owners to have a nice life, and I'll see them on the lot, okay? You tell them that for me." And, with that, I hung up the phone in disgust. I didn't know what to say. I felt Luke's arm over my shoulder. I looked up at him; he had a knowing gaze in his eyes. Luke had always been a pessimist when it came to agents and the like but had always appreciated my optimism. He watched the mortar of naiveté crumble away from my face. I'd gotten my first taste of being dumped, and it didn't feel good.

"Fuck 'em. Who needs them anyway?" he said, thumping my shoulder with his hand. "There are lots of agents in Los Angeles, and when you need one just look under a rock, or better yet, let them find you."

It wasn't easy to shake it off. I'd had a relationship with Annabella that I thought was strong. Whatever. I went back to sorting clothes and continued thinking about what I would do once I was out there.

Luke called his house and needed to get back there. He said his goodbyes and reminded me of who I was, not who I was with. I put my shit down and headed out for a while. I didn't feel like going to the habitual places, so I walked to Fourteenth Street to get on the A train heading uptown. Feeling low wasn't a frequent sensation for me, so I embraced it.

The air was choking, as I looked at the lonely faces waiting patiently for a breeze to sweep by and move their immobile lives; I just waited along with the drones. It felt like an eternity before I saw the lights coming down the tunnel. As I moved diagonally toward the incoming train a fleeting feeling came over me of leaping forwards just ending it slowly as the train flew by—my eyes connected with every window as it passed. I patiently stood waiting for the doors to open and the steam to let out with a hiss.

I entered the car and saw an open seat to my left that I ambled toward. I was practically sitting in it when an old lady—moving quicker than she should have been able to—sat down in my place. I just looked at her—her eyes, darting to the news that she opened quickly, wouldn't dare glance up to mine for fear of confrontation. I giggled to myself and turned to walk away. But that voice in my head caught the better of me as I leaned over that woman—the smell of mothballs overwhelming my senses, as her paper ruffling in my face caused a breeze. I leaned in closer, and, just when it reached an uncomfortable level, said, "I would have given you the seat anyway, you know." I just smiled as I heard the woman gasp, and I walked toward the front of the train.

There was a bold feeling when you rode between cars catching a smoke. I headed up to the first car, feeling all the eyes on me as I strode through. With hands deep in my pockets and no eye contact, I was unmistakably a New Yorker. Nobody would fuck with me. I got to the front and leaned against the faded ad on the wall—the glass scratched by a kid's tag made by a key or the like, caused a pattern that reminded me of salamanders. The train was creaky in its familiarity, banking like an old coalmine car returning to the depths below. It gave me comfort to know I could always stand there. I watched the train pull up to the next station and an onslaught of people pour in.

I got off at Fifty-ninth Street and walked up the staircase to the surface. I moved up Central Park West and hung a right at the driveway of Tavern on the Green. There were always horse-drawn carriages parked out front with tons of people milling about or eating the overpriced food served there. I continued on to the path where, years before, I'd run a race. It was only six miles, but I *was* nine.

I thought of the moment when I neared the finish line—the rain, sleeting down like spikes on my face, made my sweatsuit stick to my body like a wet burlap sack. Remembering that excruciating sensation of my legs burning—each step I stumbled forward possibly my last—made my heart jump. Just at the moment when I thought I would give up and walk the rest of the way, some consciousness came over me, and my head felt lighter. The rain—which by then had no effect on me—had been beating rhythmically, my heartbeat pulsing with every drop that fell. Hearing the music loudly, I suddenly couldn't be stopped. My legs had run numb and taken full strides—longer than I could ever have imagined being able to. I'd crossed the finish line with ease that day and never forgotten that feeling. I'd never felt it again from running, but I'd tapped into something extraordinary.

I reached Sheep's Meadow and looked around. It was a beautiful place in the park, a wide-open field where people played Frisbee or tanned themselves like lizards on rocks. I wandered around to find a comfortable spot. The scene that had played out earlier was catching up with me. It was okay; I needed the change of California more than the possibility of a career. Besides, if it was meant to be, it would happen. I lay back; the sun on my face was nice. I closed my eyes and fantasized about beaches and the women I could charm. I felt a shadow pass over and, when I opened my eyes, saw a blonde image staring down at me. "I can't believe you're here!" She sat down next to me and put her hand on mine as she spoke. "David! I heard that you were leaving but didn't know how to find you, and here you are!"

Summer was a girl I had messed around with a few times over

the years. We'd maintained a friendship. She was beautiful—her blonde hair, tied back, was falling in tendrils over her green eyes. She rarely wore a bra—which was a treat since she had great tits. I couldn't help but smile. Her body looked like love.

We caught up on the past few months and laughed. I was glad she got me out of my funk. I told her about Chase and the apartment in Venice. She was happy for me and even had some ideas. "I'm going to school with this guy whose father owns a restaurant on the ocean. I think it's in Santa Monica or something, but it's a good lead. Don't worry about all the bullshit— *annnnnnnnd*, I've got a cute girlfriend that lives out there, and she'll love you!" We laughed and talked, and all that had happened a few hours earlier appeared to melt away with the afternoon sun. California was coming closer, and the city was letting me leave.

CHAPTER 29

I T WASN'T OFTEN THAT I SAW MY FATHER with a look in his eye like he had that day. We were standing at the entrance to the terminal in silence; there wasn't a lot to say. He had his hands buried in the pockets of his shorts—I noticed him shift his toes around in the sandals he was wearing, trying to think of something a father should say. I just smiled; for me, it was the easiest way to keep from crying. I had my baseball cap on backwards—long hair tied in a ponytail, dealing with it all.

I had always valued the contrast between us: the crispness of the madras shirt my father wore, highlighted by his freshly shaven face. The only memory I had of my father with even the slightest bit of scruff was when he sat *shiva* for my grandmother. I remember being told of the tradition. One lets one's beard grow, out of respect, for the removal of vanity; why should you feel good or comfortable when someone you love is dead and uncomfortable? It made sense. I looked over at the tortoise shell sunglasses he had on that shielded his eyes from view, and as I thought of something I hoped would bring levity to the sadness, I noticed a tear rolling down his face; my grandmother's death had also been the only time I ever saw him cry.

He inhaled deeply as he reached out to embrace me; I got all choked up. I always felt comforted by my dad—but for the first time *I* was going to be truly alone, my own parent. "I love you, Tiger," I heard whispered in my ear—I hadn't heard that name used in a long time. It resonated youth, and as my father squeezed me even tighter, the Timex watch he was wearing ticked like the heartbeat of a child in my ear. I felt deep pains in my chest that resonated release; it was easy when things were like that. At some passages of my life we had seemed to touch, but barely miss; at others, when moments culminated in a perfect crescendo, we were truly peas in a pod. "I know you have to leave," he continued, thought running clear. "I always knew you would one day—but I can't tell you how much it pains me, David. God. I love you more than myself." I sniffled at the snot that was running from my nose—the smell of Grey Flannel cologne permeating my senses. We stepped away from each other, and he took the glasses off his face just long enough to wipe his eyes with his thumb and forefinger. I wiped my own with my sleeve and collected myself. I was standing on my own now, though fully supported. We strolled toward the gate, the man patting my shoulder. Whatever mistakes he and my mother had made with me certainly didn't show.

As I was getting on line to enter the plane, both his hands on my shoulders, he leaned his forehead on my back. I stood like that for a minute, then turning around to face him, said, "Dad, don't say goodbye, okay? Just say, 'See you soon,' all right?"

He didn't say a word, just looked on smiling in a kind of wonder. I started walking with my guitar in hand—I'd bought a cheap classical off my friend Brian to replace my decapitated one——making eyes at a cute chick in line. I turned once to catch a glimpse of him, but, true to form, he was already gone.

I got on the 747 and found my seat midway down the aisle as I waited for take-off. I always preferred an aisle seat—I'm one of those few people who feel the need to constantly use the bathroom; I enjoyed the freedom it brings. I liked flying but hated connections, and, naturally, there would be one in Chicago. After the This Strap or That Mask bullshit, once we were flying high at thirty-seven thousand feet, I got as comfortable as a sardine can be and tried to sleep, but images of my new home were swimming in my head. I'd never been away with any thought of permanence. Although I didn't think of it as forever, the idea of coming back didn't even enter my mind. I looked around and smiled at a brunette a few seats over. I'd once picked up a girl on a plane, so the idea wasn't that far-fetched. But I closed my eyes as sandy beaches I'd never known flooded my mind.

The stewardesses were pretty cute; I got extra peanuts, as well as a fresh blanket right out of the wrapper. I noticed one was a bit older as she hung over me, trying to reach into the compartment above. I smelled a perfume that was overwhelming but very womanly. The plane had started to bounce around a bit and I, not terribly fond of turbulence, rested my forehead against the seat in front of me. I read her nametag—*Mary Elizabeth*—when she knelt down beside me to speak. "You alright, sugar?" The southern accent reminded me of Dolly Parton.

I forced a smile. "Yeah—well, you know, I'm cool. *You* alright?" I gave her a wink, and she blushed.

"We're going to be circling over Chicago for a while. It may be a little bumpy. If you need anything, just holler, okay?"

I obliged and looked down at the Casio watch I was wearing. By my calculation, I had only twenty minutes before my connection to Los Angeles, but I figured they'd wait. I put my head back down and breathed in the recycled air deeply.

I was startled by a jolt as I felt the plane bank sharply and a voice came over the loud speaker. "This is your captain speaking. We seem to be in a pretty bad storm as we wait for clearance to land at O'Hare. Please keep your seatbelts fastened and your tray tables in their upright and locked positions, and we should be on the ground before you know it. Thank you again for flying with us—we realize there are many airlines to choose from, and we appreciate you picking us." I wished at that moment that I had chosen, not only a different airline, but a different mode of transportation altogether.

When I finally landed, I hurried off the plane only to discover that my connection to L.A. had taken off without me. I stood on a line that led to the only counter that was open and awaited my fate. When I got to talk to someone after what seemed like an eternity, I was told the airline had no intention of paying for a hotel room for passengers who missed their connection due to weather, since it was *force majeure*—an act of God. I wouldn't be able to catch a flight till seven-thirty the next morning. That was ten hours away, but I was welcome to wait in the terminal. I reached in my pocket for my wallet, but didn't find it—fuck! I ran back to the gate we'd come from and tried to board the plane. The cleaning crew was just finishing up, and I asked them if they'd seen it. I was told that, if they found everything, it would be sent back to the airport of origin's lost and found. I looked around for a phone to call my pop collect.

The phone rang and he finally answered. The first thing he asked me was, how the hell did had I forgotten my wallet in the car? He told me as soon as I had an address he's fed ex it to me, and said he'd wire me some of my money to L.A. It was nice to hear his voice. I left out the part of being stranded in Chicago, and told him I loved him. I hung up and looked in my pockets: I had my boarding pass for the next flight and twenty bucks. I didn't have enough for a hotel room, so I guess I was going to sleep on the floor of the terminal. I hunkered down and pulled my cap over my eyes.

I heard the familiar voice even before I recognized the scent. Mary Elizabeth was standing over me as I looked up. "Now, what on earth are you doing lying on that floor?" She was sweet as she knelt down, flanked by the rest of the flight crew.

"The next flight is in the morning, and I don't have the cash for a hotel. It seems safe enough here, though. Where are you guys headed?" I asked, hoping maybe a bar was in the plans; I felt a little homesick all of a sudden and could have used the company.

"We're heading to the hotel the airline provides for us. We all have flights tomorrow, too." She turned around to talk to one of the male stewards standing beside her, and then turned back to me. "All us women are sharing rooms, but Steven here's alone, and he said you're welcome to stay there if you'd like. The airline pays for it, so it wouldn't cost you a dime."

She said it with such sincerity, I found it hard to say no. I grabbed my guitar and followed the crew to an awaiting shuttle that took us to the hotel. Steven seemed like an okay guy in a geeky uniform customary for a job such as his. His hair was plastered down on his head, and his eye twitched. We spoke a little on the shuttle, and he told me he was from Houston. I talked about California and my hopes for new surroundings.

When we got to the hotel, no one was in the mood for a drink. Steven said there was usually a beer or two in the room, so we headed up. To my relief there were two beds in the room. "Take whichever one you want—I'm going to take a shower," he said as he rolled his overnight bag through the bathroom door, leaving me alone.

I looked around the room and did find a beer in the fridge. I sat on one of the beds, opened my guitar case, and started to play some blues. It felt appropriate for the moment, and the beer tasted good and cold as it went down my throat.

I took my pants off and laid them down at the foot of the bed. I finished the beer and sat cross-legged in my boxers, under the covers, playing my guitar; it always gave me comfort. I was feeling lucky to not be sleeping on the floor of the terminal, and I was getting tired.

I heard rustling from the bathroom but kept on playing my music. I heard the door open and looked over; I couldn't believe what I saw. Steven was standing in the doorway butt naked, with a hard-on, and was jerking off. I hoped it was a joke and tried to play on. He started to parade around the room to the music and continued to stroke himself.

Terrified of what might happen, my heart racing, I kept playing to stay calm. I hadn't though Steven was gay; he didn't seem to be. Maybe, I thought, he's just an exhibitionist or something and would get in his bed and quietly die. But when I saw him coming closer to my bed, I got scared. I saw the look in his eye as he inched forward, taking his hand off his manhood and reaching for me. I felt like I was twelve years old again. . .but I wasn't. In one quick movement I got up in a kneeling position and had my guitar in my hands like a baseball bat.

"Get the fuck *away* from me!" I shouted through clenched teeth. I didn't think the guy could take me, but I would break my guitar over his head if I had to. The look of surprise I saw in my assailant's eyes was not only genuine but also stunned. What did he expect me to do, let him mess with me for a hotel room? Was he out of his fucking mind?

"Are you serious?" Steven asked, hand covering his mouth.

I moved over to the other side of the bed. "Yeah, I'm fucking serious. You want to try me?" I pulled on my cap and fumbled for my pants. My heart was pounding and I wanted to cry. Steven grabbed a pillow to cover himself and withdrew to *his* bed; I sensed his fear growing. Maybe I would kill him; he'd never thought of that. Chop his body up and shove it back in his little fucking overnight bag; I'd be long gone before anyone even noticed. But at that moment, I just wanted to get out there.

"You don't have to go, you know. I won't touch you or anything," Steven said, trying to defuse the riled person standing before him with a deadly weapon. I put my guitar down just long enough to tie my shoes and grabbed my guitar case.

"Fuck you! I feel like bashing your head in for just *trying* that shit on me!" I turned toward the door, retraced them, and grabbed the other beer. As I opened the door, I heard the guy quietly say, "I really did like your playing."

I shook my head and, without turning, slammed the door behind me, glad to be safe, and headed to the elevator. The shock washed over me, and my heart slowed down. I wondered what to do. It was only midnight, and my flight wasn't for another seven hours or so. I thought of maybe trying to find Mary Elizabeth's room, but god only knew what could happen after all that. I wasn't willing to take the chance with any more people from the friendly skies and headed to the stairwell.

I moved down the carpeted floor in silent rage. Fucking people, I thought as I made my way to the stairwell door. I sat down on one of the steps. The silence was deafening. I drank the other beer and curled up like a hobo. I wanted to forget the night had ever happened. But the way I saw people had changed, maybe forever. I felt a tear run down my face, and then the light in the stairwell— on some kind of a time clock—switched off, and I was left in total darkness. I tried to calm my body and let my mind drift back to a happier place where I could be myself and not be judged.

I waited anxiously for morning to come, hoping I wouldn't run into Steven or any other of the people from the plane. I felt embarrassed for some reason, as if maybe I'd brought it upon myself. . .I knew deep within that it wasn't so, but all the same I needed the protection of sleep. I slowly drifted into unconsciousness, and as my concrete pillow softened, my trip began to harden.

CHAPTER 30

SAT IN A COFFEE-STAINED CHAIR in an office that looked like it
had been forgotten about since World War II, but I figured the
license would work since it had before in Florida, and truly
luck that we had met.

I'd been visiting my old friend Julie—I knew her from summer
camp, and she was in her first year at college. I'd showed up at her
dorm and been in awe: beautiful girls, sun, and booze. She'd introduced me around at a party one of her fraternity friends was
throwing for one of the brothers' birthday. All night at the fraternity house I'd gotten weird looks and kept being told, "You look
just like him," or "You could *be* his kid brother." I hadn't been
sure what any of it meant, but when the guy himself entered the
room, it had been uncanny, like looking in a mirror. Long hair,
pukka necklace, and all. We became fast friends and partied all
night. In the morning when I awoke from my drunken stupor and
checked to make sure I was in one piece, I found his driver's license

in my pocket; he had just turned twenty-one. Sometimes life gives you beautiful things.

I HAD NEVER TRIED USING THE LICENSE at a rental car place, and I hoped I wouldn't land in jail; you couldn't rent a car unless you were twenty-one. It'd worked for buying beer and shit, as well as at bars. I'd picked the seediest place I saw in the phone book at the airport and made sure they took cash deposits. I'd called my dad that morning and had him wire me five hundred bucks—I'd paid ten cents on the dollar for the privilege, but fuck it.

The office stank like cat shit, but I didn't care as long as I got a car. I had driven before—never legally, but that was just semantics. The guy sitting across the desk from me had a cigarette in the corner of his mouth and one going in the ashtray. The suspenders he wore were held together by a safety pin, and the ring around the collar kept his neck straight. "So, Chris, first time in Los Angeles?" he asked through yellow, smoke-stained teeth. He was going over the form I had filled out and had caught me off guard.

"Huh?" I said, remembering who I needed to be, and quickly composed myself. "Yeah, first time for a lot of things. Thinking of moving here, actually," I added with a chuckle.

"Well, now, isn't that nice! You certainly would fit right in with surfers! Long hair and all! I used to have hair down to my butt. Sixties—different time, different time." He adjusted the glasses that were sitting crookedly on his face and stood up next to me. "Well, come on, Chris, let's see what Ugly Duckling has in store for your driving future!"

He led me out onto the lot among the heaps. Could there really be this many shitty cars in one place? I asked myself as I walked down the rows of Gremlins and Pintos and broken-down Escorts. I at least understood why the place was called what it was—although wasn't an ugly duckling supposed to turn into a beautiful swan? I didn't see it happening. "You just pick whatever you want—take your time," the guy said, leaning against an old Caprice, causing its bumper to tweak as he lit another smoke. I had nearly resigned myself to driving a Pinto or such when my eyes were caught off-guard by a glimmer in the distance. I looked across the yard and spotted a white t-topped Chevy. Was I dreaming?

"What about that?" I asked, pointing at the ferocious-looking beast.

"That? You don't want that car. It'll eat through your wallet in gas alone. Been here for a while. Runs good, though."

"I'll take it!" I said without hesitation. The '78 Camaro Berlinetta had been Chevy's answer to the Pontiac Firebird, the "Smokey and the Bandit" car. It had a 5.7-liter engine, fat wheels, and just looked fast. This one was a little dinged up, but it was cool: all white, with a red-and-blue pinstripe.

I loaded my bags into the hatch, took off the t-tops, and headed out. It was a hundred a week, but I would love every minute of it. I got to a pay phone and made my first call to Chase, who was expecting me, but I needed to know where to go. He was working at the Gap in Santa Monica; and said I wasn't far away. I got some directions from a gas station attendant and headed up from Westchester through Venice, to Main Street. The sunshine on my face was like magic as the wind blew through my hair; it was a fucking commercial. I found the Gap, no problem, and pulled into the parking lot, tires screeching. Chase came out in his preppy Gap uniform and admired the car.

"What's up, man? How was your flight? Great car! I thought you were coming next month?"

I smelled bullshit but was trying to ignore it. "No, we said the seventeenth, and here I am, all ready!" I wasn't about to be played.

"Yeah, right. Well, Dave, there is a *little* problem."

He was tiptoeing around something, and I felt uncomfortable. "What do you mean, 'little' problem'?" I asked with eyebrows raised.

"The guy who was supposed to move out? My roommate? Well, he kinda had to change his plans, and. . . ."

"*What?*" I barked out in exasperation. "Are you out of your *mind?* I just packed up all my shit, flew across the country, rented a car, and expected you to live up to what you said!"

"Dave, just calm down. I'm sure there's someone you can stay with for a little—"

"I don't fucking *know* anybody in Los Angeles! Tell your fucking *roommate* to go stay with somebody! Jesus Christ! I can't believe you're saying this!"

"I'd let you stay at our place, but there isn't any *room.* I feel really bad, Dave. I'm sure I can help you out some way."

I felt victimized, but it wasn't my style, so I shifted gears. "I don't need to stay the night at your place, man. What I need is for you to talk to your roommate and give me some money. That'll make things square. I'm going to need to get a hotel room or something, and I don't have the cash. I'm not asking for a loan, I'm asking for reparations. You talk to your roommate and figure it out. You already put me out on a limb, all right? Don't break the branch." I slapped palms as I looked him in the eyes, and went to sit on my car.

I blew out a sigh. I wasn't going to be taken advantage of, but I needed to figure things out. I lit a smoke and adjusted the sunglasses on my face—the Vuarnets I wore lent a crispness to the scene. I spotted a pay phone across the street and headed over. I was sure I could fit in there among the surfers and such. I rummaged in my pocket for the piece of paper that had Marlon's phone number on it. He'd come out a week or so earlier to register for school, and I hadn't talked to him since. I dialed the number and waited.

"Hello?" answered Marlon in his usual drone.

"Ah, this is the New York city Police, Detective Mulrooney, looking for one Marlon—"

"Cut the shit, man! What's going on? . . . You *here?* How's the apartment?" Marlon was speeding even for him.

"He's fucking me around. I don't know what the fuck to do. He gave me some bullshit about his roommate can't move out and this and—"

"You're *kidding* me. What a dick! He's boning you? So what's the word?"

"I got a cool car! I told Chase he needed to cough up some bread to help me get a place." I was glad to be talking to Marlon. I noticed a beautiful brunette on roller skates.

"Dude, I can't take it at my uncle's. He's driving me fucking nuts, and I've only been here a week! Let me call my grandmother and see if she'll lend me some cash to get a place with you. Sound cool?" Marlon was always calm and thought well; it was a good solution. But since he didn't have a car, I would have to forgo my dreams of the beach. *C'est la vie.* It was more about survival than anything else. I told him I'd head in his direction and see if he could get things squared away.

In my first hour in L.A. I had rented a car, lost an apartment, and found a roommate: not bad for a city boy.

I went back across the street and saw Chase waiting at my car. He was being understandably sheepish but smiling. "All right, Dave. I feel really bad about all this, so this is what I did. I made my roommate call his parents and get some bread. I'm gonna cough up as much as I can, too. But I think I'll be able to get you, like, almost a grand. Is that cool? I know it's a bummer, man, but I'll take care of business." He sounded sincere, and I had never thought they were going to give me *that* much cash.

"Yeah, it'll get me started. I gotta go and hook up with Marlon. I'll call you tomorrow for the cash."

"No sweat, man. I really am sorry."

I shook my head. "Don't sweat it man, shit happens. I got bigger fish to fry," I said, got into my ride, and literally headed off into the sunset.

The apartment was in Studio City, but no matter how you sliced it, the valley it was. It wasn't any wonder why Marlon was losing his mind. I had been in hospital rooms less sterile: neat as a pin, with a huge Sears portrait of the folks over the mantle—Jesus, suburbia lives. I had picked up a paper on the way over, and we perused it together. I also had a few joints. Marlon hadn't smoked in a week. We went out on the balcony and lit up as we leafed through the paper—the joint moving back and forth.

"Here's one," Marlon read off. "'Sunny two bedroom, pool,

amenities, freeway views?' *Pass*." The rest had the same vibe, so it looked as though it was just the best of the worst. We wrote down a few numbers for me to call. The high felt good, but it was quickly killed when the uncle and the girlfriend came home. They had just gotten off the golf course and were dressed ridiculously. When he saw the two of us on the balcony with the glass door closed, it was pretty clear, and he wasn't amused.

"I didn't bring you into this house, Marlon, to be a pothead with your friend! I don't think your parents would like it either. Who the hell are *you?*" he asked, pointing a finger at me.

"Me? I'm—just leaving," I said, turning toward the door.

"I think that would be a good idea," the uncle said.

Marlon walked me out to the car. "Shit, man, that wasn't even funny! Do you always have to be a smartass? I gotta leave now," Marlon said as we reached the car. "Call some of those numbers and find a place. I'll get the cash, okay? Cool fucking car! Where are you gonna stay?"

For the first time, I realized I was homeless. "I'll get a hotel room or something. Don't sweat it. I'll give you a call mañana." He went back upstairs and left me alone. I got in the car and felt the chill of night coming on. It could be a hundred degrees during the day and sixty at night. When I went to a 7-Eleven and got a pack of Marlboro, I got carded; the ID worked as usual. I went back to the Camaro and lit a smoke. It was dark and getting chilly. I figured a hotel was out of the question—I'd given most of the cash to the car guy for a deposit, so it looked like the Chevy would be my bed for the time being. First night in L.A., and sleeping in a car could be worse—I could've been in another stairwell.

CHAPTER 31

I T TOOK A LITTLE WHILE, BUT I WAS SOON coming to grips with living in The Valley. Marlon and I had found an apartment in North Hollywood, and I'd gotten in touch with Luke's friend J.B., who gave me the name of an acting school—it was on the second floor of a strip mall in Hollywood off Sunset, one of those 'all-inclusive' places. It was a bit of a strain—I was going through money like crazy and still counting pennies; however, against my capital sensibility, I had my pop wire me the rest of my cash and I started there a few days later.

The Chevy *was* eating me alive in gas. I'd strolled through a couple of used cars places, seen a couple of halfway decent rides, but nothing had really excited me. I was sitting in the living room one afternoon, watching the beads of sweat roll off my forehead onto my shirt—they were drying almost instantly during the record-breaking heat wave. It was a hundred and ten when the phone rang.

"Hello?" I answered after mustering enough energy to move—it'd caught me off guard when I heard it ring; not that many people had our number.

"Hi, honey! It's your mama!" She sounded very excited as usual. Mothers can be like that—even when you don't call, they still come off unsullied. I had been remiss in calling her at least the past week, wrapped up looking for a job.

"Hey, Ma, how's it up north?" I gathered a smile that I hoped would settle her worries about her son being in a new city. It was a little strange for me to consider San Francisco as close as it was, but with shifting plates, deep beneath the earth's surface, it was all getting closer together anyway.

"It's good, honey. How are you doing? You guys getting along all right?" She always asked like a mother, but listened like a therapist.

"Sure, Ma, trying to make some moves, you know? Been hard to get a job, despite the fact that I've filled out how many applications this week? I mean, a body would think no one *wants* a waiter from New York. . .we work too fast or something." I had a tinge of despondency in my tone; I always liked to be in the thick of it. "I started that class. It seems good. Teacher's pretty cut-and-dry, which I like, don't get me wrong. But they're all caught up in this showcase that's coming up in a week or two—I got in class too late to be a part of it, but I figure in, I don't know—"

"David, I was thinking of coming down to see you, if you guys don't mind?"

Wow, *that* caught me off guard. I had to wake up for a second: Decisions were being made. "I thought it would be nice to see your place—" she fit in between my thoughts. Images of real food flashed everywhere, making my stomach rumble; in the past two weeks we'd eaten all the pizza I could take.

". . .Sure, Ma, just tell me when." I couldn't see any sound reason to fight it; the trip would be out of pure necessity for her, and I didn't mind giving in.

"I was thinking of this weekend. . . . Is that too soon?"

I was caught off guard—I hadn't thought the reality of it would slam that fast—but I recovered quickly. "Yeah, Mom, whenever you want—*mi casa es su casa*." It was decided that she'd come in on Friday, and I'd pick her up.

The major task at hand was cleaning the apartment. It amazed even me that such a disaster could have been created in so brief a time.

I was trudging across the floor with a huge black garbage bag, throwing out all the pizza boxes and beer cans, when Marlon came through the door; he plopped down on the cheesy white vinyl sofa we'd gotten from a theatre company going out of business.

"Jesus, it's *hot out there*! I mean, like *inferno* hot. And the bus? I was the only white guy on it!" His bass hit the sofa with a thud.

"My mom's coming down. I'm picking her up on Friday. She wants to see where we live," I said with a snort. Marlon chuckled at the thought himself. It was cool having the apartment with Marlon, and I was definitely a slob; who was I kidding?

WHEN I PULLED THE CAR UP TO THE CURB, I saw my mother standing there waving frantically; she was kind of hard to miss. She put her bag down as I walked around to open the door for her, and threw her arms around me. It had been a while since we'd seen each other; the hug felt good. She looked into my eyes and grabbed my face. "You look a little older," she said, smiling, a tear nearly forming in her eye.

"Aw, jeez. Come on, Ma, get in," I laughed, opening the door for her, and threw her bags in the back.

"This car doesn't seem safe, David," she said, looking around, barely able to see over the dash; she was getting white-knuckled, and I hadn't even turned the key over.

"Relax, Ma, don't you worry. I will drive ridiculously safe," I said, revving the Chevy and making a point of buckling my seatbelt.

We headed down Century Boulevard, and I hung a left on La Cienega. I wasn't too keen on freeways yet, so I stuck to surface streets. The sun was blazing, but the wind soothed as we raced down the road.

"Hey, how bout we go to the beach?" I asked as the wind, whipping at my words, made me strain my voice. She smiled; she was even enjoying the ride. Nodding, I made a quick left, adjusting for the change in plans.

When we got to the water, I parked the car, and we walked up to the beach. It was the only other time I'd been there since I picked up the money from Chase. It was nice there; the thought of people suffocating where *I* was currently living seemed lifetimes away. The gulls flew over our heads, and the water was perfect. We sat near an abandoned lifeguard station with an oceanfront view that wasn't to be believed.

The drive back to the apartment was nice, with the sun behind us; it was low in the sky, causing the clouds before us as we drove to go reddish and soft. When we got there, walking up the steps, I winced to myself about my mother's thoughts; you really only got one chance at a *first* impression of your *first* apartment.

We got to the top of the steps and opened the door. It was unusually clean. When we got inside, she clasped her hands together as she put her bag down.

"Oh, it's just *beautiful*, David." Was she looking at the same beige carpet and crappy furniture? I thought. She was just being my mother, appreciating the finish on the laminate coffee table, ignoring the squeak as she sat down on the Naugahyde sofa.

"You want something to drink? Maybe some water, Ma, or juice or something?" I asked as I spotted a roach clip on the T.V. table that was actually a nightstand. I moved subtly to stand in front of it—I didn't need to get into the 'drug' talk that very moment. Then the phone rang, I answered.

"Is, ah, David there, please?" I thought for a second, trying to place the voice. I realized it was James—we were in school together, but he worked as the class assistant to pay for it, made phone calls, copied scripts for the night; he was flat broke, but a really good actor from the little I'd seen.

"Hey, what's up, James? It's me." I didn't think I owed money that fast. I'd only been in the class for two weeks.

"Hey, man, Vince wanted me to ask if you could possibly learn a scene for the showcase on Tuesday—I know there isn't a lot of time. Something's come up with the scene that Laurie's doing." I definitely remembered Laurie—short dark hair, cut choppy; a little Goth chick. She was really cool; we'd shared a few smokes on the steps leading down from the isolated class environment to the seedy street below. He continued, "Her partner, Brian, has a family emergency and is flying back to Michigan today. Can you come by the studio to pick up a script and possibly step in for him?" I was rapidly filling with torn emotions: First, having someone telling me that I was wanted, chosen to help out in a situation, in the way only I could. But in the same moment, I was hearing the word "emergency," someone having to jump on the next plane for a loved one: The ramifications were rarely good. I didn't want the role that way but collected myself anyhow and focused on the bigger picture in the grand scheme of things.

The scene was a piece of cake for me, no big deal: Brother and sister having an argument, brother realizes sister is a vampire, very realistic. It was from some movie I had avoided the first time around. After I got off the call, my mother looked at me with that look—she'd *known* it would happen. We looked at each other after I got the news and spoke a silent language. Maybe she was a good luck charm.

I was able to get together with Laurie a handful of times before the show. We even got extra time with Vince. The whole thing was only three minutes long; how bad could we be?

THE BIG NIGHT, I PULLED BACK my ponytail and put on my favorite Hawaiian shirt. I was just about to leave for the studio when the phone rang. "Hello?" I answered.

A familiar voice came on the line. "Hey, bro, I didn't know if I would catch you," my sister said. She had gotten into a great school in the mid-West and loved life. "Mom said you had a play or something tonight, so I wanted to call and let you know I was really proud of you, and I know you'll do really great."

I was staring at my shoes while I held the phone. I didn't take compliments well sometimes; my sister and I had been too close in age when we were young to be friends at times, but then it'd just clicked. "Thanks, sis, I really appreciate it, and I feel the same about you. I know you're kicking ass at school, and I'm glad you really digging it." I had never felt regular education worked for me, but she excelled at it.

"Thanks, Dave—we turned out okay, huh?" she said with a smile in her voice.

I thought about that for a second, reminded of the way we had been raised and the people we had become. "I'd say better than okay. As a matter of fact, pretty fucking stellar," I said with a laugh. "I gotta get to the studio to run some lines, but thanks again for checking in. Love you, sis."

"You too, bro—and *you* go kick some ass," she said with a laugh. I hung up the phone, jumped in the beast, and was on my way.

When I got there, Laurie looked nervous as she stood on the balcony, chain-smoking, when I came over with some coffee.

"Thanks, I really need to relax. You're going to be great, David. I mean, you just *walked* into the scene like you belong there. Do you have anyone coming?" she asked, blowing the steam off the top, holding the cup in two hands to warm them.

"I don't really know anyone out here. My roommate might come if he can catch the bus. My mom was here over the weekend but had to get back to work." I didn't understand why a body would want anyone to see the scenes in the first place; they were pretty lame.

"Wow, that's too bad, for them! I am *sooo* glad that you were able to cover—I mean, I have an agent and a casting director coming." She was tapping her feet with excitement. At that moment, I realized people came to Los Angeles from all over to get famous. Fucking genius: *I* liked the weather, sometimes.

EVERYTHING WENT OFF WITHOUT A HITCH—I even got laughs where I was *supposed* to get them. I was standing around with a few of the other actors when James came up to my side. "David! Hey, man, nice work! You really got a good hold of that one! Just for your info, those women over there? They wanted to talk to you, when you get a chance."

"Yeah? Thanks, man." I looked over his shoulder and saw the two sitting in the first row of seats, talking to my teacher. I waited till Vince moved on and sidled over, put on my best charm, and said hello.

"Well, finally he comes over here! You were very good, young man, do you know that? And I happen to know a thing or two about a thing or two." She was brash and Jewishy and introduced herself as Barbara—she was a like a Jewish mother from Miami, which made the woman on her left seem even more attractive. *She* was more the Tina Louise type, older but sexy as hell, in her early forties and a bit quieter then her counterpart. "I never do this," Barbara said, "but I'm going to give you my card, and you give me a call tomorrow. We'll see what I can do for you. Oh, you're so cute!"

I grabbed the card and stuck it in my pocket without looking. I smiled, not knowing what the hell you were supposed to do in those situations, but as I started to turn back Ginger called out, "David, you can give *me* a call if you need to," and handed me her card as well, smiling at almost uncomfortable level. I took it, backing up, and nearly killed myself on a black box that was supposed to represent a coffee table. I had regained my composure and gone back to talking with my classmates when Vince came over. He was an older guy, sixties maybe, and he always had a smile and his hands clasped behind his back like a monk. He let go long enough to place an arm on my shoulder when he spoke. "David, you really helped out tonight. I'm glad that Barbara was here to see you. . .I've never seen her do that," he added, tapping the cards in my shirt pocket. "She's pretty big time. Just don't forget me when you're famous." I laughed at the joke, but he wasn't laughing. He left me there alone.

I turned my back—shyly pulling the cards out from my breast pocket, looking at the one who reminded me of Ginger first. *June*, it said on the card above the credits. I had figured her for an agent, but she was some kind of a casting director. I flipped to Barbara's card and was immediately stunned. It was really nice, embossed and everything: *Senior V.P, of Casting—Warner/Columbia Television*. She really was a big *macher*.

I smiled for the first time in awhile. Not really with expectation—I had been shined before in my life and was used to people being all talk; but it felt good to be noticed.

When I called Barbara the next morning, she was happy to hear from me. Her assistant put me through right away. "You know, I

298 / DAVID SHEINKOPF

never do that," she said, before a hello. "I can't believe you didn't even look at the card! I thought you might throw it *away*, for Chrissake! Listen to me. We've been looking for a character for one of our nighttime serials, and you, my young friend, fit the bill perfectly." I was floored. I'd never imagined it could be that easy to get a little part.

"Is it a big enough part for me to get a credit?" I asked: She didn't know me from Adam.

"*Big* enough? Are you *crazy*? I'm talking about one of the new series regulars! A lead, darling—a new leading role!" I was speechless for the first time in my life, speechless. "Now, you tell me, dear, do you have an agent?"

I somehow managed to utter the word *no*.

"Doesn't matter for right now, anyway. They're easy enough to find. But let's not put the cart before the horse—if it were up to me, you'd have the role, but the executive producer makes all the decisions. That's who you need to meet. How's this afternoon?" I took down the address, said thank you, and hung up the phone. I was elated at the idea of meeting someone big. I didn't know if I could get the job, but was hoping maybe I'd be remembered for some other role.

FOUR HOURS LATER, I WAS WAITING IN A LOBBY with the complimentary water a very nice-looking young woman with great legs had brought me. Just then a guy came up and greeted me. Seemed nice enough, but I felt he shook a lot of hands.

"Hi, my name is Jason Wilshire. Yeah, like the boulevard. Jerry is very excited to meet you, David. Will you please follow me?"

It turned out that Jason actually cast the show but hadn't been able to find anyone; offers were out, but nothing the network liked. We got to the outer office and waited. I smelled a cigar and saw a gold Rolex on someone's hand through the crack in the door.

I was escorted into the office, and there he was: Jerry had been an executive for longer than I'd been alive. He didn't care if the network got what they wanted, he slept well regardless. His golden tan was the clue. He was wearing a V-neck sweater over a collared shirt and looked like he'd just stepped off the back nine. He got up when I walked in to shake my hand, then sat me down.

"I heard some great stuff about you," he said to me with the look of a college scout in his eye. "You think maybe you can read something for me, do whatever Barbara saw you do again?"

I just smiled and nodded as Jason put a script in my hands and I read it as if I owned it. It wasn't hard for me to cold read; I actually liked to.

After it was over, he nodded and told me to wait outside with the secretary. I sat down on a couch and looked over at a T.V. that was showing the news.

Jason came out a few minutes later with Jerry and sat down next to me.

"Young man, it is always nice to see a fresh face with some real talent. I'd like to offer you a contract on my show," he said to me; I was smiling so fucking wide my cheeks cracked. It had been one month to the day since I moved to Los Angeles. I had something I never thought I'd get—a contract job on a television show, a real steady job for the first time in my life. Jason said it'd be worth about a hundred thousand the first year.

I glanced over their shoulders and caught a glimpse of the news-caster on the T.V. The sound was turned down, but I saw the chy-ron on the lower third the screen: *San Francisco Earthquake.* The irony of it blew my mind: I'd finally gotten a job, and the earth had shaken. It was pretty fucking cool. I had to call my mom.

David Sheinkopf

ABOUT THE AUTHOR

Growing up in New York City offered David Sheinkopf a variety of opportunities for creative expression. Modeling at a young age and moving on to television commercials and soap operas as he grew older were natural progressions, but by his late teens, he felt the need to spread his wings and move to Los Angeles. At nineteen, he was starring in the hit series *Falcon Crest*. He appeared in more television shows until he worked in the Disney film *Newsies, which* put him on the big screen. With a voiceover career that grew as a strong sideline to hosting and design work, he felt life was going smoothly. His work as a writer has given him the voice he has looked for all his life, and becoming an executive producer has been the perfect way to turn that voice into reality.

CPSIA information can be obtained
at www.ICGtesting.com
Printed in the USA
LVHW101536290322
714719LV00004B/76